THE 100 GREATEST AMERICAN FILMS

A Quiz Book

THE 100 GREATEST AMERICAN FILMS

A Quiz Book

~

Andrew J. Rausch

CITADEL PRESS
Kensington Publishing Corp.
www.kensingtonbooks.com

CITADEL PRESS BOOKS are published by

Kensington Publishing Corp.
850 Third Avenue
New York, NY 10022

All Kensington titles, imprints, and distributed lines are available at special quantity discounts for bulk purchases for sales promotions, premiums, fund-raising, educational, or institutional use. Special book excerpts or customized printings can also be created to fit specific needs. For details, write or phone the office of the Kensington special sales manager: Kensington Publishing Corp., 850 Third Avenue, New York, NY 10022, attn: Special Sales Department, phone 1-800-221-2647.

First printing: June 2002

10 9 8 7 6 5 4 3 2 1

Printed in the United States of America

Library of Congress Control Number: 2001099896

ISBN 0-8065-2337-9

To Steve Spignesi,
a good friend and teacher whose assistance
has been invaluable and whose work continues
to inspire and influence my own writing.

Contents

Foreword

Here's a sobering thought. As I was reading through Andy Rausch's entertaining quiz book, the one you now hold in your hands, I asked myself a private-quiz question—how many of the questions could I have answered if only I knew how to operate the filing system in my head, that place of gnarled synapses and tidbits of information stuck like Post-its all over the place? Why couldn't I have been blessed with total recall? Why does becoming a *Jeopardy* contestant seem like a more remote goal by the day?

This really struck me as I was reading Quiz No. 95 on *Pulp Fiction*. As the author of a biography on Quentin Tarantino, you'd think I could easily answer all twenty-five questions, especially considering that Andy lists my book as one of his sources. Certainly I remember what Fabienne likes for breakfast and what book John Travolta's character was reading on the commode. But much of the information that is readily accessible about a movie on the screen, or from interviews conducted about it, gets lost and muddled over time like dropouts in a digital-cell-phone signal. One minute, you're sure you know every inch of a movie. The next, you're sneaking a peek at the answer key at the back of this book and saying, "Ah, yes, I knew that. It was on the tip of my tongue."

Reading this book is like gazing, mesmerized, into a campfire. Each chapter induces a reverie about the movie in question. It's not just because movie trivia is fun (although it certainly is that). It's also because we love movies so much we just want to be around them, rubbing up against anything that has to do with them like a mad cow with scrapie. We bask in the afterglow of movies, remembering the good parts, the uncanny parts, the gossip from behind the scenes—everything including what Fabienne likes for breakfast. Knowing the answers to trivia questions gives us a sense of part ownership of something a lot bigger than us. While I have always found it odd, even unseemly, when knee-high boys can recite baseball RBIs the way students in another time had to commit Latin verbs to memory, it is somehow never surprising to run across a movie fan who knows that the set of *Rear Window* was the largest ever built at Paramount Studios or that the models for King Kong were clad in rabbit fur.

This book is disarming precisely because the questions here represent more than just a parlor game. They are a way to get to know more about a particular movie, and ultimately, about movies themselves. To call Andy's book educational might be the kiss of death, like calling a nonfiction film the "d" word—"documentary." But there you have it: it would be impossible to read this interactive book without learning more about some of the greatest movies ever made. (Naturally, I have a few quibbles with the official American Film Institute (AFI) list on which this book is based, but on the whole, we certainly are talking about great movies.)

Andy Rausch loves movies. He offers this book as a gift to those who share his enthusiasm. Do not be discouraged if you can't answer all the questions herein. Believe me, I am not fast on the draw with these things myself. I expect every reader to know the name of Citizen Kane's sled, but you are forgiven if you did not know that Gloria Swanson's car was towed onto the Paramount lot in *Sunset Boulevard* because her "chauffeur," Erich von Stroheim, did not know how to drive.

Life is full of great unanswerables, but thankfully, this book is not. I invite you to jump in, twenty-five questions at a time, and enjoy some of the greatest movies ever made.

—Jami Bernard

Author's Note

My intention with *The 100 Greatest American Films: A Quiz Book* was to craft something that is both academic and fun—two words which rarely go hand-in-hand. To avoid the inevitable arguments concerning which films deserve the designation top one hundred films in the history of American cinema, I opted to use the one hundred films selected by the American Film Institute in 1998. While this list is in some ways problematic, in both its acceptance of overrated crowd-pleasers and its definition of an *American* film, it also contains many truly spectacular works. If not actually a volume on the one hundred *greatest* American films in terms of artistic merit, this book certainly covers one hundred of the most-*beloved* films of all time.

The quizzes cover all aspects of each film, from its plot and characters to the details of its production. This is an academic work on the history of film in America, as well as a pass-the-time-on-a-trip quiz book. While a few people may know all the answers to one or two quizzes, I guarantee you that no one will know the answers to all the questions in this book. Before researching for this project, I certainly did not.

Consider this an open-book test if you'd like. It is my sincere hope that *The 100 Greatest American Films: A Quiz Book* sparks interest in you to rewatch these classic gems and rediscover their beauty and to track down the films covered here that you still have not seen. (Shame on you for not having seen them yet.) The quizzes in *The 100 Greatest American Films* were designed to be fun, challenging, and educational.

So, if you have your number-two pencils ready, you may now turn over your test and begin. Good luck.

—Andrew J. Rausch, March 2001

Note: All these films are available on both VHS and DVD, except for *Sunset Boulevard* and *E.T. The Extra-Terrestrial*, which are available on VHS only.

Quiz No. 1:
Citizen Kane (1941)

Screenplay by Herman J. Mankiewicz and Orson Welles
Directed by Orson Welles
Starring Orson Welles, Joseph Cotten, and Agnes Moorehead
RKO Pictures

> ***I've been asked many times if those of us working on* Kane *realized at the time that we were making something . . . that would be thought of fifty years later as perhaps the greatest picture ever made, and I have to say no, none of us did. I don't even think that Orson—who had a pretty good-sized ego—felt that. But you couldn't look at those dailies coming in every day and not realize you were getting something quite extraordinary.***
>
> —Editor Robert Wise

Widely regarded as the finest film ever made, Orson Welles's directorial debut, *Citizen Kane,* is the story of newspaper mogul Charles Foster Kane (Welles). The story begins with Kane's end; in the opening moments of the film, Kane dies, uttering but a final word, "Rosebud." But what is Rosebud? Can a single word sum up the whole of a man's existence? As a news reporter seeks to unlock the mystery of Kane's final utterance in the hopes of finding out who Charles Foster Kane truly was, Welles shows us the story of Kane's life through the memories of those he tormented.

Despite Hollywood's view of Welles as a brash young outsider, the Academy still recognized his achievements by nominating *Kane* for nine Academy Awards: Best Picture (Welles), Best Director (Welles), Best Original Screenplay (Welles and Herman J. Mankiewicz), Best Actor (Welles), Best Black-and-White Cinematography (Gregg Toland), Best Black-and-White Art Direction–Set Decoration (Perry Ferguson, Al Fields, Van Nest Polglase, and Darrell Silvera), Best Film Editing (Robert Wise), Best Original Score (Bernard Herrmann), and Best Sound (John Aalberg). However, the Academy was not yet ready to reward Welles for his work. The film received only one Oscar, awarded for Best Original Screenplay; in truth, this was likely intended more as a reward for journeyman cowriter Mankiewicz than Welles. Tellingly, Welles's film took top honors in nonindustry awards; both the New York Film Critics Circle and the National Board of Review named *Citizen Kane* "Best Film."

1. What real-life newspaper mogul served as the inspiration for *Citizen Kane*?
2. What is the name of Kane's lavish compound?
3. At the film's conclusion, Rosebud is being burned. What is Rosebud?
4. According to an essay written by Gore Vidal, Rosebud was, in real life, a pet name for what?
5. In 1999, an HBO telefilm was made about Orson Welles's battle to make *Citizen Kane.* In this Benjamin Ross–directed film, actor Liev Schreiber portrays auteur Kane. What is the name of this film?
6. Celebrated cinematographer Gregg Toland left *Citizen Kane* before filming was completed to work on another film. What is this film?
7. What is the name of the theater group that included Orson Welles, Joseph Cotten, and Agnes Moorehead?
8. During the montage of newspaper headlines that tells of Kane's death, which newspaper proclaims ENTIRE NATION MOURNS GREAT PUBLISHER AS OUTSTANDING AMERICAN?
9. At the time of Kane's death, how many newspapers does he control?
10. What was the cost of building the Chicago Municipal Opera House?
11. According to the narrator, what was the cost for construction of Kane's home?
12. What are the names of Kane's two wives?
13. At the age of twenty-six, Orson Welles became the youngest person to contend for an Oscar for Best Director. This record stood until 1992 when a twenty-four-year-old director was nominated. Who was this?
14. How many sources does reporter Jerry Thompson find to discuss Kane, and who are they?
15. In what year does Mr. Thatcher say he first encountered Kane?
16. At what age is Kane given control of his trust fund?

17. According to Thatcher, how much money will Charles's parents receive yearly?

18. As a child, Kane received a sled from Mr. Thatcher. What is the name of the sled?

19. Why does Kane initially say he's interested in operating the *Inquirer*?

20. Kane tells correspondent Wheeler, "You provide the prose poems. I'll provide the war!" This closely parallels a real-life statement. Who made the statement and to whom was it made?

21. At the rate of one million dollars lost per year, in how many years does Kane conclude he will be forced to sell the newspaper?

22. Kane's first editorial is a declaration of what?

23. While making *Kane,* Orson Welles repeatedly screened the film he considered the closest thing to cinematic perfection. What was this film?

24. In Herman J. Mankiewicz's first draft of the screenplay, the leading character had a different surname that Orson Welles later changed to Kane. What was this?

25. Many people have stated that the film's biggest flaw is that Kane dies alone, so no one should know what his final words are. Is this theory true or false, and why or why not?

Quiz No. 2:
Casablanca (1942)

Screenplay by Julius J. Epstein, Philip G. Epstein, and Howard Koch
Directed by Michael Curtiz
Starring Humphrey Bogart, Ingrid Bergman, and Paul Henreid
Warner Bros.

> *In* Casablanca, *I would say I had very little complaints. If I could have chosen the performers that made the film, I wouldn't have changed any of them. That's what made the film so great! The performers were so tremendous at what they did in this film! They were born for these roles! Could you imagine anybody else playing those parts?*
>
> —Screenwriter Howard Koch

Director Michael Curtiz's *Casablanca* features screen-icon Humphrey Bogart as Rick Blaine, an exiled American freedom fighter turned nightclub owner in a World War II way station known as Casablanca. The shrewd, cynical nightclub owner comes into the possession of two letters of transit given to him by a small-time hustler only moments before being captured by local authorities. When Czechoslovakian underground figurehead Victor Laszlo (Paul Henreid) arrives in Casablanca after thwarting the Nazis on more than one occasion, he finds Nazi major Strasser (Conrad Veidt) awaiting him. Here, they tell him he will meet his end. So, the letters of transit that Rick possesses become Laszlo's only means of escape. The only catch is that Laszlo's wife, the beautiful Ilsa (Ingrid Bergman), is Rick's former lover. Rick is bitter toward Ilsa, who ran out on him without a word in Paris, just as the Nazis stormed in. Although Blaine appears to be double-crossing Laszlo, blocking his escape in the name of vengeance, we slowly see his cynicism and self-minded nature eroding away, exposing a compassionate human being.

In 1943, *Casablanca* received eight Academy Award nominations: Best Picture (Hal B. Wallace), Best Director (Curtiz), Best Adapted

Screenplay (Julius J. Epstein, Philip G. Epstein, and Howard Koch), Best Actor (Bogart), Best Supporting Actor (Claude Rains), Best Cinematography (Arthur Edeson), Best Film Editing (Owen Marks), and Best Original Score (Max Steiner). From its eight nominations, *Casablanca* was awarded three Oscars—for Best Picture, Best Director, and Best Adapted Screenplay.

1. The much ballyhooed letters of transit that the story revolves around are historically inaccurate. In what way?
2. According to screenwriter Julius Epstein, how many of the studio's seventy-five writers tried to figure out an ending for *Casablanca*?
3. While shooting the film, actress Ingrid Bergman repeatedly voiced one major complaint. What was this?
4. What number does Rick instruct the young Bulgarian husband to bet on at the roulette table?
5. According to legend, a prankster once changed the characters' names, locations, and title of the *Casablanca* script and submitted it as an original screenplay to every major studio in Hollywood. What is said to have been the result?
6. Why is media mogul Ted Turner sometimes called "the man who ruined *Casablanca*"?
7. Dooley Wilson, who plays Sam the piano player, was a professional musician in real life. What instrument did Wilson play?
8. Ingrid Bergman was not producer Hal B. Wallace's first choice for the role of Ilsa. Who was?
9. A line of dialogue, which is shown in early-theatrical trailers, was removed from the scene in which Rick shoots Major Strasser. Before shooting Strasser, what did Rick originally say?
10. In 1944, producer Hal B. Wallace was awarded an Oscar for Best Picture for *Casablanca*. That same year, another Wallace-produced film was nominated for Best Picture. What was this film?
11. Composer Max Steiner, who scored *Casablanca*, was adamantly against the use of what in the film?
12. Before Humphrey Bogart was cast, what actors were considered for the role of Rick?
13. What actor, on loan from Selznick International, did not want to appear in *Casablanca* and did so against his will?
14. In 1983, a short-lived television series based on *Casablanca* was produced. In that series, who appeared in the role of Rick Blaine?

15. What is the name of the *Casablanca*-continuation novel penned by Michael Walsh?

16. How many times in the film does Rick say, "Play it again, Sam"?

17. What is the inaccurate translation of "Here's looking at you, kid" that appears in the German version of *Casablanca*?

18. In 1987, a special re-edited version of *Casablanca* prepared by Joao Luiz Albuquerque was screened at the Rio Film Festival. How does this version of the film end?

19. What is the name of the play *Casablanca* is based upon?

20. What 1944 film reunited *Casablanca* actors Humphrey Bogart, Claude Rains, Sydney Greenstreet, and Peter Lorre with director Michael Curtiz?

21. What legendary filmmaker directed the montages in *Casablanca*?

22. *Flash Gordon* scribe Frederick Stephani once presented a treatment for a proposed *Casablanca* sequel to producer Hal B. Wallace. What is the name of Stephani's would-be sequel?

23. When *Casablanca* was initially released in Germany, approximately twenty minutes of the film had been excised. What were these scenes?

24. At one point the producers considered changing the character Sam into a woman. What actress were they interested in casting?

25. In a January 17, 1942, memo to Warner Bros., what did Joseph Breen of the Hays Office insist the filmmakers could not hint at in *Casablanca*?

Quiz No. 3:
The Godfather (1972)

Screenplay by Francis Ford Coppola and Mario Puzo
Directed by Francis Ford Coppola
Starring Marlon Brando, Al Pacino, and Diane Keaton
Paramount Pictures

> *The old [Mafia] guys were men of honor. They had family values, but I don't know if that exists anymore because it was based on a patriarchal view of society. That's all changed as the families became more Americanized. The Mob chiefs in the 1930s didn't want their kids to go into the business. They wanted their kids to be better than them, to be more than them. They sent them to West Point, sent them to the best schools. It was a variation of the American dream."*
>
> —Screenwriter Mario Puzo

Gangster movies, such as the classic Warner Brothers productions of the thirties, have long been a staple of American cinema. However, *The Godfather* completely reinvented the genre and elevated it to a higher artistic level with its beautifully framed cinematography, wonderful direction, and exquisite acting. The lush three-hour epic tells the story of one man's struggle to balance his gangster family with his real-life family, and his vow not to become like his powerful father, a Mafia boss. However, in the end, Michael Corleone (Al Pacino) cannot escape his destiny and becomes the head of the crime organization. The film turned Francis Ford Coppola, known prior for "B" movies he had directed for producer Roger Corman, into a well-respected superstar overnight.

In 1973, *The Godfather* received eleven Academy Award nominations: Best Picture (Albert S. Ruddy), Best Director (Coppola), Best Adapted Screenplay (Coppola and Mario Puzo), Best Actor (Marlon Brando), Best Costume Design (Anna Hill Johnstone), Best Film-Editing (William Reynolds and Peter Zinner), Best Original Score

(Nino Rota), Best Sound (Charles Grenzbach, Christopher Newman, and Richard Portman), and an impressive three Best Supporting Actor nods for Al Pacino, James Caan, and Robert Duvall. Out of its eleven Oscar bids, the film was awarded three: Best Picture, Best Adapted Screenplay, and Best Actor.

1. How many times does the word "Mafia" appear in *The Godfather*?
2. Just before Sonny is murdered, what is he listening to on the radio?
3. When Marlon Brando won the Oscar for Best Actor, why did he decline to accept it?
4. At the Academy Awards ceremony, who showed up to receive Brando's Oscar?
5. The character Michael Corleone appears as a minor secondary character in another novel written by Mario Puzo. What is the name of this novel?
6. Who appears as the infant in the baptism scene?
7. Screenwriter Mario Puzo lobbied hard for Marlon Brando as Vito Corleone. What comedian did Paramount want cast in the role?
8. What is Vito Corleone's familial connection to Bonasera's daughter?
9. What position does Tom Hagen hold under Vito Corleone?
10. Before enlisting, where did Michael Corleone attend college?
11. The story of Vito Corleone was modeled loosely on the life of what notorious Mobster?
12. Singer Johnny Fontane was meant to parallel a real-life star. Who was this?
13. When making the bandleader the "offer he couldn't refuse," how much did Vito wind up paying for Fontane's release?
14. How many directors were offered *The Godfather* before Coppola?
15. What actors were considered for the role of Michael Corleone before Pacino was cast?
16. What role in *The Godfather* did Robert De Niro test for?
17. What role in *The Godfather* did Robert De Niro land?
18. Who does Vito Corleone send to the bar to meet with Bruno Tattaglia?
19. While Michael is in Sicily, where does Kay move to?

20. Just before Sollozzo is gunned down in the restaurant, what meal does he recommend as “the best in the city”?

21. What was shipped to the set of *The Godfather* packed in dry ice inside a metal container?

22. After receiving Vitelli’s permission, Michael pays a visit to Apollonia in her father’s home. What gift does he present her with?

23. According to Francis Ford Coppola, how many times was he fired while filming *The Godfather*?

24. When Michael meets with Moe Greene in Las Vegas, what does Fredo do that foreshadows his traitorous actions in *The Godfather: Part II*?

25. What happens each time oranges are shown in *The Godfather*?

Quiz No. 4:
Gone with the Wind (1939)

Screenplay by Sidney Howard
Directed by Victor Fleming
Starring Vivien Leigh, Clark Gable, and Olivia de Havilland
Metro-Goldwyn-Mayer

> ***It's a marvelous film, and every time I see it, it's as if I were seeing it for the first time. I notice things I didn't notice before. For example, I didn't care much for the character of Rhett Butler for many years, but then I noticed what was going on in the scene where he's going off to join the soldiers. Rhett was becoming a complete man by becoming partly Ashley.***
>
> —Actress Olivia de Havilland

Often called "the most beloved film of all time," *Gone with the Wind* is the story of Scarlett O'Hara (Vivien Leigh), a selfish Southern belle who must face a world ravaged by war, the fires of Atlanta, and carpetbaggers. Because of her stubbornness, Scarlett refuses to admit her love for ladies' man Rhett Butler (Clark Gable) and eventually loses him because of this denial. Shocking in its day, *Gone with the Wind* features some of the finest performances ever captured on film. With five filmmakers contributing to its direction, as well as various second-unit directors, the epic film uniquely disputes the adage that "too many cooks spoil the broth." Much of the credit for this goes to the singular vision of producer David O. Selznick.

In 1940, *Gone with the Wind* received thirteen Academy Award nominations: Best Picture (Selznick), Best Director (Victor Fleming), Best Adapted Screenplay (Sidney Howard), Best Actor (Gable), Best Actress (Leigh), Best Art Direction (Lyle R. Wheeler), Best Color Cinematography (Ernest Haller and Ray Rennahan), Best Film Editing (Hal C. Kern and James E. Newcom), Best Effects (Fred Albin, Jack Cosgrove, and Arthur Johns), Best Original Score (Max Steiner), Best Sound Recording (Thomas T. Moulton), and Best Supporting Actress nods for both Hattie McDaniel and Olivia de Havilland. The film won in eight categories, losing in its bids for Best Actor, Best Effects, Best Original Score, Best Sound Recording, and Best Supporting Actress (De Havilland). The film was also awarded two special achievement Oscars for William Cameron Menzies's "outstanding achievement in the use of color" and Don Musgrave's "pioneering in the use of coordinated equipment."

1. What was the significance of Hattie McDaniel's Oscar win?

2. Why wasn't screenwriter Sidney Howard present to accept his Best Adapted Screenplay Oscar?

3. Although Victor Fleming is the only filmmaker credited, four other directors greatly contributed to *Gone with the Wind.* Who were they?

4. In 1978, Academy Award–winning screenwriter James Goldman was hired to write a sequel to *Gone with the Wind.* The screenplay was adapted from Anne Edwards's unpublished novel, *Tara: A Continuation of Gone with the Wind.* What was the name of Goldman's screenplay?

5. What does Scarlett throw at Jonas Wilkerson when he attempts to buy her out?

6. Screenwriter Sidney Howard was the first writer to win both the Pulitzer Prize and the Academy Award. For what 1925 play had Howard been awarded the Pulitzer Prize?

7. Who does Scarlett believe to be a "goody-goody"?

8. What does John Wilkes say is the "only thing that lasts"?

9. How does Scarlett handle the Union deserter who attempts to loot Tara?

10. What sickness claims the life of India Wilkes?

11. True or false: Producer David O. Selznick purchased the rights to *Gone with the Wind* with actress Vivien Leigh in mind for the role of Scarlett.

12. What actor plays Rhett Butler in the 1994 Emmy-winning sequel, *Scarlett?*

13. Producer David O. Selznick was fined for not complying with the Hollywood Production Code. What was the questionable scene that warranted the fine?

14. Which of the actors from the film was not allowed to attend its premiere?

15. Why does Dr. Mende refuse to assist with Melanie's childbirth?

16. Susan Hayward failed two screen tests for the role of Scarlett O'Hara. Eleven years later, she appeared in a blatant *Gone with the Wind* ripoff playing a character named Morna Dabney. What is this film?

17. Mammy teases Scarlett by saying that it's not proper for a woman to expose her bosom before what time?

18. What movie did Victor Fleming make just before working on *Gone with the Wind*?

19. How much does Rhett bid to dance with Scarlett?

20. How long does Scarlett proclaim that she will hate Ashley?

21. When does Rhett say he generally develops a weakness for lost causes?

22. George Reeves plays the role of Stuart Tarleton. However, he is credited with the wrong part. What character is Reeves credited as playing?

23. Upon the orders of Clark Gable, director George Cukor was fired one week into the filming of *Gone with the Wind*. Why?

24. In their first conversation, what does Scarlett conclude that Rhett is not?

25. In a 1940 parody of *Gone with the Wind*, cartoon character Elmer Fudd plays Nett Cutler. What is the name of this Friz Freleng–directed cartoon?

Quiz No. 5:
Lawrence of Arabia (1962)

Screenplay by Robert Bolt
Directed by David Lean
Starring Peter O'Toole, Omar Sharif, and Anthony Quinn
Columbia Pictures

> ***I can understand how most of the great religious leaders came out of the desert because, when you're there, you feel terribly small and, in a strange way, very big. Because this vastness . . . it's sort of pitilessness combined with enormous beauty.*** —Director David Lean

David Lean's epic, *Lawrence of Arabia,* is the true story of T. E. Lawrence, the eccentric Englishman who assisted the Arabs in their struggle for liberation. With a remarkable script by first-time screenwriter Robert Bolt and a then-unknown leading man named Peter O'Toole, Lean crafted a masterpiece. *Lawrence of Arabia* exemplifies everything filmmaker Lean would become known for and also features the finest performance of actor O'Toole's long and respectable career.

In 1963, *Lawrence of Arabia* received ten Academy Award nominations: Best Picture (Sam Spiegel), Best Director (Lean), Best Adapted Screenplay (Bolt), Best Actor (O'Toole), Best Supporting Actor (Omar Sharif), Best Color Art Direction–Set Decoration (John Box, Dario Simoni, and John Stoll), Best Color Cinematography (Freddie Young), Best Film Editing (Anne V. Coates), Best Substantially Original Score (Maurice Jarre), and Best Sound (John Cox). The film was awarded seven Oscars, but O'Toole, Sharif, and Bolt all lost in their bids.

1. Who suggested actor Peter O'Toole for the role of Lawrence after seeing him perform in *The Long and the Short and the Tall* at London's Royal Court Theatre?
2. What does Brighton conclude of British and Arab interests?

3. What is the title of T. E. Lawrence's autobiographical account upon which the film is based?

4. Screenwriter Robert Bolt wrote *Lawrence of Arabia* on a yacht named the *Mulhane*. Who owned the yacht?

5. Who does Gasim say Allah favors?

6. Before Peter O'Toole came on board, another actor had been cast in the leading role. Director David Lean once commented of this actor, who quit after only four days of work, "One of the big advantages is that this boy really looks like the portraits of Lawrence." Who was this actor?

7. Two films had already been made about Lawrence's exploits when *Lawrence of Arabia* was filmed, and both featured the real-life T. E. Lawrence. What are the names of these films?

8. What does Lawrence say is the trick to putting out a burning match with one's fingers?

9. Despite David Lean's well-documented hatred for second-unit directors, producer Sam Spiegel insisted that he use them on *Lawrence of Arabia*. Two of the four assistant directors are now accomplished filmmakers in their own right. Who are they?

10. What is the title of the *Lawrence of Arabia* sequel featuring Ralph Fiennes as T. E. Lawrence?

11. Screenwriter Robert Bolt recommended a Joseph Conrad novel to director David Lean. In 1985, Lean began working on the film for Warner Brothers with Steven Spielberg acting as executive producer. However, the film was later aborted. What is the name of this project?

12. When Lawrence agrees to execute the offender who murdered one of Auda's men, who does he find himself forced to kill?

13. In 1961, producer Sam Spiegel announced that actor Cary Grant was expected to appear in *Lawrence of Arabia*. What role was Grant to have played?

14. How many wounds does Auda abu Tayi claim to carry?

15. Director David Lean and screenwriter Robert Bolt discussed making another biopic for nearly twenty years. Bolt wrote a forty-page treatment that Lean liked quite a bit. However, Lean disliked Bolt's first draft of the screenplay, and he aborted the project. Who was the subject of this biopic?

16. Director David Lean and screenwriter Robert Bolt collaborated on three films, beginning with *Lawrence of Arabia*. What were Lean and Bolt's other two collaborations?

17. In 1963, Peter O'Toole lost in his bid for Best Actor. What actor did O'Toole lose to?

18. What is the name of the real-life journalist Jackson Bentley is modeled after?

19. On February 18, 1960, the *Hollywood Reporter* announced that an actor had been cast to portray T. E. Lawrence. A. W. Lawrence, the brother of the film's subject, concluded, "It seems a mistake. I think it will almost inevitably mean that the film will be a flop—in England at least." Who was this actor?

20. How many lives does Auda claim his hands have taken?

21. *Lawrence of Arabia* was the first of four films actors Peter O'Toole and Omar Sharif have appeared in together through 2001. What are the other three films?

22. Before Robert Bolt was hired to rewrite the screenplay, another scribe had spent a year-and-a-half writing a first draft, which David Lean rejected. Who was this screenwriter?

23. Who makes a brief cameo in the film as the cyclist who hails Lawrence from across the Suez Canal asking, "Who are you?"?

24. How many female speaking roles are there in *Lawrence of Arabia*?

25. According to actress Katharine Hepburn, what did Peter O'Toole have cosmetically altered to make him look more like T. E. Lawrence?

Quiz No. 6:
The Wizard of Oz (1939)

Screenplay by Noel Langley, Florence Ryerson, and Edgar Allan Woolf
Directed by Victor Fleming
Starring Judy Garland, Jack Haley, and Ray Bolger
Metro-Goldwyn-Mayer

> ***People say, "It must have been fun making that picture." Fun? Like hell it was fun! It was a lot of hard work! It was not fun at all. There was nothing fun about it.*** —Actor Jack Haley

The fantasy film, *The Wizard of Oz,* adapted from author L. Frank Baum's popular children's book, is the most watched film in the history of American cinema. Despite a crazed shooting schedule involving multiple directors and the fact that *The Wizard of Oz* is a remake, it's a nearly flawless film. Noted film critic Leonard Maltin has called it "the perfect cast in the perfect fantasy."

In 1940, *The Wizard of Oz* received six Academy Award nominations: Best Picture (Mervyn LeRoy), Best Art Direction (Cedric Gibbons and William A. Horning), Best Color Cinematography (Harold Rosson), Best Effects (A. Arnold Gillespie and Douglas Shearer), Best Original Score (Herbert Stothart), and Best Song (Harold Arlen and E. Y. Harburg). The film was awarded two Oscars for Best Original Score and Best Song.

1. In 1939, Victor Fleming was the sole credited director on two epic color films, although both projects were the collaborative efforts of numerous filmmakers. One of these films is *The Wizard of Oz.* What is the other film?
2. What directors worked on *The Wizard of Oz* but did not receive credit?
3. Although most people don't realize it, *The Wizard of Oz* is a re-

make. How many versions were produced prior to this most famous one?

4. Actor Jerry Maren claims the midgets working in the film received less pay than Terry the terrier. The Munchkins earned fifty dollars per week. According to Maren, how much did the dog make?

5. What two actresses were initially approached to play Dorothy?

6. Buddy Ebsen was slated to play two different roles at different stages of production. What are these?

7. Two primary cast members would later have children who would marry. Who were they?

8. What is the name of the 1978 *Wizard of Oz* remake that features Richard Pryor as the Wizard?

9. Some theorize that Baum's tale contained social and political satire. In this theory, what politician is the cowardly lion said to represent?

10. Actress Betty Jaynes's role was cut from the screenplay after she was hired. What character was Jaynes hired to play?

11. What Pink Floyd album has been discovered to synchronize perfectly with *The Wizard of Oz*?

12. In 1981, Warner Bros. produced a horrible comedy about the midgets who appeared in *The Wizard of Oz*, which featured Chevy Chase and Carrie Fisher. What is the name of this film?

13. What do Professor Marvel, the Emerald City Gatekeeper, the Cabbie, the Wizard's Guard, and the Wizard himself all have in common?

14. What was created with a thirty-foot muslin stocking?

15. Margaret Hamilton, who appears as Almira Gulch, and Terry the terrier, who appears as Toto, reunited on another film three years after *The Wizard of Oz*. What is this film?

16. After reuniting in *Thousands Cheer* (1943), Judy Garland and Frank Morgan would later work together on a third film, only to see each of their scenes cut from the film. What is this film?

17. What is Dorothy's last name?

18. How does the Wicked Witch of the East die?

19. What is the only thing the Scarecrow claims to fear?

20. When Dorothy finds the Tin Woodsman, he cannot move. Why?

21. What kind of animals does the Tin Woodsman believe the woods are inhabited by?

22. Why doesn't the Lion count sheep?

23. Where is the Scarecrow's straw refilled?

24. According to the song, what turns a slave into a king?

25. Who tears the Scarecrow apart, prompting the Lion to tease, "They sure knocked the stuffing out of you"?

Quiz No. 7:
The Graduate (1967)

Screenplay by Buck Henry and Calder Willingham
Directed by Mike Nichols
Starring Dustin Hoffman, Anne Bancroft, and Katharine Ross
Embassy Pictures

> ***I was always taken by the love story part of it. A story about one guy's desperation to connect to one person. It's very corny, but when Dustin's sitting and writing her name over and over again, it affects me every time. I suppose it's because it's something I've done.***
>
> —Screenwriter Buck Henry

Director Mike Nichols's *The Graduate* is one of the most revered movies of the late sixties. The comedy, based on the novel of the same title by Charles Webb, tells the story of Benjamin Braddock (Dustin Hoffman), a listless college grad with no aim or ambitions in life. For lack of having anything better to do, Benjamin becomes involved in an adulterous fling with the wife of his father's business partner. Benjamin soon finds trouble in paradise when he comes to the realization that he's in love with the woman's daughter.

In 1968, *The Graduate* received seven Academy Award nominations: Best Picture (Lawrence Turman), Best Director (Nichols), Best Adapted Screenplay (Buck Henry and Calder Willingham), Best Actor (Hoffman), Best Actress (Anne Bancroft), Best Supporting Actress (Katharine Ross), and Best Cinematography (Robert Surtees). The film won only one Oscar, awarded to Mike Nichols for Best Director.

1. What future movie star appears in an uncredited cameo as a boardinghouse neighbor?
2. The year before winning an Academy Award for Best Director with *The Graduate,* Mike Nichols was nominated for another film. What was the film?

3. There are two versions of Benjamin and Mrs. Robinson's first encounter. In the original version, Benjamin says, "Jesus Christ" and then, "Oh, my Christ." In another version of the film, these lines have been redubbed. What does Ben say in lieu of these lines in the altered version?

4. Who makes a cameo in the film as the hotel-desk clerk?

5. The film's memorable title sequence shows Benjamin standing on the moving walkway at the airport, oblivious to the world around him. In this scene, what song plays over the soundtrack?

6. What 1997 film pays homage to *The Graduate* by re-creating the title sequence by placing its own title character on a moving walkway as music plays?

7. When Mr. McGuire tells Benjamin that he would like to offer him just one word, what is this word?

8. When Benjamin offers Mrs. Robinson his keys to drive herself home, where does she promptly deposit them?

9. According to Mrs. Robinson, where was Elaine conceived?

10. What is the hotel room number where Benjamin and Mrs. Robinson rendezvous?

11. What is the name of the hotel where Benjamin and Mrs. Robinson meet?

12. How much of the film's screenplay was written by screenwriter Calder Wittingham?

13. What is the name of Elaine's preppy pipe-smoking boyfriend?

14. At what college were the Berkeley scenes filmed?

15. As Benjamin shows up at the wedding, Mrs. Robinson says, "It's too late." What is Elaine's response?

16. What is the name of the family holding the party in the hotel ballroom?

17. What is the occasion of the party at which Benjamin dons scuba gear and jumps into the swimming pool?

18. In what 1992 film is screenwriter Buck Henry shown pitching a sequel to *The Graduate* to a studio executive?

19. When Benjamin telephones Mrs. Robinson for their first meeting, how long does she say she will be?

20. What position did Benjamin hold on his college newspaper during his senior year?

21. Director Mike Nichols and screenwriter Buck Henry initially envisioned Benjamin Braddock looking quite different than he does in the film. What kind of man did they envision in the role?

22. When Mrs. Robinson enters Elaine's room behind Benjamin, in what is her naked body reflected?

23. Before allowing him to leave, what does Mrs. Robinson send Benjamin downstairs to retrieve?

24. When Elaine and Benjamin go on their first date, he tries to scare her away. Where does he take her?

25. What blond actress turned down the role of Mrs. Robinson before Anne Bancroft was cast?

Quiz No. 8: On the Waterfront (1954)

Screenplay by Budd Schulberg
Directed by Elia Kazan
Starring Marlon Brando, Karl Malden, and Lee J. Cobb
Columbia Pictures

> ***We finally get to see [Darryl] Zanuck and he starts talking about widescreen Technicolor pictures. And I thought, uh oh, because our script was specifically in black and white. Finally, Zanuck comes clean and says he doesn't like a single thing about it. And we ask why not. And I will never forget his reply, "Who's going to care about a bunch of sweaty longshoremen?"***
> —Screenwriter Budd Schulberg

A highly controversial film at the time of its release, Elia Kazan's *On the Waterfront* examines the corruption of workers' unions and the problems found on New Jersey's waterfront docks. The social commentary, written by Budd Schulberg with uncredited contributions by Kazan, was immediately met with critical acclaim. As film critic Andrew Howe wrote in *Film Written* magazine, "Everyone should see the Mona Lisa at least once in their lifetime, and so should they see this film."

In 1955, *On the Waterfront* received twelve Academy Award nominations: Best Picture (Sam Spiegel), Best Director (Kazan), Best Screenplay (Schulberg), Best Actor (Marlon Brando), Best Black-and-White Cinematography (Boris Kaufman), Best Film Editing (Gene Milford), Best Black-and-White Art Direction–Set Decoration (Richard Day), Best Supporting Actress (Eva Marie Saint), Best Original Score (Leonard Bernstein), and an astounding three Best Supporting Actor nods for the performances of Karl Malden, Lee J. Cobb, and Rod Steiger. The film was awarded eight Oscars, losing only for Bernstein's score and the three Best Supporting Actor nominations.

1. Why did Arthur Miller decline when asked to write the screenplay for *On the Waterfront*?

2. What actor appears uncredited in the role of Slim?

3. Slim says his real name is Malden Skulovich. What is the significance of this name?

4. What actor appears uncredited in the role of Gilette?

5. What is the significance of composer Leonard Bernstein's contributions to the film?

6. Marlon Brando was awarded a Best Actor Oscar for his turn in *On the Waterfront*. How many career Academy Award nominations has Brando received through the year 2001?

7. Actors Marlon Brando and Karl Malden appear in three films together. One of these is *On the Waterfront*. What are the other two?

8. What is the significance of both Brando and Malden's being nominated by the Academy for *On the Waterfront*?

9. One of the thugs laments that Joey Doyle could sing. What does he then conclude that Joey could *not* do?

10. Marlon Brando angrily walked off the set after filming the "I coulda been a contender" scene, stating that he was annoyed by Rod Steiger. Why?

11. Where does Father Barry suggest the longshoremen discuss their grievances?

12. What occupation is Edie studying to go into?

13. What is Charlie's nickname?

14. A demand in Marlon Brando's contract allowed the actor to leave the set at four P.M. each day. Why did Brando need to leave at this time?

15. How many pages is the deposition of testimony Kayo Dugan gave to the crime commission?

16. When Kayo Dugan dies, whose jacket is he wearing?

17. What is the name of the thug who throws a banana at Father Barry?

18. What is the love that Father Barry believes to be the problem with the waterfront?

19. What boxer does Charlie compare Terry to?

20. What does Charlie offer Terry in exchange for his silence?

21. Where does Terry believe Charlie gave him a one-way ticket to?

22. While testifying, what does Big Mac claim happened to the union's financial records?

23. A famous singer was initially attached to the film for the role of Terry Malloy. However, director Elia Kazan couldn't find complete financing for the film with him in the role. Who was this?

24. What is the name of the newspaper shown with the headline proclaiming Johnny Friendly the "waterfront murder boss"?

25. What is the gift from "Uncle" Johnny that Terry receives?

Quiz No. 9:
SCHINDLER'S LIST (1993)

Screenplay by Steven Zaillian
Directed by Steven Spielberg
Starring Liam Neeson, Ben Kingsley, and Ralph Fiennes
Universal Pictures

> ***I have been searching the way the characters in* Citizen Kane *searched for the meaning of "Rosebud." I have been searching for the meaning of Oskar Schindler for over a decade now. And I am no closer today, having made the movie, to discovering it than I was when I first read the book.***
> —DIRECTOR STEVEN SPIELBERG

Schindler's List is director Steven Spielberg's masterpiece; the finest piece of work in a career brimming with brilliance. The story of Oskar Schindler, a businessman who saved the lives of many Jews during the Holocaust, *Schindler's List* is based on Thomas Keneally's 1982 novel *Schindler's Ark*. The film parallels the lives of two men, Schindler, portrayed by Liam Neeson, and his evil Nazi counterpart, Goeth, played by Ralph Fiennes.

In 1993, *Schindler's List* received twelve Academy Award nominations: Best Picture (Branko Lustig, Gerald R. Molen, and Spielberg), Best Director (Spielberg), Best Adapted Screenplay (Steven Zaillian), Best Actor (Neeson), Best Supporting Actor (Fiennes), Best Art Direction–Set Decoration (Ewa Braun and Allan Starski), Best Cinematography (Janusz Kaminski), Best Film Editing (Michael Kahn), Best Original Score (John Williams), Best Costume Design (Anna B. Sheppard), Best Makeup (Judith A. Cory, Matthew W. Mungle, and Christina Smith), and Best Sound (Ron Judkins, Scott Millan, Andy Nelson, and Steve Pederson). The film was awarded seven Oscars, losing in its bids for Best Actor, Best Supporting Actor, Best Costume Design, Best Makeup, and Best Sound.

1. Novelist Thomas Keneally was awarded the prestigious literary award known as the Booker Prize for *Schindler's Ark,* which the film is based upon. What does Keneally see as being "one of the most overlooked ironies" regarding this award?

2. *Schindler's List* won an Oscar for Best Picture. Prior to this, what was the last black-and-white film to accomplish this feat?

3. Why did Martin Scorsese decline when offered the chance to direct *Schindler's List*?

4. In 1982 and 1985, coproducer Branko Lustig produced two other Holocaust-themed films. What were these?

5. According to director Steven Spielberg, coproducer Branko Lustig approached him, saying, "These are my credentials." To what was he referring?

6. Ralph Fiennes put on considerable weight for the role of Goeth. How did he gain the weight?

7. In the first scene of the film, who appears in a cameo as the nightclub maitre d'?

8. How many elected Jews serve on the Jewish Council?

9. Before casting Liam Neeson, director Steven Spielberg attended a Broadway production featuring the actor. What was the play Spielberg attended?

10. Warren Beatty read for the part of Oskar Schindler. Why did Steven Spielberg decide not to cast him in the role?

11. Steven Spielberg initially considered making *Schindler's List* a non-English-speaking film with subtitles. In what two languages would the film's dialogue have been?

12. As Schindler interviews women for the secretarial positions, a painter is brushing his title on the office door. What is the title as it appears on the door?

13. Before hiring cinematographer Janusz Kaminski for *Schindler's List,* Steven Spielberg hired him to shoot a pilot he was executive producing. What is the name of this pilot?

14. What brand of champagne does Schindler seek to acquire from the Poles?

15. What are the three things Oskar Schindler's father believed one needs in life?

16. What is the name of Oskar Schindler's wife?

17. What, according to Oskar Schindler, is the sole purpose of his 350 employees?

18. What is the fate of the one-armed machinist?
19. What university did Diana Reiter attend?
20. What occurs on March 13, 1943?
21. What is the name of Goeth's maid?
22. What does Schindler threaten he will do if Elsa Krause weeps?
23. What, according to Goeth, is always the right answer?
24. Steven Zaillian was awarded an Oscar for Best Screenplay for *Schindler's List*. This was Zaillian's second Best Screenplay nomination. For what film did he receive his first?
25. According to the film's postscript, what was Oskar Schindler declared by the Council of Yad Vashem in 1958?

Quiz No. 10:
Singin' in the Rain (1952)

Screenplay by Betty Comden and Adolph Green
Directed by Stanley Donen and Gene Kelly
Starring Gene Kelly, Donald O'Connor, Debbie Reynolds, and Jean Hagen
Metro-Goldwyn-Mayer

> ***Stanley, Betty, Adolph, and I thought musicals were a real, legitimate art form. We were as serious as Monet was about painting.***
>
> —Codirector Gene Kelly

Produced during MGM's most creative period, Stanley Donen and Gene Kelly's *Singin' in the Rain* is an extraordinary achievement and remains one of the most revered musicals ever filmed. Although the film's premise was inspired by *Once in a Lifetime* (1932)—the Moss Hart–George S. Kaufman adaptation about the film industry's transition from silent films to talkies—*Singin' in the Rain* was an original story rather than the standard Broadway musical adaptation.

At the time of its release, the film was largely critically dismissed. The film received two Academy Award nominations in 1953: Best Scoring of a Musical Picture (Lennie Hayton) and Best Supporting Actress (Jean Hagen). However, the film was awarded no Oscars.

1. Who choreographed the film?
2. Although Donald O'Connor would play the role of Cosmo in the film, the role was originally written with another actor in mind. Who was this?
3. What film recycled several costumes from *Singin' in the Rain* two years later?
4. In what year is the film set?
5. What film was the title song composed for originally?
6. *Singin' in the Rain* opens at a premiere for a Monumental Pictures release starring Don Lockwood and Lina Lamont. What is the name of the film?

7. What Judy Holliday role served as the inspiration for the character Lina?

8. In a great bit of irony, as Debbie Reynolds's character, Kathy, overdubs Lina's singing voice, Reynolds's own voice was overdubbed. Who provided the singing voice for Debbie Reynolds in *Singin' in the Rain*?

9. In filming the movie's most memorable sequence, in which Gene Kelly dances in the rain while singing the title song, the actor was actually quite ill. What was wrong with him?

10. What is the name of the magazine that asks LOCKWOOD AND LAMONT—REEL LIFE OR REAL LIFE ROMANCE?

11. In 1993, *Singin' in the Rain* collaborators Arthur Freed, Betty Comden, and Adolph Green worked on a musical starring Fred Astaire, which featured the catalogue of composer Irving Berlin. When Freed died, the project was aborted. What was the name of this unfilmed project?

12. Who is the Monumental Pictures studio chief?

13. What is the name of Lina's diction coach?

14. According to the diction exercise, what does "Moses supposes"?

15. What move does Simpson predict will result in Warner Brothers losing their shirts?

16. As with most Arthur Freed musicals, what was the major difficulty screenwriters Betty Comden and Adolph Green faced when they began writing the story line for the film?

17. What is the name of Monumental Pictures's first talking film?

18. Don conceives a fourteen-minute extravaganza for the film. What is the name of this ballet?

19. In what film did Cosmo's "Make 'Em Laugh" sequence originate?

20. Who does Don call a rattlesnake?

21. Codirectors Stanley Donen and Gene Kelly would later each marry a woman who appeared in an uncredited role in *Singin' in the Rain* and also served as assistant choreographer. Who was this?

22. What does Don say he'd rather kiss than Lina?

23. Who does Lina falsely quote as being "wildly enthusiastic" about her singing?

24. Why does Cosmo say Lina is a "triple threat"?

25. According to Don, five-hundred-thousand watts of what is added to each film?

Quiz No. 11:
It's a Wonderful Life (1946)

Screenplay by Frances Goodrich, Albert Hackett, and Frank Capra
Directed by Frank Capra
Starring James Stewart, Donna Reed, and Lionel Barrymore
RKO Pictures

> ***This was the first picture we made with Liberty Films and it was my production. And to me, that's a great film. I love that film. It's my favorite film, and in a sense it epitomizes everything I'd been trying to do and say in the other films. Only it does it very dramatically with a very unique story. The importance of the individual is the theme—and no man is a failure. If he's born, he's born to do something, he's not born to fail.***
>
> —Director Frank Capra

Frank Capra's *It's a Wonderful Life* is the story of George Bailey (James Stewart), a man of vision, who sacrifices his dreams to help others. When eight thousand dollars is misplaced at the building and loan where he works, George faces jail time. George's many regrets intensify and he begins to question the value of his existence. He decides to end it all and kill himself. But before he can, he is saved by a mysterious man named Clarence who claims to be an angel. Clarence then shows him what fates would have befallen his beloved town of Bedford Falls, and those he loves the most, had he never been born.

In 1947, *It's a Wonderful Life* received five Academy Award nominations: Best Picture (Capra), Best Director (Capra), Best Actor (Stewart), Best Film Editing (William Hornbeck), and Best Sound (John Aalberg). However, the film was awarded no Oscars.

1. Clarence is said to have the IQ of what animal?
2. What is the book Clarence is reading?
3. What organization included *It's a Wonderful Life* in its list of subversive films in 1947?

4. In the Charleston scene, George cuts in on Mary and another man, played by Carl Switzer. Nearly twenty years before *It's a Wonderful Life,* Switzer had found tremendous success as a child actor. What famous role had Switzer played as a child?

5. Nonoriginal music composed by Alfred Newman appears in *It's a Wonderful Life*. From what 1939 film does the music originate?

6. What is the name of the business founded by George's father and his Uncle Billy?

7. Todd Karns, the actor who plays Harry Bailey, had worked with actress Donna Reed before *It's a Wonderful Life*. Karns would later recall, "Donna Reed was very pretty and very mature. I was young and looked maybe fifteen. I had a crush on her, but in the romance department she didn't look my way." What is the name of this first film featuring Karns and Reed?

8. After agreeing to stay in Bedford Falls and accept his father's position at the building and loan, what does George do with the money he's saved for college?

9. Before casting *It's a Wonderful Life,* director Frank Capra submitted a detailed list of casting ideas to the studio. Henry Travers, the actor who appears in the film as Clarence, was listed as a possible candidate for three roles. What were they?

10. What does George say are the three most exciting sounds in the world?

11. The film is an adaptation of Philip Van Doren Stern's short story, "The Greatest Gift." Where did this story first appear?

12. How much on every dollar does Henry Potter offer to pay for the Building and Loan shares?

13. *It's a Wonderful Life* was remade into a not so wonderful telefilm in 1977 that featured Cloris Leachman and Orson Welles. In this remake, how does George Bailey's character differ from the original film?

14. Actors James Stewart and Lionel Barrymore appear together in five films. One of these is *It's a Wonderful Life*. What are the other four films the two actors appear together in?

15. Who does Potter believe hates the Building and Loan almost as much as he does?

16. What *Sesame Street* characters were later named after characters in *It's a Wonderful Life*?

17. In 1942, James Stewart narrated a short film about the Army Air Corps, which was produced by the Office of War Information. Its

title coincidentally describes Clarence's plight in *It's a Wonderful Life*. What is the name of this film?

18. Who shoots down fifteen planes in the war, winning the Congressional Medal of Honor?

19. A newspaper headline reads SMITH WINS NOMINATION. This is a reference to another film. What is this film?

20. Frank Capra said the character Henry Potter should have the same characteristics as a man he saw in a painting. What was this famous painting?

21. Although James Stewart appears in the film, RKO had purchased the rights to Philip Van Doren Stern's short story as a vehicle for another actor. Who was the actor?

22. Three screenwriters tried unsuccessfully to adapt "The Greatest Gift" before Frances Goodrich and Albert Hackett were hired. Who were the three screenwriters?

23. *It's a Wonderful Life* was the first Liberty Films production. Liberty Films was a coventure between production executive William Briskin, Frank Capra, and two noted film directors. Who were they?

24. James Stewart was reluctant to make *It's a Wonderful Life* so shortly after his return home from World War II. However, he was convinced to do the film by a close friend. Who convinced him?

25. As George runs down the street in Bedford Falls, a theater marquee advertises *The Bells of St. Mary's* (1945). Which *It's a Wonderful Life* actor appears as Horace P. Bogardus in that film?

Quiz No. 12: Sunset Boulevard (1950)

Screenplay by Charles Brackett, D. M. Marshman, Jr., and Billy Wilder
Directed by Billy Wilder
Starring William Holden, Gloria Swanson, and Erich von Stroheim
Paramount Pictures

> ***The final mad scene raised problems. I had to descend down a grand staircase crowded with extras and a few people like Hedda Hopper in a state of derangement, and Billy Wilder wanted me to come down on the side of the stairway where the steps were narrowest. On high heels I would have tripped for sure. I played the scene barefoot. I imagined a steel ramrod in me from head to toe holding me together and descended as if in a trance.***
>
> —Actress Gloria Swanson

As *Sunset Boulevard* opens, we see the corpse of screenwriter Joe Gillis (William Holden) floating in a swimming pool. The dead man then serves as narrator, sharing the tale of his six months with a washed-up silent screen actress named Norma Desmond (Gloria Swanson). Gillis met Desmond while attempting to hide his car from repossession, and then became sucked into her world of disillusionment. With the advent of the talking motion picture thirteen years before, Desmond has become an unwanted relic from an earlier era. However, the actress is convinced that she is still adored by legions of fans and is planning to stage a big comeback. When Gillis attempts to leave, he finds himself floating in the pool face down. Billy Wilder's dark film is a masterwork. As *The New York Times* proclaimed when the film was released, "*Sunset Boulevard* is that rare blend of pungent writing, expert acting, masterly direction and unobtrusive artistic photography which quickly casts a spell over an audience and holds it enthralled to a shattering climax."

In 1951, *Sunset Boulevard* received eleven Academy Award nominations: Best Picture (Charles Brackett), Best Director (Wilder), Best

Screenplay (Wilder, Brackett, and D. M. Marshman, Jr.), Best Actor (Holden), Best Actress (Swanson), Best Supporting Actor (Erich von Stroheim), Best Supporting Actress (Nancy Olson), Best Black-and-White Cinematography (John F. Seitz), Best Black-and-White Art Direction–Set Decoration (Sam Comer, Hans Dreier, John Meehan, and Ray Moyer), Best Original Score (Franz Waxman), and Best Film Editing (Duane Harrison and Arthur P. Schmidt). The film was awarded in only three categories, taking home Oscars for Best Screenplay, Best Art Direction–Set Decoration, and Best Original Score.

1. What actresses were offered the role of Norma Desmond before Gloria Swanson?

2. Cowriters Billy Wilder and Charles Brackett received an Academy Award nomination for Best Screenplay for *Sunset Boulevard*. This was the fifth time the duo was nominated for Best Screenplay. What are the other four films Wilder and Brackett received nominations for?

3. Prior to William Holden's involvement on the project, another actor was signed to play Joe Gillis. However, the actor backed out two weeks before filming was to begin, saying, "I don't think I can be convincing making love to a woman twice my age." Who is this actor?

4. Who directed the unreleased 1929 film that Norma and Joe screen, which features actress Gloria Swanson?

5. Joe and Betty discuss a screenplay about a couple who never sees each other. Although unfilmed, this screenplay actually exists. Who wrote it?

6. The initial cut of *Sunset Boulevard* opened with Joe Gillis lying in the morgue, talking with another corpse. Why was this scene cut?

7. The Desmond Mansion was located at 3810 Wilshire Boulevard in Los Angeles. In real life, who owned the mansion?

8. In early drafts of the screenplay, Joe Gillis's character had a different name. What was it?

9. The pool where Joe Gillis is found dead appears in another film, which was made five years after *Sunset Boulevard*. What is this film?

10. What is the name of Joe's baseball-themed screenplay?

11. What name does the film's cold-hearted producer character share with a cold-hearted executive in director Billy Wilder's *The Apartment* (1960)?

12. Billy Wilder was verbally attacked after a studio screening of

Sunset Boulevard. "You bastard," he was told. "You have disgraced the industry that made you and fed you! You should be tarred and feathered and run out of Hollywood!" Who said this?

13. In 1951, two films starring William Holden were nominated for Best Picture. One of them was *Sunset Boulevard.* What was the other film?

14. Cowriter D. M. Marshman, Jr., was a film critic. For what publication did Marshman write?

15. Who first suggested casting Gloria Swanson in the role of Norma Desmond?

16. Norma tells Joe, "I am big." What does she say "got small"?

17. Due to the nature of the picture, director Billy Wilder didn't want the studio to know anything about the film he was making. A nondescript shooting title was used to conceal the nature of the project. What was this?

18. When Max drives Norma onto the Paramount lot to speak with Cecil B. DeMille, her Isotta-Franschini is actually being pulled by a rope offscreen. Why was this done?

19. Cecil B. DeMille agreed to appear in *Sunset Boulevard* for ten thousand dollars. After shooting the scenes with DeMille in them, director Billy Wilder realized he needed another close-up. When he mentioned this to DeMille, the veteran director agreed to do the close-up for more money. How much money did DeMille request for the close-up?

20. When Norma visits Cecil B. DeMille on stage eighteen, he is shooting a film. What is this film?

21. *Sunset Boulevard* lost three Oscars—Best Picture, Best Director, and Best Supporting Actor—to the same film. What was this film?

22. What does Max say the Maharaja did with Norma's stockings?

23. What actor appears in *Sunset Boulevard* as Artie Green?

24. What headline does Joe envision regarding Norma's suicide?

25. In *Sunset Boulevard,* Cecil B. DeMille refers to Norma Desmond as "Young Fellow." This was a nickname DeMille had actually given to an actress while filming *Don't Change Your Husband* (1918). Who was this actress?

Quiz No. 13: The Bridge on the River Kwai (1957)

Screenplay by Pierre Boulle, Carl Foreman, and Michael Wilson
Directed by David Lean
Starring Alec Guiness, William Holden, and Sessue Hayakawa
Columbia Pictures

> ***My relationship with Mr. Lean was particularly good. Of necessity he is something of a solitary traveler in his profession. In his role of director, he sees not only the fragments which, woven together, make the whole composition of a film, but the entirety as well. We never found ourselves in opposition, but he was less than slightly beloved by some of his associates being boiled in the hot sun and infernal humidity.***
>
> —Actor Sessue Hayakawa

The Bridge on the River Kwai, David Lean's adaptation of Pierre Boulle's 1954 opus of the same title, examines the futility of war and the similarities between two seemingly different cultures. The film tells the story of British prisoners of war in World War II. The Japanese, led by Colonel Saito (Sessue Hayakawa), order the prisoners to construct a railway bridge under their supervision. After squaring off against their captors, the prisoners decide to take over the operation and show the Japanese just what British soldiers can do.

In 1957, *The Bridge on the River Kwai* received eight Academy Award nominations: Best Picture (Sam Spiegel), Best Director (Lean), Best Adapted Screenplay (Boulle), Best Actor (Alec Guiness), Best Supporting Actor (Hayakawa), Best Cinematography (Jack Hildyard), Best Film Editing (Peter Taylor), and Best Original Score (Malcolm Arnold). The film was awarded seven Oscars, losing only in its bid for Best Supporting Actor.

1. Novelist Pierre Boulle was the only credited screenwriter on

The Bridge on the River Kwai, despite his having nothing to do with the writing of the screenplay. Why is this?

2. Just before attaching himself to *The Bridge on the River Kwai,* director David Lean had worked on another project about a Japanese prisoner of war. An adaptation of a novel by Richard Mason, it was aborted. What is the name of this project?

3. Carl Foreman did not receive screenwriter credit on *The Bridge on the River Kwai,* causing him to petition the Writers Guild. According to director David Lean, how much of the finished script was written by Foreman?

4. What does Saito call "fruit juice of Scotland"?

5. Saito studied in Europe for three years. Where?

6. Three noted directors were offered *The Bridge on the River Kwai* before David Lean, and all of them declined. Who were they?

7. What is the name of the film's sequel starring Timothy Bottoms, Chris Penn, and George Takei?

8. What does Shears call the corrugated-metal box Nicholson is placed in?

9. Why didn't Alec Guiness attend the Academy Awards in 1957?

10. Why does Colonel Nicholson say his officers cannot perform manual labor?

11. What real-life British officer was Colonel Nicholson modeled after?

12. Alec Guiness claimed that David Lean greeted him at Colombo Airport by informing him that he'd wanted another actor for the role of Colonel Nicholson. Who was this actor?

13. Only two men remain from the original group of prisoners who built the camp. One of these is Shears. Who is the other prisoner?

14. Actor William Holden appears in four AFI Top 100 films. One of these is *The Bridge on the River Kwai.* What are the other three films?

15. What will Saito be forced to do if the bridge is not completed on time?

16. Nicholson says two things happen when an officer loses respect. What are these?

17. Although "The Colonel Bogey March" appears in the film, director David Lean had envisioned the soldiers whistling a different tune. However, producer Sam Spiegel could not secure the rights. What song was this?

18. What happens when the river's water level decreases?

19. Saito gives his prisoners a day of rest to honor the anniversary of a historical event. What is this?

20. Which of the following actors was not considered for the role of Shears: Humphrey Bogart, Cary Grant, or Marlon Brando?

21. Who does Shears say are two-of-a-kind, both "crazy with courage"?

22. Why did Shears trade uniforms with a dead officer?

23. While aiding Force 316, what is Shears's "simulated rank"?

24. Producer Sam Spiegel, director David Lean, and actor Alec Guiness would all reunite on another film five years later. What is this film?

25. Laurence Olivier was initially approached to play the role of Colonel Nicholson. However, Olivier turned down the project for another film. What is this film?

Quiz No. 14:
Some Like It Hot (1959)

Screenplay by I.A.L. Diamond and Billy Wilder
Directed by Billy Wilder
Starring Marilyn Monroe, Tony Curtis, and Jack Lemmon
United Artists

> ***I'm the only director who ever made two pictures with [Marilyn] Monroe. It behooves the Screen Directors Guild to award me a Purple Heart.***
> —Director Billy Wilder

Billy Wilder's outrageous comedy, *Some Like It Hot,* finds Joe (Tony Curtis) and Jerry (Jack Lemmon), two down-on-their-luck musicians, in the hot seat when they witness a gangland shooting. With the Mob on their trail, they disguise themselves as women and travel as part of an all-girl band. Soon, Joe falls for a gorgeous blonde named Sugar (Marilyn Monroe), who doesn't know he's a man. Meanwhile, Jerry has his own problems when he finds himself the object of another man's affections.

In 1960, *Some Like It Hot* received six Academy Award nominations: Best Director (Wilder), Best Adapted Screenplay (I.A.L. Diamond and Wilder), Best Actor (Lemmon), Best Black-and-White Cinematography (Charles Lang), Best Black-and-White Costume Design (Orry-Kelly), and Best Black-and-White Art Direction–Set Decoration (Edward G. Boyle and Ted Haworth). The film was awarded one Oscar for Orry-Kelly's costume designs.

1. What is the title of the German film *Some Like It Hot* is loosely based upon?
2. Who did actor Tony Curtis liken kissing Marilyn Monroe to?
3. In 1960, Jack Lemmon was nominated by the Academy for Best Actor for his turn in *Some Like It Hot*. This was one of eight Oscar

nominations Lemmon has received through the year 2001. What are the other seven films Lemmon has been nominated for?

4. What is the significance of George Raft's asking the coin-flipping thug in the film, "Where did you pick up that cheap trick?"

5. What was the film's working title?

6. Jack Lemmon won a Golden Globe Award for *Some Like It Hot*. The following year, Lemmon won the award again. What film did he receive this second Golden Globe Award for?

7. What is the film's famous tagline?

8. What is the name of the agency operated by Sid Poliakoff?

9. Joe suggests that he and Jerry pawn their coats to place a bet on a greyhound. What is the name of this dog?

10. The scene in which Spats threatens to stuff a grapefruit into one of the goons' faces was lifted from another film. What was the film?

11. *Some Like It Hot* was the second film actress Marilyn Monroe appeared in for director Billy Wilder. What was the first?

12. Where is the Valentine's Day dance Joe and Jerry are hired to perform at?

13. What number is Daphne's berth on the train?

14. Director Billy Wilder came quite close to casting a famous musician in the role of Jerry. After this musician failed to show up for a lunch with Wilder, the director nixed the idea. Who was this?

15. Sugar asks Joe whether water polo is dangerous. What is his response?

16. Billy Wilder and cinematographer Charles Lang collaborated on four films. One of these is *Some Like It Hot*. What are the other three films?

17. Osgood introduces himself as Osgood Fielding the Third. Who does Daphne jokingly introduce herself as?

18. What does Sugar conclude millionaires get weak eyes from reading?

19. In one scene, Jerry imitates actor Cary Grant's voice. However, this never could have happened in real life. Why?

20. Marilyn Monroe was not Billy Wilder's first choice for the role of Sugar. Who was?

21. How many takes were required for Marilyn Monroe to correctly recite the simple line, "It's me, Sugar"?

22. What does Joe say he would do if he weren't a coward?

23. What city does Daphne say she wouldn't be caught dead in?

24. When Jerry asks why a man would want to marry another man, what is Joe's one-word response?

25. Actors Tony Curtis and Jack Lemmon appear together in three films. One of these is *Some Like It Hot.* What are the other two films?

Quiz No. 15: STAR WARS (1977)

Screenplay by George Lucas
Directed by George Lucas
Starring Mark Hamill, Harrison Ford, Alec Guiness, and Carrie Fisher
Twentieth Century–Fox

> ***We'd come into a scene and we're faced with dialogue straight from Buck Rogers. I mean, I used to threaten George [Lucas] with tying him up and making him repeat his own dialogue!***
>
> —ACTOR HARRISON FORD

A mixture of 1950s sci-fi serials and Errol Flynn swashbuckling tales, George Lucas's *Star Wars* is the story of an adventure-seeking farm boy named Luke Skywalker (Mark Hamill). With two droid robots and a wise sage known as Obi-Wan Kenobi (Alec Guiness) for traveling companions, Skywalker soon finds himself in the middle of a war between rebel forces and an evil emperor who is constructing a space station capable of destroying entire planets. Along the way, Skywalker finds unlikely friendship in a bootlegger named Han Solo (Harrison Ford), and falls in love with a beautiful princess named Leia (Carrie Fisher).

In 1978, *Star Wars* received ten Academy Award nominations: Best Picture (Gary Kurtz), Best Director (Lucas), Best Original Screenplay (Lucas), Best Supporting Actor (Guiness), Best Art Direction–Set Decoration (John Barry, Roger Christian, Leslie Dilley, and Norman Reynolds), Best Costume Design (John Mollo), Best Visual Effects (Robert Blalack, John Dykstra, Richard Edlund, Grant McCune, and John Stears), Best Film Editing (Richard Chew, Paul Hirsch, and Marcia Lucas), Best Sound (Derek Ball, Don MacDougall, Bob Minkler, and Ray West), and Best Original Score (John Williams). The film was awarded six Oscars, losing in its bids for Best Picture, Best Director, Best Screenplay, and Best Supporting Actor.

1. What Akira Kurosawa film does George Lucas credit as the inspiration for *Star Wars*?

2. During the final battle, the radio asks, "Red Six, can you see Red Five?" Red Six promptly answers. What's wrong with his response?

3. When Han and Luke dress as stormtroopers to transfer Chewbacca, what is the cell-block number where the wookie is being kept, and what is its significance?

4. When rereleased, what was added to the crawling text at the beginning of the film?

5. Denis Lawson, the actor who plays Wedge Antilles, is the uncle of what actor?

6. What was Luke's surname in early drafts of the screenplay?

7. What did George Lucas add to the cantina gunfight for the 1997 special edition?

8. In 1980, Roger Corman produced a *Star Wars* knockoff, which was written by John Sayles and features actors Robert Vaughn, John Saxon, and Sybil Danning. What is the name of this similarly titled imitation?

9. Inside the Death Star, Han comments that they should be able to escape if they can "avoid any more" what?

10. What is the name of the campy 1978 *Star Wars* television special directed by Steve Binder, significant because it features the first appearance of the character Boba Fett?

11. Han brags about having made the Kessel Run in less than twelve parsecs. By definition, what's wrong with this statement?

12. When R2D2 and Chewbacca are playing chess, C3PO offers his sidekick some advice. What is it?

13. Princess Leia's home planet is destroyed before her eyes. What is the name of this planet?

14. What does Ben say his experience has taught him about luck?

15. What are the names of Luke's aunt and uncle on Tatooine?

16. James Earl Jones supplied the voice for Darth Vader, but who wore the suit?

17. In what two non–*Star Wars* films do actors James Earl Jones and Harrison Ford appear together?

18. What language does Luke's uncle inquire if C3PO can speak?

19. What are the small hooded creatures who sell the droids to Luke and his uncle called?

20. In what wars did Anakin and Obi-Wan fight together?

21. In the rereleased special edition of the film, what crew member appears in an uncredited cameo as a stormtrooper?

22. What does Han conclude that "hokey religions and ancient weapons" are no match for?

23. What vehicle does Luke say he drove when he wanted to "bull's-eye womp rats"?

24. What is the name of the spaceport where Ben and Luke meet Han?

25. Today, actress Carrie Fisher is a respected screenwriter. What George Lucas–produced project was Fisher hired to write?

Quiz No. 16:
All About Eve (1950)

Screenplay by Joseph L. Mankiewicz
Directed by Joseph L. Mankiewicz
Starring Bette Davis, Anne Baxter, and George Sanders
Twentieth Century–Fox

> ***Dear boy, have you gone mad? This woman will destroy you. She will grind you down to a fine powder and blow you away. You are a writer, dear boy. She will come to the stage with a thick pad of long yellow paper. And pencils. She will write. And then she, not you, will direct. Mark my words.***
>
> —EDMUND GOULDING'S WARNING TO JOSEPH MANK-IEWICZ REGARDING BETTE DAVIS

All About Eve follows the story of a fading theater star named Margo Channing (Bette Davis) and Eve Harrington (Anne Baxter), her biggest fan. The calculating Eve lands a job as Margo's understudy after working her way into the actress's life. When Margo inevitably misses a performance, theater critic Addison DeWitt (George Sanders) praises the young starlet, Eve, while writing scathing remarks about the aged Margo. Addison soon becomes Eve's mentor, but also begins to see through her treachery and deceit.

In 1951, *All About Eve* received fourteen Academy Award nominations: Best Picture (Darryl F. Zanuck), Best Director (Joseph L. Mankiewicz), Best Screenplay (Mankiewicz), Best Actress (Davis), Best Actress (Baxter), Best Supporting Actor (Sanders), Best Supporting Actress (Celeste Holm), Best Supporting Actress (Thelma Ritter), Best Black-and-White Cinematography (Milton R. Krasner), Best Original Score (Alfred Newman), Best Black-and-White Art Direction–Set Decoration (George W. Davis, Thomas Little, Walter M. Scott, and Lyle R. Wheeler), Best Black-and-White Costume Design (Edith Head and Charles La Maire), Best Film Editing (Barbara McLean), and Best Sound (individual recipient not specified). The film was awarded six

Oscars for Best Picture, Best Director, Best Screenplay, Best Black-and-White Costume Design, Best Sound, and Best Supporting Actor.

1. What is the name of the radio play, written by Mary Orr, that *All About Eve* is based upon?
2. What was the film's working title?
3. The clinging sweater-dress Marilyn Monroe wears in the hotel sequence belonged to the actress. In fact, she had already worn it in two films. What were these?
4. *All About Eve* was nominated for fourteen Oscars. Through 2001, only one other film has been nominated as many times. What is this film?
5. The film depicts a rivalry between an older actress, played by Bette Davis, and a young newcomer, played by Anne Baxter. Ironically, in a case of life imitating art, Davis was later replaced on a project by Baxter. What was this project?
6. What actress was initially cast as Margo Channing?
7. In 1970, *All About Eve* was adapted into the successful Broadway musical *Applause*, featuring Lauren Bacall as Margo Channing. When Bacall left the show, who took over the role?
8. The film's editor, Barbara McLean, was a standout editor and pioneer who was nominated for seven Academy Awards. How many times did McLean and director Joseph L. Mankiewicz work together?
9. *All About Eve* has been praised as one of the finest screenplays ever written. How long did it take Joseph L. Mankiewicz to write it?
10. What actor does Bill conclude that everyone cannot be?
11. What role does Addison DeWitt say Margo was unforgettable as, and must soon play again?
12. How many AFI Top 100 films does actress Marilyn Monroe appear in?
13. What name does Bill say he's never been called?
14. Director Joseph L. Mankiewicz cast Marilyn Monroe after seeing her in another film. What was this film?
15. What does Margo suggest Eve put where her heart once was?
16. What actor receives screen credit, but does not appear in *All About Eve*?
17. Who did producer Darryl F. Zanuck want cast in the role of Addison DeWitt?
18. What does Margo say Bill did five years ago, and will do twenty years from now, causing her to say, "I hate men"?

19. How much was Marilyn Monroe paid for her brief appearance in the film?

20. Mary Orr had patterned the character Margo Channing after a real spot-stealing Broadway actress. Who was this?

21. Margo made her stage debut at the age of four. What was the play in which she appeared?

22. Who proclaims himself "essential to the theater"?

23. In 1951, Joseph L. Mankiewicz's *All About Eve* screenplay was published by Random House. What is the significance of this?

24. When does Karen Richards say she developed her cynicism?

25. Eight years after *All About Eve* was released, *The New York Times* erroneously reported: PRODUCER JOSEPH L. MANKIEWICZ KILLED IN CRASH. Mankiewicz said the newspaper's reporting him as dead didn't bother him, but something else did. What was this?

Quiz No. 17:
The African Queen (1951)

Screenplay by James Agee and John Huston
Directed by John Huston
Starring Humphrey Bogart, Katharine Hepburn, and Robert Morley
United Artists

> ***They weren't sure who they were going to have for the man. At first, John [Huston] felt it should be an authentic cockney. But when they began to think of Bogie, there was no one who could compete with him in personality or looks. They had him be a Canadian. Can you imagine anyone else in that part? He was perfection.***
>
> —Actress Katharine Hepburn

In their only pairing, Humphrey Bogart and Katharine Hepburn turn in rich, powerful performances, displaying a strong chemistry in director John Huston's *The African Queen*. The film—the story of two unlikely traveling companions, Charlie and Rose, who find themselves first in a battle of wills, and later in love, fighting for their lives—was adapted from C. S. Forester's novel of the same title. Screenwriters James Agee and Huston deftly combine humor, romance, and adventure.

In 1952, *The African Queen* received four Academy Award nominations: Best Director (Huston), Best Screenplay (Agee and Huston), Best Actor (Bogart), and Best Actress (Hepburn). The film received only one Oscar, awarded for Bogart's performance. (The award would be the only Oscar of Bogart's career.)

1. What is the name of Rose's brother?
2. *The African Queen* was the first of three John Huston–directed films actor Robert Morley appears in. What are the two subsequent films?
3. Charlie reads a newspaper advertisement for a humorous product. What is the name of this product?

4. What does Rose offer as proof that God has not forsaken East Africa?

5. What does Rose pour into the river, infuriating Charlie?

6. *The African Queen* was remade for television in 1977. In this remake, what actor appears in the role of Charlie Allnut?

7. Where is the German fort with the sharpshooting guards located?

8. When Charlie advises, "Don't wear yourself out," what is Rose doing?

9. How does Rose's brother die?

10. How many cigarettes does Charlie say he has onboard the African Queen?

11. How does Charlie think his "dear old mother" would assess Rose?

12. Who does Rose accuse Charlie of failing to assist "in her hour of need"?

13. What does Charlie conclude to be the trouble with Rose?

14. What is the name of the German warship that patrols the river?

15. To what punishment do the Germans sentence Charlie and Rose?

16. Who was the first actor approached to play Charlie?

17. Who did director John Huston tell Katharine Hepburn to model Rose's behavior after?

18. What is Charlie's motto?

19. When Charlie finally agrees to travel down the river, who does he say will be happy to see them coming?

20. What is the name of the church were Charlie finds Rose?

21. Bette Davis was offered the role of Rose twice. When she was first approached in 1938, David Niven was cast as her costar. Nine years later, she was approached again. What actor was cast to play Charlie this time?

22. What does Charlie believe Rose has ten of for each one of his?

23. Charlie explains that something has been dropped down the steam-pump safety valve. What was it?

24. What river does Charlie call "death a dozen times over"?

25. Katharine Hepburn appears in four AFI Top 100 films. One of them is *The African Queen*. What are the other three films?

Quiz No. 18:
Psycho
(1960)

Screenplay by Joseph Stefano
Directed by Alfred Hitchcock
Starring Anthony Perkins, Janet Leigh, and Vera Miles
Paramount Pictures

> ***I believe that every audience wants to grab on to somebody almost from the first frame; they want to care about someone. And in this film, it was going to be this young woman who steals the forty thousand dollars and then is killed unexpectedly. This was the shocker.***
>
> —Screenwriter Joseph Stefano

Based on Robert Bloch's novel of the same title, Alfred Hitchcock's *Psycho* is the story of two people, both desperate to escape the realities of their lives. Tired of the hand life has dealt her, Marion Crane (Janet Leigh) steals forty thousand dollars from the real-estate office she works in and takes to the road. Overcome by fatigue, Marion pulls into the dilapidated Bates Motel. Finding that she's the motel's lone tenant, she agrees to have dinner with the manager, a troubled young man named Norman Bates (Anthony Perkins). After dinner and a little conversation, the exhausted Marion goes back to her room for a shower . . .

In 1961, *Psycho* received four Academy Award nominations: Best Director (Hitchcock), Best Supporting Actress (Leigh), Best Black-and-White Cinematography (John L. Russell), and Best Black-and-White Art Direction–Set Decoration (Robert Clatworthy, Joseph Hurley, and George Milo). *Psycho* lost in all four categories.

1. In 1987, the pilot for a *Psycho*-related television series aired on NBC. However, the show was never picked up. What is the name of this pilot?
2. What is Norman Bates's middle name?
3. Three years after making *Psycho,* Alfred Hitchcock approached screenwriter Joseph Stefano to pen the screenplay for another film.

However, Stefano passed, saying he had no interest in this project. What film was this?

4. How many cabins are there at the Bates Motel?

5. What actress appears in the film as Caroline?

6. What did director Alfred Hitchcock insert into the final shot of the film?

7. How was the sound of a blade penetrating human flesh simulated?

8. What did Alfred Hitchcock substitute for blood during the famed shower scene?

9. Why does Caroline believe Cassidy didn't flirt with her?

10. Marion's license plate reads "NFB418." What is the significance of the first three letters?

11. Who makes an uncredited cameo appearance as a prison guard?

12. How did Norman's mother die?

13. Under what identity does Marion register at the motel?

14. What does Norman say a son is "a poor excuse for"?

15. Actor Viggo Mortensen appears in the 1998 remake of *Psycho*. That same year, Mortensen appeared in another remake of an Alfred Hitchcock classic. What is this film?

16. In one scene, a man wearing a cowboy hat stands outside the realty office. Who is this?

17. Robert Bloch's novel *Psycho* is loosely based upon real-life serial killer Ed Gein. In 1974, another film based upon Gein's story was produced. What is this film?

18. Censors asked director Alfred Hitchcock to remove one word from *Psycho*. What is this word?

19. What is the room number where Marion and Sam meet?

20. *Psycho* was the second Alfred Hitchcock–directed film actress Vera Miles appeared in. What was the first?

21. What is the newspaper that Marion purchases?

22. Two prominent *Psycho* cast members reprised their roles in *Psycho II* (1983). One of them is Anthony Perkins. Who is the other?

23. Where does the police officer suggest Marion might be safer?

24. What is Arbogast's first name?

25. What does Sam notice missing from cabin one at the Bates Motel?

Quiz No. 19: Chinatown (1974)

Screenplay by Robert Towne
Directed by Roman Polanski
Starring Jack Nicholson, Faye Dunaway, and John Huston
Paramount Pictures

> *I finished the film and I looked at the rough cut, and as usual the rough cut is this very depressing moment for a director. And a director who does not have experience with it is close to suicide at that stage. But even knowing that very difficult moment would pass, I still was tremendously depressed seeing the rough cut. I showed it to a friend of mine . . . and was so ashamed when the lights came up. And he said, "What a great movie!" I said, "Is there something wrong with him?" I truly didn't think that he could be right.*
>
> —Director Roman Polanski

In 1973, screenwriter Robert Towne was offered $175,000 by Paramount Pictures to pen an adaptation of F. Scott Fitzgerald's *The Great Gatsby*. However, Towne was already working on a pet project he called *Chinatown,* and he convinced Paramount to purchase it for a meager $25,000. *Chinatown* is a modern-day film noir, which pays homage to the hard-boiled detective films of the past, combining mystery, suspense, humor, and romance. The film also marked the return of director Roman Polanski after a five-year hiatus.

In 1975, *Chinatown* received eleven Academy Award nominations: Best Picture (Robert Evans), Best Director (Polanski), Best Original Screenplay (Towne), Best Actor (Jack Nicholson), Best Actress (Faye Dunaway), Best Cinematography (John A. Alonzo), Best Art Direction–Set Decoration (W. Stewart Campbell, Ruby R. Levitt, and Richard Sylbert), Best Costume Design (Anthea Sylbert), Best Film Editing (Sam O'Steen), Best Original Score (Jerry Goldsmith), and Best Sound (Charles Grenzbach and Lawrence Jost). The film received only one Oscar, awarded to screenwriter Towne.

1. The film's assistant director is the son of a famous screenwriter. Who is this?

2. What is the name of Jake's detective agency?

3. *Chinatown* is one of three AFI Top 100 films screenwriter Robert Towne contributed to. What are the other two films?

4. What is the name of *Chinatown*'s sequel?

5. What actress was initially considered for the role of Evelyn Mulwray?

6. According to director Roman Polanski, producer Bob Evans didn't want actress Faye Dunaway cast for the role of Evelyn Mulwray. Why?

7. At one point, Jake tells Curly, "I only brought it up to illustrate a point." Because this was a reference to dialogue that had been cut from the film, this doesn't make much sense. What was the dialogue that had been cut here?

8. Roman Polanski and screenwriter Robert Towne stopped talking after *Chinatown* because of their many artistic disagreements. However, the two later patched things up and collaborated on a film in 1988. What is this film?

9. Two screenwriters wrote the film's final scene. Robert Towne was not one of them. Who were they?

10. *Chinatown* is one of five films actor Jack Nicholson and screenwriter Robert Towne collaborated on. What are the other four films?

11. A hood slices Jake's nose open. Who is the actor who plays the hood?

12. What 1969 event led to director Roman Polanski's five-year hiatus prior to *Chinatown*?

13. The undertaker says that Hollis Mulwray's death is rather ironic. How so?

14. There is one word Evelyn Mulwray says she dislikes. What is this?

15. John Huston appears in the film as Noah Cross. In 1985, actor Jack Nicholson would appear in another film with Huston. What is this film?

16. In a scene cut from the film, Jake travels to Noah Cross's home by seaplane. During the flight, the pilot drops a few hints regarding Evelyn Mulwray's troubled past. What veteran actor played the pilot?

17. How does Jake tell Yelburton he injured his nose?

18. *Chinatown* is one of three AFI Top 100 films actress Faye Dunaway appears in. What are the other two films?

19. What does Jake say is unusual concerning Jasper Lamar Crabb's recent land purchase?

20. Screenwriter Robert Towne and director Roman Polanski had a huge argument regarding the film's ending. In the film, Evelyn is killed in front of her daughter, Katherine. In Towne's original screenplay, how did the film end?

21. Three years after directing *Chinatown*, Roman Polanski fled the United States when he was charged with a crime, and he has never returned. What was the crime Polanski was charged with?

22. What are Walsh's final words to Jake?

23. What is the shiny object Jake sees in Evelyn Mulwray's fish pond?

24. In a scene cut from the film, Noah Cross says, "[I] love the smell of it. A lot of people do, but of course they won't admit it." What is Cross referring to?

25. Where does Evelyn shoot her father?

Quiz No. 20:
One Flew Over the Cuckoo's Nest (1975)

Screenplay by Bo Goldman and Lawrence Hauben
Directed by Milos Forman
Starring Jack Nicholson, Louise Fletcher, and William Redfield
United Artists

> ***The secret to** Cuckoo's Nest, **and it's not in the book . . . my secret design for it was this guy's a scamp who knows he's irresistable to women and in reality expects Nurse Ratched to be seduced by him. This is his tragic flaw. This is why he ultimately fails.***
>
> —Actor Jack Nicholson

Based on Ken Kesey's best-selling novel, director Milos Forman's *One Flew Over the Cuckoo's Nest* is a touching, and at times outrageously funny, indictment of mental institutions in the 1960s and those who cared for the patients. In what is arguably his best performance, Jack Nicholson's over-the-top Randle Patrick McMurphy is easily one of American cinema's most colorful and memorable characters. Not quite sane, yet not quite nuts, McMurphy's observations are dead-on in their accuracy and poignancy.

In 1976, *One Flew Over the Cuckoo's Nest* received nine Academy Award nominations: Best Picture (Saul Zaentz and Michael Douglas), Best Director (Forman), Best Adapted Screenplay (Bo Goldman and Lawrence Hauben), Best Actor (Nicholson), Best Actress (Louise Fletcher), Best Supporting Actor (Brad Dourif), Best Cinematography (Bill Butler and Haskell Wexler), Best Film Editing (Richard Chew, Sheldon Kahn, and Lynzee Klingman), and Best Original Score (Jack Nitzsche). The film was awarded five Oscars and was the first film in forty years to sweep all five of the major categories.

1. What well-known actor served as a producer on *One Flew Over the Cuckoo's Nest*?

2. Who appears in a brief cameo as the boat's captain onshore?

3. What actor was first offered the role of McMurphy?

4. At the 1976 Academy Awards, *One Flew Over the Cuckoo's Nest* triumped in the five most significant categories (Best Picture, Best Director, Best Screenplay, Best Actor, and Best Actress); it was only the second film to accomplish this feat. What was the first?

5. Before it was filmed, Ken Kesey's novel was first adapted into a stage play. What well-known actor originated the role of McMurphy on Broadway?

6. What did author Ken Kesey say about the film after viewing it for the first time?

7. *One Flew Over the Cuckoo's Nest* was filmed on location in a real mental institution. Where was this institution located?

8. How old is Randle Patrick McMurphy?

9. What future director appears in the role of Martini?

10. McMurphy was charged with statutory rape. How old was the girl he slept with?

11. What is McMurphy's argument to justify his five fistfights?

12. What does McMurphy say he doesn't want slipped into his medications?

13. When McMurphy and Nurse Ratched square off over the television, what does McMurphy want to watch?

14. Actors Jack Nicholson and Danny DeVito appear in five films together. One of these is *One Flew Over the Cuckoo's Nest*. What are the other four films?

15. What nickname is Harding given?

16. Of the eighteen patients, how many votes does McMurphy receive in the second vote to change the television channel (excluding the Chief, whose vote doesn't count)?

17. What type of game does McMurphy say Nurse Ratched likes?

18. What's the name of the prostitute McMurphy picks up on the outing?

19. Who does McMurphy convince the harbor manager that the escaped patients are?

20. On their outing, McMurphy tells Martini that he's no longer a "goddamn looney." What does McMurphy say he now is?

21. After breaking the windows, what does McMurphy take from the nurse's station?

22. Who does McMurphy sneak into the hospital for a party?

23. Actors Christopher Lloyd, Jack Nicholson, and Danny DeVito all reunited on another project in 1978. What is this film?

24. Scatman Crothers and Jack Nicholson appear together in four films. One of these is *One Flew Over the Cuckoo's Nest*. What are the other three films?

25. McMurphy tells Chief Bromden that basketball is an old Indian game. What does he say it's called?

Quiz No. 21:
THE GRAPES OF WRATH (1940)

Screenplay by Nunnally Johnson
Directed by John Ford
Starring Henry Fonda, Jane Darwell, and John Carradine
Twentieth Century–Fox

> ***I was only interested in the Joad family as characters. I was sympathetic to people like the Joads, and contributed a lot of money to them, but I was not interested in* Grapes *as a social study. I admire John Steinbeck and enjoyed working on it. I bucked to do that picture and put everything I had into it. Before all else, it is the story of a family, the way it reacts, how it is shaken by a serious problem which overwhelms it. It is not a social film on this problem, it's a study on a family.***
>
> —DIRECTOR JOHN FORD

Film critic Andrew Sarris once called John Ford's *The Grapes of Wrath* the film "that was singlehandedly to transform [Ford] from a storyteller of the screen to America's cinematic poet laureate." *The Grapes of Wrath* tells the story of Oklahoman Tom Joad (Henry Fonda), who returns home after four years to find his homeland ravaged by the Depression. When the Joads lose their home, they pack up their belongings and begin a long, arduous trek across the country to California in search of a better life. Along the way, the family is faced with many trials and tribulations, but refuses to give up.

In 1941, *The Grapes of Wrath* received seven Academy Award nominations: Best Picture (Nunnally Johnson and Darryl F. Zanuck), Best Director (Ford), Best Screenplay (Nunnally Johnson), Best Actor (Fonda), Best Supporting Actress (Jane Darwell), Best Film Editing (Robert L. Simpson), and Best Sound (Edmund H. Hansen). The film won two Oscars, awarded for Best Director and Best Supporting Actress.

1. When Tom tries to hitch a ride at the beginning of the film, the driver points to a decal. What does the decal say?

2. Tom has been away for four years. Where has he been?

3. What does Tom observe that the driver is "about to bust a gut" to know?

4. When Casey was a minister, what does he say he saw women as?

5. In 1938, actor Charlie Grapewin announced his retirement. However, he was convinced to work for one week on another film. This soon lead to more projects, including *The Grapes of Wrath*. What was the film Grapewin had returned to work on initially?

6. What are referred to as "the cats"?

7. Who calls himself "an old-graveyard ghost"?

8. Tom remembers his mother beating a peddler. What did she beat him with?

9. How many workers does the handbill advertise as being wanted in California?

10. Upon first seeing him, what does each of Tom's relatives ask him?

11. What's the name of Sharon's husband?

12. *The Grapes of Wrath* was remade as a made-for-television movie in 1991. In this telefilm, what actor appears as Tom Joad?

13. What does Casey believe will be a "miracle out of scripture"?

14. What is Grandpa's coffee spiked with to make him more tolerant of the trip?

15. What kind of man does Tom conclude that the government often cares the most about?

16. Who does Mrs. Joad say "sure sings purty"?

17. Actor Henry Fonda and director John Ford collaborated on nine films. *The Grapes of Wrath* is one of these. What are the other eight films?

18. What four varieties of pie are available at the gas station where the Joads stop to purchase bread?

19. Why does the gas-station attendant say the Joads "got a lot of nerve"?

20. One character observes that a "human being couldn't live the way they do." Who is this character referring to?

21. One year before the release of *The Grapes of Wrath,* audiences were treated to another film directed by John Ford and featuring actors Henry Fonda, John Carradine, and Ward Bond. What is this film?

22. When Grandma gets sick, who does she repeatedly ask for?

23. A policeman says, "If I've seen one of those things, I've seen ten thousand." What is he referring to?

24. Casey and Tom knock out a policeman at the transient camp. Why?

25. During his eulogy for Grandpa, who does Casey suggest prayers should be said for?

Quiz No. 22:
2001: A Space Odyssey (1968)

Screenplay by Arthur C. Clarke and Stanley Kubrick
Directed by Stanley Kubrick
Starring Keir Dullea, William Sylvester, and Leonard Rossiter
Metro-Goldwyn-Mayer

> ***I tried to create a visual experience, one that bypasses verbalized pigeonholing and directly penetrates the subconscious with an emotional and philosophical content. I intended the film to be an intensely subjective experience that reaches the viewer at an inner level of consciousness, just as music does. You're free to speculate as you wish about the philosophical and allegorical meaning of the film.***
>
> —Director Stanley Kubrick

Based on a short story by Arthur C. Clarke, director Stanley Kubrick's *2001* is a masterpiece that is unlike any film made before or since. "While reviewers will try to lend answers and interpretation to *2001,* it is ultimately a very personal film to many," *BBC Online* critic Almar Haflidason observes. "Its triumph lies in its scope of cinematic splendor and the attempt to marry some of man's most beautiful music to the infinite mystery of space."

In 1969, *2001: A Space Odyssey* received four Academy Award nominations: Best Director (Kubrick), Best Original Screenplay (Kubrick and Clarke), Best Effects (Kubrick), and Best Art Direction–Set Decoration (Ernest Archer, Harry Lange, and Anthony Masters). The film won only one Oscar, awarded for Best Effects.

1. What is the title of the unpublished short story by Arthur C. Clarke on which the film is based?
2. What are the three titled sections of *2001*?

3. What Richard Strauss arrangement does the film open with?

4. What composer was initially hired to score the film?

5. In both Stanley Kubrick's screenplay and the subsequent novel by Arthur C. Clarke, HAL's birthdate is January 12, 1997. However, a different date appears in the film. What is this?

6. What Pink Floyd song was deliberately timed and arranged to synchronize with the fourth segment of *2001*?

7. Who appears in a brief cameo as Dr. Floyd's daughter?

8. What is the Jupiter explorer's serial number?

9. In the film's sequel, *2010* (1984), the American president and the Russian premier are shown on the cover of *Time* magazine. Who are the two men who appear as the U.S. president and the Russian premier?

10. In Arthur C. Clarke's novel, what is the name of the man-ape played by Michael Richter in the film?

11. In what book can readers learn how to use the zero-gravity toilet shown in *2001*?

12. What is Dr. Floyd the chairman of?

13. What is the British news program that the astronauts watch in space?

14. The blue spacesuit is the only suit not used in either *2001* or *2010.* However, it was later used in two episodes of a sci-fi television series. One of the episodes is titled, "War Without End." What is this television series?

15. When an astronaut is in hibernation, how many times per minute does his heart beat?

16. When the letters of HAL's name are extrapolated, what do they become?

17. HAL's name was derived from two words. What are they?

18. When HAL discovers the malfunction in the AE35 component, how many hours does it conclude will pass before reaching 100-percent failure?

19. The chess moves shown in the film were taken from a famed real-life match. What was this match?

20. How many days was Nicholas Rain, the actor who voiced HAL, present on the set of *2001*?

21. Before his dialogue was replaced, another actor had read HAL's lines. Who was this?

22. Under what false pretenses do Dave and Frank attempt to speak where HAL cannot hear them?

23. What, according to Frank, sounds like famous last words?

24. While Dave is outside the ship, what does HAL "terminate" inside?

25. Where is the HAL plant located?

Quiz No. 23:
The Maltese Falcon (1941)

Screenplay by John Huston
Directed by John Huston
Starring Humphrey Bogart, Mary Astor, and Gladys George
Warner Bros.

> ***Is there any chance we can get Dashiell Hammett to write a sequel to*** **The Maltese Falcon?** ***What I mean by this is can he take all the characters, with the exception naturally of Mary Astor, as she is supposed to receive a death sentence, and go right from the end of our picture. If Hammett would be interested in this type of proposition, let me know quick. We would use Bogart, [Sidney] Greenstreet, and the rest of [the] cast. However, we don't want to interfere with Hammett's adaptation of*** **Watch on Rhine.** ***This can all happen afterwards.***
> —Memo from Jack Warner to New York Story Editor Jacob Wilk

Based on the novel by Dashiell Hammett, John Huston's *The Maltese Falcon* is the story of a gumshoe named Sam Spade (Humphrey Bogart) who becomes a murder suspect when his partner, Miles, is slain following a lead. In trying to clear his name, Spade becomes entangled in a web of lies and deceit when he meets three parties who will each stop at nothing to obtain a priceless golden statue. *Movie Review UK* critic Damian Cannon observes, "For those who like to dissect the enchantment of cinema . . . any film can be boiled down to a marriage of precursor elements. To create a film, merely mix together the necessary quantities of action, image, dialogue, and montage. That's one argument. On the other hand, there's *The Maltese Falcon,* a movie in which these ingredients are inextricably bound, linked together at every level. Sure, the film is superb in each of these individual areas, but it is in their synthesis that *The Maltese Falcon* becomes great."

In 1942, *The Maltese Falcon* received three Academy Award nominations: Best Picture (Hal B. Wallace), Best Screenplay (Huston), and

Best Supporting Actor (Sydney Greenstreet). However, the film was awarded no Oscars.

1. Dashiell Hammett's novel had already been adapted twice. What two actors appeared as detective Sam Spade in these earlier versions?

2. In 1942, Mary Astor was not nominated for her performance in *The Maltese Falcon*. However, she won Best Supporting Actress for her turn in another film. What is this film?

3. George Raft was originally cast as Sam Spade but declined to make the film. Why?

4. What actor appears in a cameo as Captain Jacobi?

5. The 1936 adaptation of this story, *Satan Met a Lady*, and *The Maltese Falcon* share one primary production-crew member. Who was this?

6. One year after making *The Maltese Falcon*, director John Huston made another film featuring Humphrey Bogart, Mary Astor, Elisha Cook, Jr., Sydney Greenstreet, Walter Huston, and Peter Lorre. What is this film?

7. In the alley where Miles's body is found, a movie poster is visible on the brick wall behind the detectives. What film does it feature?

8. In the film, Wilmer is said to be a "gunsel." What is a gunsel?

9. Actors Sydney Greenstreet and Peter Lorre appear together in six films. One of these is *The Maltese Falcon*. What are the other five films?

10. In 1941, John Huston also wrote the screenplay for a film directed by Raoul Walsh that starred Humphrey Bogart. What is this film?

11. In what room at the Coronet Apartments is Ruth Wonderly staying in?

12. In Dashiell Hammett's novel, *The Maltese Falcon*, who is described as having the appearance of a "blond satan"?

13. Joel Cairo has a theater ticket in his pocket. What theater is the ticket for?

14. In what hotel is Joel Cairo staying?

15. As Spade leaves his office, the Bailey Theatre marquee is visible behind him. What film is advertised on the marquee?

16. When Cairo exclaims, "This is the second time you've laid hands on me," what is Sam Spade's infamous response?

17. In the earlier adaptation of *The Maltese Falcon*, *Satan Met a*

Lady, the characters are not chasing after a golden falcon. What are they instead chasing after?

18. As referenced in the quotation at the top of page 64, Warner Bros. was interested in filming a sequel to *The Maltese Falcon*. Production executives even came up with a title for this would-be sequel. What was the title?

19. What is the real name of the Fat Man?

20. In 1975, actors Elisha Cook, Jr., and Lee Patrick reprised their roles in a film Leonard Maltin describes as a "horrendously bad, unfunny takeoff on *The Maltese Falcon*." What is the name of this film?

21. On November 13, 1986, eighty-year-old director John Huston—sick and dying of emphysema—held a *Maltese Falcon*–related press conference. Why?

22. In what year is the golden bird said to have been created?

23. In what year did the Falcon "turn up again in Sicily"?

24. Who does Sam suggest as the logical fall guy for the murders?

25. Actor Ward Bond appears in seven AFI Top 100 films. One of these is *The Maltese Falcon*. What are the other six?

Quiz No. 24:
RAGING BULL (1980)

Screenplay by Mardik Martin and Paul Schrader
Directed by Martin Scorsese
Starring Robert De Niro, Joe Pesci, and Frank Vincent
United Artists

> ***When I saw the film I was upset. I kind of look bad in it. Then I realized it was true. That's the way it was. I was a no-good bastard.***
>
> —BOXER JAKE LA MOTTA

Director Martin Scorsese's biopic, *Raging Bull,* tells the story of boxer Jake La Motta's (Robert De Niro) ascent to stardom and his tragic undoing, caused by his paranoid obsession with his wife, an uncontrollable rage, and a self-destructive lifestyle. *Newsweek* film critic Jack Kroll praised "De Niro's great performance captures the humanity in the bull and the tragic excitement in his rage. . . . There is terror, irony, and a grim humor in De Niro's depiction."

In 1981, *Raging Bull* received eight Academy Award nominations: Best Picture (Irwin Winkler and Robert Chartoff), Best Director (Scorsese), Best Actor (De Niro), Best Supporting Actor (Joe Pesci), Best Supporting Actress (Cathy Moriarty), Best Cinematography (Michael Chapman), Best Film Editing (Thelma Schoonmaker), and Best Sound (David J. Kimball, Lee Lazarowitz, Donald O. Mitchell, and Bill Nicholson). The film won two Oscars, which were awarded to De Niro and Schoonmaker.

1. *Raging Bull* was the fourth collaboration between director Martin Scorsese and actor Robert De Niro. What were the three films the duo had already made together?
2. Who is the Mobster Salvy tries to convince Jake to let control his career?

3. Jake says he can't be the best because of his hands. What kind of hands does Jake say he has?

4. Robert De Niro and Martin Scorsese met at a Christmas party thrown by a mutual friend. Who was this person?

5. Who first suggested that Martin Scorsese adapt *Raging Bull*?

6. At one stage, Martin Scorsese envisioned adapting *Raging Bull* into both a film and a stage play. What was the proposed title of the project at this stage?

7. While playing miniature golf, Vickie loses her golf ball under a small church. She then asks Jake what this means. What is Jake's response?

8. What year is Jake's first match with Sugar Ray Robinson?

9. On Labor Day weekend, 1978, director Martin Scorsese was hospitalized after suffering a physical collapse. At this point, he still wasn't sure he wanted to make the film, but a close friend visited him, asking, "Can you live without making *Raging Bull*?" This conversation led to Scorsese's decision to make the film. Who was this friend?

10. After drafts of the screenplay had been written by Mardik Martin and Paul Schrader, the final draft was written by two screenwriters who did not receive credit. Who were these writers?

11. How does Jake contain his lust for Vickie during training?

12. Whose wedding was Jake and Vickie's rooftop ceremony modeled after?

13. After seeing them together in another film, director Martin Scorsese cast Joe Pesci and Frank Vincent in *Raging Bull*. What was the film Scorsese saw the two actors in?

14. After their fight, what does Jake boast that Janiro "ain't . . . no more"?

15. Where does the reconciliation occur that Tommy Como organizes between Joey and Salvo?

16. Who is the fight promoter for the Fox-Lamotta fight?

17. What scene was removed from Paul Schrader's screenplay to avoid an "X" rating?

18. When Jake asks Vickie where she's been, she says that she's been to the theater. What film did she see?

19. Martin Scorsese and editor Thelma Schoonmaker repeatedly studied a film directed by Michael Powell during editing. What is this film?

20. At the bar, how does Jake make two underaged girls prove that they're twenty-one?

21. How much money is Jake told he will need to bribe his way out of the charges against him?

22. What does Jake remove from his championship belt?

23. What writers' work is featured in *An Evening with Jake La Motta,* Jake LaMotta's nightclub act?

24. While *Raging Bull* was being filmed in 1979, another boxing film produced by Irwin Winkler was released. What is this film?

25. The film is dedicated to Haig P. Manoogian. Who is this?

Quiz No. 25:
E.T. The Extra-Terrestrial (1982)

Screenplay by Melissa Mathison
Directed by Steven Spielberg
Starring Dee Wallace Stone, Henry Thomas, and Peter Coyote
Universal Pictures

> ***E.T. is my most personal film, and my greatest gratification has been to see how the film and E.T. became so loved all over the world.***
> —Director Steven Spielberg

Steven Spielberg's *E.T. The Extra-Terrestrial* is the story of a ten-year-old boy named Elliot who makes an unusual friend when a group of aliens visits the earth, accidentally leaving one of their comrades stranded three million light-years from home. As Elliot and his new friend, E.T., learn to communicate with each other, they develop an unusually strong bond.

In 1983, *E.T.* received nine Academy Award nominations: Best Picture (Kathleen Kennedy and Spielberg), Best Director (Spielberg), Best Original Screenplay (Melissa Mathison), Best Cinematography (Allen Daviau), Best Sound-Effects Editing (Ben Burtt and Charles L. Campbell), Best Film Editing (Carol Littleton), Best Visual Effects (Dennis Muren, Carlo Rambaldi, and Kenneth Smith), Best Original Score (John Williams), and Best Sound (Gene S. Cantamessa, Don Digirolamo, Robert J. Glass, and Robert Knudson). The film was awarded four Oscars for its sound, score, and the two effects categories.

1. Michael, Steve, Greg, and Tyler play a game, but refuse to let Elliot play. What is the game they are playing?
2. What is the name of Elliot's dog?
3. What acclaimed screenwriter wrote an early unfilmed draft of *E.T.* entitled, *Night Skies*?

4. When Elliot first tells his family about the alien, no one believes him. Who does Elliot insist would believe him if he were present?

5. In a very blatant instance of product placement, Elliot feeds E.T. candy and a soft drink. What brands of candy and cola does he feed him?

6. What George Lucas–produced film is given a nod through Elliot's action figures, and later, through a neighbor's Halloween costume?

7. What does E.T. do to the dying geranium?

8. When E.T. downs a can of beer, what reaction does Elliot experience at school?

9. What is the name of the film starring John Wayne that E.T. watches on television?

10. What two *E.T.* costars would later pose nude in *Playboy*?

11. What does E.T. observe that makes him aware of the telephone?

12. What talking toy does the alien use to construct a communicator?

13. What does the sign on Elliot's door say?

14. What is the name of the scientist with the jingling keys?

15. In the boys' game, who is the Game Master, with absolute power?

16. What does E.T. observe, causing Elliot to kiss a girl at school?

17. What is the name of the documentarian who directed *The Making of* E.T. The Extra-Terrestrial (1996), as well as documentaries about the making of Steven Spielberg's *Jaws* (1975), *Close Encounters of the Third Kind* (1977), *1941* (1979), and *The Lost World* (1997)?

18. What does Elliot toss into the toolshed, only to see it thrown back?

19. Elliot's father is in Mexico with his girlfriend. What is her name?

20. How does Elliot fake sickness?

21. According to director Steven Spielberg, what is *E.T.* "really about"?

22. When Elliot explains the toy car to the alien, what does E.T. attempt to do?

23. Elliot's mother observes of his bedroom, "This is no room." What does she say it is?

24. What does Elliot do to the frogs at school?

25. What causes E.T. to throw a can of beer at the television screen?

Quiz #26:
Dr. Strangelove or: How I Learned to Stop Worrying and Love the Bomb (1964)

Screenplay by Stanley Kubrick, Terry Southern, and Peter George
Directed by Stanley Kubrick
Starring Peter Sellers, George C. Scott, and Sterling Hayden
Columbia Pictures

> [Columbia Pictures] *continued to distance itself from the film. Even when* Strangelove *received the infrequent good review, it dismissed the critic as a pinko nutcase, and on at least one occasion the publicity department defended the company against the film by saying it was definitely "not anti-U.S. military," but "just a zany novelty flick which did not reflect the views of the corporation in any way." This party line persisted, I believe, until about five years ago, when the Library of Congress announced that the film had been selected as one of the fifty greatest American films of all time . . . Who said satire was "something that closed Wednesday in Philadelphia"?*
>
> —Screenwriter Terry Southern

Dr. Strangelove is director Stanley Kubrick's provocative satire of life during the Cold War, examining those given the power to wage war with modern weapons of mass destruction. The film is a cynical parody of nuclear paranoia, as well as a frightening "what-if," depicting those final moments when the nation is put on red alert. As in *Lolita* (1962), which Kubrick directed two years prior, actor Peter Sellers appears in multiple roles, brilliant in each of them. As *Austin Chronicle* critic Jason Zech observes, "*Dr. Strangelove* is one of the funniest and most poignant political satires ever made. . . . And while there are several fine performances, Peter Sellers dominates the film in three different parts with true comic genius."

In 1965, *Dr. Strangelove* received four Academy Award nominations: Best Picture (Kubrick), Best Director (Kubrick), Best Adapted Screenplay (Kubrick, Terry Southern, and Peter George), and Best Actor (Sellers). Because of *Dr. Strangelove*'s reputation as being subversive, the film was awarded no Oscars.

1. *Dr. Strangelove* is an adaptation from a novel. What is the title of this novel?
2. Peter Sellers appears in three roles. What are they?
3. Screenwriter Terry Southern cowrote two AFI Top 100 films. One is *Dr. Strangelove*. What is the other?
4. What *Bonanza* regular was approached for the role of Major T. J. Kong?
5. On what island are the Russians developing the doomsday device?
6. The second H-bomb is labeled "Dear John." What was the bomb named in the original Peter George novel the film is adapted from, and why did director Stanley Kubrick opt to retitle it?
7. In the film, Peter Sellers appears in three roles. However, he was originally cast to appear in a fourth role. What was this role?
8. Stanley Kubrick originally intended to end the film with the Russians and the Americans battling in the War Room. In this scenario, what had Kubrick intended the two sides to use as weapons?
9. When Major Kong discusses the survival kit, the word "Las Vegas" was overdubbed in the film. What was the original location Kong mentioned, and why was it changed?
10. A director's trademark, the number 114 appears in most Stanley Kubrick films. Where does the number 114 rear its head in *Dr. Strangelove*?
11. At the end of the film, what Vera Lynn tune is played over various shots of explosions?
12. Who is the centerfold in Major Kong's *Playboy* magazine?
13. According to the narrator, how many megatons of bomb-load can each B-52 deliver?
14. What is Lieutenant Goldberg's nickname?
15. What Air Force base does General Ripper command?
16. According to the motto of the SAC, what is "our profession"?
17. What are the three rules General Ripper gives in his address?
18. Prior to *Dr. Strangelove*, director Stanley Kubrick worked for more than a year in preproduction on another film featuring Slim

Pickens. However, Kubrick was removed from the film and was replaced by actor Marlon Brando. What is this film?

19. Who did Clemenceau believe war was too important to be left to?

20. What is the title on the three-ring binder General Ripper has regarding bomb targets?

21. What nickname does Turgidson's secretary give him?

22. In 1968, Buck Henry, best known for writing *The Graduate* (1967), adapted a novel written by *Dr. Strangelove*–scribe Terry Southern. This film stars Marlon Brando, James Coburn, Richard Burton, and John Huston. What is the name of this film?

23. During production, director Stanley Kubrick said, "I feel like Elisha Cook in one of those early Warner films. You know, when you learn there's a contract out on you, and all you can do is wait for the hit. They're ruthless." To whom was Kubrick referring?

24. What does Ripper conclude that a "commie" will not drink?

25. In a scene cut from the film, Dr. Strangelove rises to his feet and proclaims, "Mein Führer, I can walk!" What does Strangelove then do?

Quiz No. 27: BONNIE AND CLYDE (1967)

Screenplay by David Newman and Robert Benton
Directed by Arthur Penn
Starring Warren Beatty, Faye Dunaway, and Michael J. Pollard
Warner Bros.

> ***You have to put the film in its proper social context. Young people were resisting the government, the draft, in a collective revolt, and they recognized themselves in Clyde Barrow and Bonnie Parker. That self-recognition swept the film along.*** —DIRECTOR ARTHUR PENN

Bonnie and Clyde was a highly controversial film when it was released in 1967. While updating the classic crime genre, it also set a new high-water mark for cinematic violence. The film follows two naive bandits who fall in love and get in way over their heads, becoming folk heroes along the way. While other films, such as *They Live by Night* (1967), had been made about the real-life duo, their story had never been told in such a way before. The film captured the imagination of an entire generation and paved the way for films such as *The Wild Bunch* (1969), released only two years later. *Chicago Sun-Times* critic Roger Ebert observes, "Today, the freshness of *Bonnie and Clyde* has been absorbed in countless other films, and it's hard to see how fresh and original it felt in 1967—just as the impact of *Citizen Kane,* in 1941, may not be obvious to those raised in the shadow of its influence."

In 1968, *Bonnie and Clyde* received ten Academy Award nominations: Best Picture (Warren Beatty), Best Director (Arthur Penn), Best Original Screenplay (Robert Benton and David Newman), Best Actor (Beatty), Best Actress (Faye Dunaway), Best Supporting Actor (Gene Hackman), Best Supporting Actor (Michael J. Pollard), Best Supporting Actress (Estelle Parsons), Best Cinematography (Burnett Guffey), and Best Costume Design (Theadora Van Runkle). The film was awarded two Oscars for Best Supporting Actress and Best Cinematography.

1. Complete this famous tagline: "They're young, they're in love, and . . ."
2. What acclaimed screenwriter performed an uncredited rewrite of the screenplay?
3. Cinematographer Burnett Guffey received his fifth Academy Award nomination for *Bonnie and Clyde,* winning his second Oscar. For what film did Guffey receive his first?
4. In 1990, actors Warren Beatty and Michael J. Pollard would reunite on another film. What is this film?
5. Who produced *Bonnie and Clyde*?
6. The character C. W. Moss is a composite of two real-life members of the Barrows Gang. Who are they?
7. What was actress Morgan Fairchild's involvement with *Bonnie and Clyde*?
8. Scenes containing sexual tension between two characters were ultimately excised from the script in its final draft. Which two characters was this sexual tension between?
9. One year after *Bonnie and Clyde* was released, a low-budget knockoff was produced. This film features narration by Burl Ives. What is the name of this film?
10. Clyde is attacked by a grocer while attempting a robbery. What weapon does the grocer wield?
11. When the Mineola bank manager climbs on to the running board of the Barrows Gang's car, he becomes Clyde's first murder victim. Where does Clyde shoot him?
12. What does C. W. Moss have tattooed on his chest?
13. What is the occupation of Blanche's father?
14. While shooting at bottles, Clyde says, "I'm not good." What does he say he is?
15. Why do the robbers leave the Farmers State Bank empty-handed?
16. Before he joins the Barrows Gang, what is C. W. Moss's occupation?
17. After Clyde shoots the Mineola bank manager, the robbers go to the movies. What film do they see?
18. While dancing before the mirror, what song does Bonnie sing?

19. C. W. Moss's obsession with actress Myrna Loy was based on a real gangster's infatuation with her. Who was this?

20. What is the name of the establishment in which Captain Hamer and C. W.'s father plan the ambush?

21. Bonnie writes a poem about the Barrows Gang's exploits and sends it to a newspaper. What is the name of this poem?

22. After *New York Times* film critic Bosley Crowther gave *Bonnie and Clyde* scathing reviews, the studio applied pressure to the newspaper and Crowther was handed his walking papers. However, in a book on important films, critic-turned-author Crowther would later celebrate the film as one of the most significant films ever made saying, "No film turned out in the 1960s was more clever in registering the amoral restlessness of youth in those years. This is why it is so popular and is a landmark film today." What is the title of this book?

23. While in prison, what did Clyde do to "get off work detail"?

24. How many people does the film say the Barrows Gang killed?

25. What is Bonnie's response to the suggestion that she find a rich man?

Quiz No. 28:
APOCALYPSE NOW (1979)

Screenplay by John Milius and Francis Ford Coppola
Directed by Francis Ford Coppola
Starring Martin Sheen, Marlon Brando, and Robert Duvall
United Artists

> *My film is not about Vietnam. It is Vietnam. It's what it was really like. It was crazy. And the way we made it is very much like the Americans were in Vietnam: we were in the jungle, there were too many of us, we had access to too much money, too much equipment, and little by little we went insane.*
>
> —DIRECTOR FRANCIS FORD COPPOLA

Francis Ford Coppola's *Apocalypse Now* captures the horrors of war like no other film before or since. The film's tumultuous shoot, documented in the film, *Hearts of Darkness: A Filmmaker's Apocalypse* (1991), is the stuff of legend. While filming in the Philippines, Coppola fired the film's leading man, Harvey Keitel. Then, when actor Marlon Brando arrived on location, he was substantially overweight, underprepared, and threatened to leave the production at any minute unless his strict demands were met. The scheduled seventeen-week $12-million shoot ballooned into a thirty-five week $31-million nightmare. As the Hollywood trades began questioning, "Apocalypse When?," Coppola was forced to sink every penny he owned into financing the picture. When it took two and a half years for Coppola and his three editors to piece the film together, its prospects did not look good. So, understandably, when the film was released and immediately hailed as a masterpiece, it surprised many Hollywood insiders.

In 1980, *Apocalypse Now* received eight Academy Award nominations: Best Picture (Coppola, Gray Frederickson, Fred Roos, and Tom Sternberg), Best Director (Coppola), Best Adapted Screenplay (John

Milius and Coppola), Best Supporting Actor (Robert Duvall), Best Cinematography (Vittorio Storaro), Best Sound (Richard Beggs, Mark Berger, Nathan Boxer, and Walter Murch), Best Art Direction–Set Decoration (Angelo P. Graham, George R. Nelson, and Dean Tavoularis), and Best Film Editing (Lisa Fruchtman, Gerald B. Greenberg, Richard Marks, and Walter Murch). The film received two Oscars, awarded for its cinematography and sound.

1. *Apocalypse Now* is an adaptation. What is the name of the novella the film was adapted from?

2. What legendary filmmaker had planned to adapt this same novella for his directorial debut, but instead directed another AFI Top 100 film?

3. Harvey Keitel was initially cast in the role of Willard, but was fired during production. He was then replaced by Martin Sheen. Ironically, Keitel and Sheen appeared together in another film the year *Apocalypse Now* was released. What is this film?

4. Before Harvey Keitel (and later Martin Sheen) was cast, a number of actors were offered the role of Willard and passed. Which of the following actors was *not* offered the role: Robert De Niro, Steve McQueen, Al Pacino, Robert Redford, Jack Nicholson, or James Caan?

5. How old was actor Laurence Fishburne when filming began in 1976?

6. George Lucas was initially enlisted to direct the film for Warner Bros. During this time, Lucas and company came up with a way to make the film. However, the studio did not approve. Screenwriter John Milius remembers, "I think Warner Bros. finally backed off because they figured most of us would be killed." What was this plan Milius is referring to?

7. In the filmed alternate ending, how does the film close?

8. During filming, Martin Sheen was hospitalized. Why?

9. The character G. D. Franklin plays in the film is named after a famous filmmaker. Who is this?

10. In the film, there is a director filming a documentary on the Vietnam War. Who appears in the film as the director?

11. In the 70-millimeter version of the film, what conventional device was noticeably absent, resulting in the distribution of pamphlets before screenings?

12. In 1998, Marlon Brando and Martin Sheen reunited in a horrendous straight-to-video turkey. What is this film?

13. What are Kurtz's last words as he dies?

14. During Kurtz's ritualistic decapitation, what rather fitting song plays over the soundtrack?

15. Just before being attacked, Chef is reading a newspaper. What is the subject of the piece?

16. What are placed on posts, decoratively surrounding Kurtz's compound?

17. How does Willard describe the odor of Kurtz's lair?

18. As Kurtz prepares to murder Dennis Hopper's character, he recites a poem. What is the name of this poem?

19. Why does Kurtz say he wants men who will kill without judgment?

20. During filming, one of the members of the film crew threatened to commit suicide on numerous occasions. Who was this?

21. In Kurtz's grisly story, what do Vietcong guerrillas do after Vietnamese children are inoculated for polio?

22. What happened to the sets during filming, causing the shoot to be delayed?

23. What composer scored the film?

24. According to Willard, what does Charlie do every minute he squats in the bush?

25. What does Willard compare charging someone with murder in Vietnam to?

Quiz No. 29:
Mr. Smith Goes to Washington (1939)

Screenplay by Sidney Buchanan
Directed by Frank Capra
Starring James Stewart, Jean Arthur, and Claude Rains
Columbia Pictures

> ***The film was outrageous, exactly the kind of picture that dictators and totalitarian governments would like to have their subjects believe exists in a democracy.***
>
> —Senator James F. Byrnes (D), South Carolina

Ludicrously viewed as subversive at the time of its release, Frank Capra's *Mr. Smith Goes to Washington* is the story of an idealistic young senator named Jefferson Smith (James Stewart). While trying to establish a national boys' camp, the naive senator quickly discovers the shortcomings of the American political process, making enemies with state political chief Jim Taylor (Edward Arnold) in the process. Although the film was so controversial in United States' political circles that it brought director Capra under scrutiny from the FBI, in London's *Sunday Graphic,* film critic James Hilton called the film "just about the best American patriotic film ever made."

In 1940, *Mr. Smith Goes to Washington* received eleven Academy Award nominations: Best Picture (Capra), Best Director (Capra), Best Original Story (Lewis R. Foster), Best Screenplay (Sidney Buchanan), Best Actor (Stewart), Best Supporting Actor (Harry Carey), Best Supporting Actor (Claude Rains), Best Art Direction–Set Decoration (Lionel Banks), Best Film Editing (Al Clark and Gene Havlick), Best Original Score (Dimitri Tiomkin), and Best Sound Recording (John P.

Livadary). The film received only one Oscar, awarded for Foster's original story.

1. Claude Rains appears in three AFI Top 100 films. One of these is *Mr. Smith Goes to Washington*. What are the other two films?
2. *Mr. Smith Goes to Washington* is one of six films in which actor James Stewart appeared in 1939. What are the other five?
3. What is the name of the hospital where Senator Sam Foley dies?
4. Who is the political sidekick present when Foley dies?
5. Director Frank Capra and James Stewart made three films together. One of these is *Mr. Smith Goes to Washington*. What are the other two?
6. A newspaper headline reads GOVERNOR HOPPER'S CHOICE IS EAGERLY AWAITED. What is the name of this newspaper?
7. Who is said to be a "born stooge"?
8. The discouraged Jefferson Smith visits one of the many monuments in Washington, D.C. Which one is it?
9. What does Jefferson Smith say his constituents need permanent relief from?
10. *Mr. Smith Goes to Washington* was adapted from a novel written by Lewis R. Foster. What is the title of Foster's novel?
11. Before actor James Stewart was hired, the film had a different title. What was it, and why was it changed?
12. Who has Jefferson Smith often heard calling Joseph Paine the finest man he ever knew?
13. What is the name of the only publication in Montana that Smith can convince to print the truth?
14. Saunders says they were "fools who pressed on, despite the odds against them." To whom is she referring?
15. What is the nickname that Saunders gives Smith?
16. When referring to his "feathered friends," what type of bird is Jefferson Smith talking about?
17. What is Nosey Parker's occupation?
18. Susan Paine is raising money for a fund. What is this fund?
19. Frank Capra was nominated for Best Director for *Mr. Smith Goes to Washington*. This was one of six Best Director nominations for Capra. What are the other five films Capra was nominated for?
20. As a coproducer, Capra was also nominated for Best Picture.

This was one of four Best Picture nominations Capra received. What are the other three films Capra was nominated for?

21. What is the name of Saunders's press secretary?
22. In 1977, *Mr. Smith Goes to Washington* was loosely remade in a film directed by Tom Laughlin. What is the name of this film?
23. Who does Saunders call a "gorilla in man's clothing"?
24. What is Saunders's first name?
25. Who are called "ambulance chasers" in the film?

Quiz No. 30: The Treasure of the Sierra Madre (1948)

Screenplay by John Huston
Directed by John Huston
Starring Humphrey Bogart, Tim Holt, and Walter Huston
Warner Bros.

> [The Maltese Falcon] *was simply a matter of editing Dashiell Hammett's book. It's his book on the screen, and it took me all of three weeks to write the screenplay. On the other hand, all the elements in the film* The Treasure of the Sierra Madre *are in the book, but they are organized quite differently from the way that [author B.] Traven wrote them. Gold hat, for instance, goes right through the picture, whereas he was just an episode in the book.*
>
> —Director John Huston

In 1948, screenwriter-director John Huston and actor Humphrey Bogart collaborated on two memorable films: *Key Largo* and *The Treasure of the Sierra Madre*. The story of three unlikely partners on a quest for gold, *The Treasure of the Sierra Madre* is a study of greed and its effect on a man's character. While the three prospectors—played by Bogart, Tim Holt, and Huston's father, Walter—begin their journey with the best of intentions, they find themselves slowly changed: transformed and corrupted by the gold they seek. "It's Bogart's best film," Edinburgh University Film Society's Steven Cox observes. "His portrayal as a callous, miserly disloyal son-of-a-bitch was a marked contrast to the smooth benevolence of Rick in *Casablanca* (1942) which is why the film flopped at the box office—the audience didn't want the actor they wanted the stereotype."

In 1949, *The Treasure of the Sierra Madre* received four Academy Award nominations: Best Picture (Henry Blanke), Best Director (Huston), Best Screenplay (Huston), and Best Supporting Actor (Walter

Huston). The film was awarded three Oscars, losing in its bid for Best Picture.

1. *The Treasure of the Sierra Madre* won three Oscars. What is the significance of these?

2. At the start of the film, Dobbs repeatedly hounds a "fellow American" for his spare change. Who is the actor playing this man?

3. What is the first thing Dobbs plans to do with his share of the gold?

4. What are the wages promised to Dobbs and Curtin by Pat McCormick?

5. B. Traven, the author of the novel the film was adapted from, was invited to the set. The reclusive author decided to send an associate to the set rather than come himself. Whom did he send?

6. After cleaning up, what problem does Dobbs experience with his fedora?

7. What famed Alfonso Bedoya line was later used in a number of other films, including *Blazing Saddles* (1974)?

8. Howard plans to do some reading after returning with the gold. What does he plan to read?

9. Dobbs, laughing maniacally, proposes a bet to Curtin regarding which of them will fall asleep first. How much does Dobbs want to bet?

10. As Cody sleeps outside the tent, who volunteers for the first shift of guard duty?

11. Dobbs suggests that Cody visit a nearby club if he's looking for some American company. In what city is this club located?

12. When the federales catch two of the train robbers, where do they lead them?

13. In 1999, *Natural Born Killers* cowriter David Veloz was hired by Warner Bros. to pen a screenplay for a proposed remake of *The Treasure of the Sierra Madre*. The character of Curtin is changed dramatically in Veloz's script. How so?

14. How much money does Howard say is more than enough to last him the rest of his lifetime?

15. What do the bandits offer Dobbs for his rifle?

16. Cody offers the miners three possible options for dealing with him. What are these?

17. How many of the train robbers does Dobbs claim to have killed?

18. Dobbs laments that if he were a native, he would purchase something and go into business. What is this?

19. What musical instrument does Howard play?

20. Dobbs says he mistook Howard for being "an ordinary human being." After reconsidering, what does Dobbs say he now believes Howard is?

21. When Curtin pays Dobbs the gold powder he owes him (plus interest), what does Dobbs do with it?

22. Where is Cody from?

23. What is the name of Cody's son?

24. When they first meet, what line of work does Curtin tell Cody he's in?

25. Dobbs claims he shot five foxes and a lion. Where does he say he shot them?

Quiz No. 31:
ANNIE HALL (1977)

Screenplay by Woody Allen and Marshall Brickman
Directed by Woody Allen
Starring Woody Allen, Diane Keaton, and Tony Roberts
United Artists

> ***[I] felt instinctively that a picture where I addressed the audience directly and talked about myself personally would interest them, because I felt many people in the audience had the same feelings and the same problems. I wanted to talk to them directly and confront them.***
>
> —DIRECTOR WOODY ALLEN

Annie Hall is the quintessential Woody Allen film, displaying all the characteristics his work has since become known for. Largely autobiographical, as is much of Allen's work, the lines become blurred between the character that he portrays and the artist himself. *Annie Hall* is Allen's masterpiece, a modern romance brimming with endlessly quotable one-liners, Freudian analyses of life and sex, and monologues addressed directly to the audience.

In 1978, *Annie Hall* received five Academy Award nominations: Best Picture (Charles H. Joffe), Best Director (Allen), Best Original Screenplay (Allen and Marshall Brickman), Best Actor (Allen), and Best Actress (Diane Keaton). The film was awarded four Oscars, losing only in its bid for Best Actor.

1. What does Alvy say is the "only cultural advantage" to living in Los Angeles?
2. What actress made her acting debut in a nonspeaking role as Alvy's date outside the theater?
3. The character Annie Hall was modeled after an ex-girlfriend of Woody Allen's. Who is this?

4. Woody Allen was not present the night *Annie Hall* won the Triple Crown at the Academy Awards. Where was he?

5. On what talk show does Alvy talk about his not being accepted into the military?

6. What is the name of the Marcel Ophuls documentary that Alvy and Annie see several times in the film?

7. Cowriter Marshall Brickman would later direct a film featuring actress Diane Keaton. What is this film?

8. According to Woody Allen, *Annie Hall* began as a completely different type of screenplay. What genre did Allen and Marshall Brickman initially set out to write?

9. What type of person does Alvy say he does not consider himself?

10. Alvy begins the film with two jokes. Who does he attribute the second joke to?

11.In a flashback scene depicting Alvy's school life, "Tuesday, Dec. 1" is scrawled on the blackboard. What is the significance of this date?

12. What fixture was Alvy's childhood home located under?

13. Alvy jokes that *My Sexual Problem* sounds like the sequel to a novel. What is this novel?

14. When Alvy is stopped on the street and asked who he is, what is his response?

15. Where is Annie from?

16. Alvy is shown doing standup at a presidential candidate's fundraiser. Who is this presidential hopeful?

17. Alvy produces Marshall McLuhan to set the blowhard in the movie line straight. However, McLuhan was not director Woody Allen's first choice. Who was?

18. Prior to *Annie Hall,* Woody Allen and Marshall Brickman had already cowritten one film. What is this film?

19. What book do Annie and Alvy discuss during his first visit to her apartment?

20. What composer scored *Annie Hall*?

21. Alvy jokes that the Gestapo could easily get information from Annie by doing one thing. What is this?

22. Screenwriters Woody Allen and Marshall Brickman met while working together in a cabaret. What two instruments did Brickman play?

23. Alvy says that his grandmother never gave him gifts because she was too busy. What does he say she was too busy doing?

24. Alvy and Annie go to the theater to view a John Huston film. What is this film?

25. For *Annie Hall,* Woody Allen was nominated in three categories. This record would be broken the following year by another ex-boyfriend of actress Diane Keaton. Who was this?

Quiz No. 32:
THE GODFATHER PART II (1974)

Screenplay by Francis Ford Coppola and Mario Puzo
Directed by Francis Ford Coppola
Starring Al Pacino, Robert De Niro, and Robert Duval
Paramount Pictures

> ***I always wanted to write a screenplay that told the story of a father and a son at the same age in parallel action; let's say that they were both in their thirties, and you would interrelate the two characters***
>
> —DIRECTOR FRANCIS FORD COPPOLA

The Godfather Part II is the rarest of films: a sequel that is at least as good as its predecessor, if not better. *The Godfather Part II* continues the saga of the Corleone crime family and its young leader, Michael Corleone (Al Pacino). Here, director Francis Ford Coppola pulls off an extraordinary feat in simultaneously telling the stories of both Michael's expansion of the family in the 1950s and his father, Vito (Robert De Niro), establishing it in the early 1900s.

In 1975, *The Godfather Part II* received eleven Academy Award nominations: Best Picture (Coppola, Gray Frederickson, and Fred Roos), Best Director (Coppola), Best Adapted Screenplay (Coppola and Mario Puzo), Best Actor (Pacino), Best Supporting Actor (De Niro), Best Supporting Actor (Michael V. Gazzo), Best Supporting Actor (Lee Strasberg), Best Supporting Actress (Talia Shire), Best Art Direction–Set Decoration (Dean Tavoularis, George R. Nelson, and Angelo P. Graham), Best Original Score (Carmine Coppola and Nino Rota), and Best Costume Design (Theodora Van Runkle). The film was awarded six Oscars for Best Picture, Director, Screenplay, Art Direction–Set Decoration, Score, and Supporting Actor for De Niro's performance.

1. When Robert De Niro was awarded the Oscar for Best Supporting Actor, he became the first actor to beat out his acting teacher for an Academy Award. Who was his acting teacher?

2. Who does Michael say will not live to see the new year?

3. What famed filmmaker makes a cameo in the film as Senator No. 2?

4. Who makes an uncredited cameo as the little girl on the boat in the Statue of Liberty scene?

5. A future Academy Award–nominated AFI Top 100 screenwriter served as a location assistant on *The Godfather Part II* after working as a babysitter for the Coppola's children. Who is this?

6. What actor playing a primary Corleone family member appears in both installments of *The Godfather,* but is uncredited in *The Godfather Part II*?

7. Fanucci says he wants just enough of Vito's six-hundred-dollar cut to "wet his beak." How much does Fanucci ask for?

8. Robert De Niro and Al Pacino do not share a scene in *The Godfather Part II* and would not appear onscreen together until 1995. What is the film that brought them together?

9. When Michael goes to Fredo and "forgives" him, he looks across the room at Al Neri. What is the significance of this action?

10. Robert De Niro won an Oscar for his turn in *The Godfather Part II.* In doing so, he achieved a feat that only Sofia Loren, Roberto Benigni, and Benicio del Toro have matched. What is this?

11. Mario Puzo was adamant against one element of the film's storyline. What was this?

12. This was the last film in the United States ever printed using a certain printing process. What is this process called?

13. Who is called "The Black Hand"?

14. While Michael is away on business, he must place someone else in charge. Who does he choose?

15. Who does Hyman Roth refer to as "small potatoes"?

16. Tony Rosato strangles Frank Pantangeli. Who is the actor who appears as Tony Rosato?

17. The Hail Mary segment is based on someone's real-life fishing experiences. Whose?

18. Vito's older brother is murdered by Don Ciccio. What is his name?

19. Vito's surname is changed to Corleone at Ellis Island. What is it before it's changed?

20. What is the name of the ship that brings Vito to the United States?

21. Who is the "special guest" at Anthony's party?

22. What does Hyman Roth brag that he always does for his partners?
23. What future regular from *The Sopranos* appears as Johnny Ola?
24. What is the significance of oranges in the film?
25. At what hotel were scenes of Michael's stay in Havana filmed?

Quiz No. 33:
High Noon (1952)

Screenplay by Carl Foreman
Directed by Fred Zinneman
Starring Gary Cooper, Thomas Mitchell, and Grace Kelly
Paramount Pictures

> ***I've always been fascinated by the idea of conscience. To photograph that conflict as expressed in the actions or choices a person makes is very photogenic.***
> —Director Fred Zinneman

High Noon is director Fred Zinneman's classic tale of good versus evil. The film tells the story of a small-town marshal bound by a sense of duty and honor to protect the very people who have abandoned him. As *DVD Verdict* critic Sean McGinnis observes, "This film is a masterwork of the genre. In essence, it is an anti-Western. Contrary to the Western films of the period, and for that matter, the Western period in general, the film is slow moving, evenly paced and deliberate in presentation. Most Westerns are shoot-'em-up action flicks. Not this one. Much like *Unforgiven,* this Western tells a story, something Hollywood has always been good at when it puts its mind to it."

In 1953, *High Noon* received seven Academy Award nominations: Best Picture (Stanley Kramer), Best Director (Zinneman), Best Screenplay (Carl Foreman), Best Actor (Gary Cooper), Best Film Editing (Harry W. Gerstad and Elmo Williams), Best Score (Dimitri Tiomkin), and Best Song (Tiomkin and Ned Washington). The film won four Oscars, but lost in the three most significant categories—Best Picture, Best Director, and Best Screenplay.

1. What are Will Kane's first words in the film?
2. On May 14, 1961, what did the front page of the *Sunday News* proclaim that actor Gary Cooper had done at high noon?

3. What do Frank Miller, Will Kane, and Harvey Pell have in common?

4. What is actor Lee Van Cleef's most famous line in *High Noon*?

5. What actor makes an uncredited cameo in the film as Charlie?

6. Legendary Western-director Howard Hawks once commented that in *High Noon* "Gary Cooper ran around trying to get help and no one would give him any. And that's a rather silly thing for a man to do, especially since at the end of the picture he is able to do the job by himself." With this in mind, Hawks set out to make a Western that is "just the opposite" of *High Noon*. What is this film?

7. What is the name of the town where Will Kane is the marshal?

8. What actress appears in her first starring role as Amy Fowler?

9. Another actor was offered the role of Will Kane before Gary Cooper, but turned it down. Who was this?

10. What does Fred manufacture for a living?

11. What is Amy's ultimatum to Will?

12. At his trial, what did Frank Miller vow to do?

13. A made-for-television sequel was produced in 1980. In this sequel, Lee Majors appears as Will Kane. What is the name of this film?

14. What is the "personal trouble" between Will and Frank Miller?

15. What actor appears in an uncredited cameo as Johnny?

16. What does Helen believe will happen if Will Kane dies?

17. *High Noon* was remade in 2000. Who plays Will Kane in this remake?

18. What does Helen say she would do if Will Kane was her man?

19. At the end of the film, what does Will throw into the dirt?

20. *High Noon* is one of two films that were produced by Stanley Kramer and directed by Fred Zinneman in 1952. What is the other film?

21. When Jimmy Trumbull asks why he hasn't arrested Frank Miller's henchmen, what is Will Kane's reasoning?

22. A traumatic event in Amy's past has turned her into a pacifist. What was this?

23. What is the name of the town drunk?

24. The former marshal is now retired and lives with an Indian woman. What is his name?

25. Who is the first man killed in the gunfight?

Quiz No. 34:
To Kill a Mockingbird (1962)

Screenplay by Horton Foote
Directed by Robert Mulligan
Starring Gregory Peck, John Megna, and Frank Overton
Universal Pictures

> ***I know that authors are supposed to knock Hollywood and complain about how their works are treated here, but I just can't manage it. Everybody has been so darn nice to me and everything is being done with such care that I can't find anything to complain about.***
>
> —Novelist Harper Lee

Adapted from Harper Lee's Pulitzer Prize–winning novel of the same title, *To Kill a Mockingbird* is the story of Atticus Finch (Gregory Peck), a weary lawyer raising two children by himself in a small Southern town. When a black man is accused of raping a white woman, Atticus defends him, despite the ever-increasing sentiment that the man is guilty. While defending the doomed man, he is scorned by the white townsfolk, but gains newfound respect from the town's black population and his own children. Film critic Harvey O'Brien praises, "Well cast, superbly acted, beautifully photographed in rich black and white, evocatively designed and scored, the film is marvelously crafted on every level."

In 1963, *To Kill a Mockingbird* received eight Academy Award nominations: Best Picture (Alan J. Pakula), Best Director (Robert Mulligan), Best Adapted Screenplay (Horton Foote), Best Actor (Peck), Best Supporting Actress (Mary Badham), Best Black-and-White Art Direction–Set Decoration (Henry Bumstead, Oliver Emert, and Alexander Golitzen), Best Black-and-White Cinematography (Russell Harlan), and Best Substantially Original Score (Elmer Bernstein). The film was awarded three Oscars for its screenplay, art direction–set decoration, and for Gregory Peck's unforgettable turn as Atticus Finch.

1. In what town does this story take place?
2. How old is Scout?
3. Seven years after working together on *To Kill a Mockingbird,* director Robert Mulligan and actor Gregory Peck collaborated on another film. What is this film?
4. What does Atticus forbid Scout to do?
5. What historical figure was Bob Ewell named after?
6. According to Aunt Stephanie, what does Mrs. Lafayette keep hidden beneath her shawl?
7. Who was the real-life owner of the watch Atticus Finch carries?
8. Harper Lee won the Pulitzer Prize for *To Kill a Mockingbird.* How many other novels did Lee publish?
9. In one scene, Atticus shoots a dog. Why?
10. Who was the character Dill modeled after?
11. Who does Jem call the "meanest man that ever took a breath of life"?
12. Where does Dill believe they will find "instruments of torture"?
13. In 1962, Robert Mulligan directed two films. One of these is *To Kill a Mockingbird.* The other stars Rock Hudson, Burl Ives, and Gena Rowlands. What is this film?
14. What does the inscription on Atticus's watch read?
15. What does Jem say is the "most exciting thing" that has ever happened in town?
16. In the courtroom, Bob Ewell claims that someone is trying to take advantage of him. Who is this?
17. Atticus tells Scout that someday his watch will belong to Jem. What does he say he will give to her?
18. Who does Sheriff Tate say should be allowed to bury the dead after Bob Ewell's death?
19. What is the "evil assumption" Atticus says Bob Ewell believed the jury would make?
20. Who kills Bob Ewell?
21. Why does Tom Robinson say he did Mayella's chores for free?
22. Atticus proclaims that Mayella broke a "rigid and time-honored code." What did she do?
23. How did Tom Robinson injure his left arm when he was twelve-years old?

24. According to Mayella, how long did it take her to save seven nickels?

25. One year after the release of *To Kill a Mockingbird,* actors Gregory Peck and Robert Duvall made another film together. What is this film?

Quiz No. 35:
It Happened One Night (1934)

Screenplay by Robert Riskin
Directed by Frank Capra
Starring Clark Gable, Claudette Colbert, and Walter Connolly
Columbia Pictures

> ***Comedies were not "the thing" in that glamorous era, but I loved comedy, having played it on Broadway. And as Paramount was putting me in rather dull "nice women" roles, I jumped at this gay prospect of looking at [Clark] Gable every day and getting paid besides!***
>
> —Actress Claudette Colbert

This Frank Capra–directed screwball comedy tells the story of a spoiled, wealthy heiress (Claudette Colbert), who runs away from her controlling father because he won't allow her to marry her fiancé, King Westley (Jameson Thomas). On a bus bound for New York City, she meets a down-on-his-luck reporter named Peter Warne (Clark Gable). The two instantly dislike each other, but later find themselves in love.

In 1935, *It Happened One Night* received five Academy Award nominations: Best Picture (Harry Cohn), Best Director (Capra), Best Adapted Screenplay (Robert Riskin), Best Actor (Gable), and Best Actress (Colbert). The film was awarded Oscars for all five nominations, becoming the first film to sweep the five major categories.

1. *It Happened One Night* was later remade as a musical starring Jack Lemmon. What is the name of this film?
2. This film was adapted from a short story written by Samuel Hopkins Adams. What is the name of this story?
3. In 1985, Rob Reiner helmed another remake of *It Happened One Night*. This film stars John Cusack, Anthony Edwards, and Daphne Zuniga. What is this film?
4. What actor appears in an uncredited role as the bus driver?

5. Who did Harry Cohn want to cast in the role of Ellie Andrews?

6. In 1934, Clark Gable appeared in five films. One of them was *It Happened One Night*. What are the other four films?

7. In 1935, Claudette Colbert received the first of three Academy Award nominations for *It Happened One Night*. What are the other two films she was nominated for?

8. One scene featuring Clark Gable would later serve as the inspiration for the mannerisms of a well-known cartoon character. Who is this?

9. How much is the reward Mr. Andrews offers for Ellie?

10. Peter says he won't accept the reward. How much money does he ask for?

11. After Ellie's bag is stolen, how much money is she left with?

12. Six years after *It Happened One Night*, Clark Gable and Claudette Colbert appeared together in another film. What is this film?

13. Who does Peter call the "pill of the century"?

14. What does Peter say is an art?

15. How much do hamburgers cost at the rest stop?

16. What is the name of Peter's editor?

17. Prior to this film, director Frank Capra and Claudette Colbert had already made one film together. What is this film?

18. In the telegram Peter sends Mr. Andrews, what does he say are "a-toppling"?

19. What does Ellie say she comes from a long line of?

20. What kind of woman does Shapely say he likes meeting?

21. Whom does Ellie say she'd trade places with any day?

22. In 1934, two films directed by Frank Capra were released. One of these is *It Happened One Night*. The other movie features Warner Baxter and Myrna Loy. What is this film?

23. *It Happened One Night* was the first of three films to date that have swept the five major categories at the Academy Awards. What are the other two films that have accomplished this feat?

24. Robert Riskin cowrote the screenplay with another writer who did not receive credit. Who was this?

25. After turning down the role of Ellie, one actress offered to purchase the screenplay. She planned to have it rewritten to her specifications as a vehicle for her. Who is this actress?

Quiz No. 36:
Midnight Cowboy (1969)

Screenplay by Waldo Salt
Directed by John Schlesinger
Starring Dustin Hoffman, Jon Voight, and Sylvia Miles
United Artists

I've always been into rather dark subjects.

—Director John Schlesinger

Following his Oscar-nominated performance as Benjamin Braddock in *The Graduate* (1967), actor Dustin Hoffman turned a complete 360, portraying a filthy vagrant with homosexual tendencies in *Midnight Cowboy*. The film, which was slapped with an "X" rating at the time of its release, follows Texas stud Joe Buck (Jon Voight), lost in the streets of New York City. The would-be gigolo meets up with fellow-loser Ratso Rizzo (Hoffman), and the two become unlikely partners.

In 1970, *Midnight Cowboy* received seven Academy Award nominations, which were unheard of for an "X"-rated film: Best Picture (Jerome Hellman), Best Director (John Schlesinger), Best Adapted Screenplay (Waldo Salt), Best Actor (Hoffman), Best Actor (Voight), Best Supporting Actress (Sylvia Miles), and Best Film Editing (Hugh A. Robertson). The film received three Oscars, awarded for Best Picture, Best Director, and Best Adapted Screenplay.

1. *Midnight Cowboy* won an Oscar for Best Picture. What is the significance of this?
2. In 1969, two films starring Dustin Hoffman were released. One of these is *Midnight Cowboy*. In the other film, Hoffman appears opposite Mia Farrow. What is this film?
3. Before Jon Voight was hired, another actor had been cast in the role of Joe Buck. Who was this?

4. What is the name of the restaurant where Joe Buck washes dishes?

5. As Joe passes the Rio Theatre, the marquee advertises a film starring John Wayne. What is this film?

6. The film was theatrically rereleased in 1994. Who was this rerelease dedicated to?

7. In what year was the film reevaluated and given an "R" rating?

8. What does Ratso believe are the two things necessary to sustain life?

9. What is Ratso's real name?

10. Who does Joe Buck offer as proof that cowboys are not "fags"?

11. Who raised Joe Buck?

12. When Cass and Joe Buck have sex, what symbolic image is shown as they climax?

13. What illness does Ratso suffer from?

14. Joe Buck tells himself, "You know what you gotta do, Cowboy." What is he referring to?

15. Who is the pimp Ratso introduces Joe Buck to?

16. How much money does Cass take for cab fare?

17. After his eviction, Joe Buck goes to eat in a diner where he feasts on crackers. What does he eat on his crackers?

18. What did actor Dustin Hoffman do to make his limp look more realistic in the film?

19. What two items does Joe Buck purchase for Ratso?

20. How does Ratso describe his father's signature?

21. Why was Ratso's father buried with gloves on his hands?

22. What is the significance of Sylvia Miles' Best Supporting Actress Academy Award nomination?

23. Ratso says the landlord cannot collect rent for his apartment. Why?

24. Seven years after making *Midnight Cowboy,* Dustin Hoffman and director John Schlesinger collaborated on another film. What is this film?

25. Why does Joe Buck become angry with Shirley?

Quiz No. 37: The Best Years of Our Lives (1946)

Screenplay by Robert E. Sherwood
Directed by William Wyler
Starring Myrna Loy, Fredric March, and Dana Andrews
Goldwyn Pictures Corporation

> The Best Years of Our Lives *was a great film. However, I personally always had a slight—not exactly dislike—but somehow I couldn't quite go along with the girl I played, which people sometimes think is strange. I think it summed itself up in the scene with the mother and father, where this girl Peggy, who is supposed to be a mature girl and understanding and sensitive and intelligent . . . she's defending her right to break up a marriage which she decided is not good, [and] she turns on her parents and says, 'You've forgotten what it's like to be in love.'*
>
> —Actress Teresa Wright

A gritty, unflinching examination of three American servicemen who return home after World War II and the struggles each of them faces, *The Best Years of Our Lives* is a breathtaking film. The film serves as a reminder of what each American GI—wounded, maimed, or otherwise—sacrificed to defend this nation. Each of the three servicemen returns home to find that his time spent languishing overseas would ultimately be "the best years of our lives." After the war, they find contempt, ostracism, unemployment, and suffer bouts with alcoholism.

In 1947, *The Best Years of Our Lives* received eight Academy Award nominations: Best Picture (Samuel Goldwyn), Best Director (William Wyler), Best Screenplay (Robert E. Sherwood), Best Actor (Fredric March), Best Supporting Actor (Harold Russell), Best Film Editing (Daniel Mendell), Best Score (Hugo Friedhofer), and Best Sound (Gordon Sawyer). The film received seven Oscars, losing only for Best

Sound. In addition, Harold Russell was given a special Oscar for inspiring hope in World War II veterans.

1. What famed director appears in an uncredited cameo as an army corporal?
2. Nine years after making *The Best Years of Our Lives,* director William Wyler and actor Fredric March would collaborate on another film. What is this film?
3. The film was adapted from a novel written by MacKinlay Cantor. What is the title of this novel?
4. Fredric March received an Oscar for Best Actor for his turn in *The Best Years of Our Lives.* This was his second Oscar. For what film had March received his first Oscar?
5. What is the significance of the two Oscars actor Harold Russell received for his turn in *The Best Years of Our Lives*?
6. How many servicemen are transported on the B-57 Fred Derry takes home?
7. William Wyler discovered Harold Russell, an army sergeant who lost both hands in a dynamite accident, after seeing him in a military-training film. What is the name of this training film?
8. What is the name of Parrish's girlfriend?
9. The role of Homer Parrish was originally written as a spastic, and another actor had been cast before director William Wyler discovered Harold Russell. Who was this actor?
10. Gregg Toland, who worked on *The Best Years of Our Lives,* is one of the most celebrated cinematographers in the history of American cinema. Prior to this film, how many projects had he and director William Wyler collaborated on?
11. Two sisters appear in an uncredited cameo as the girls at the soda fountain. Who are they?
12. In 1981, one of the film's cast members wrote an autobiography titled, *The Best Years of My Life.* Who was this?
13. What is the name of Fred Derry's stepmother?
14. Fred Derry finds that his wife Marie has moved from his parent's home in his absence. Where does she now reside?
15. Al Stephenson gives Rob a flag. Where did he find the flag?
16. The Camerons ask Homer if he met someone overseas. Who is this?

17. Three years before the release of *The Best Years of Our Lives*, actress Teresa Wright was nominated by the Academy for Best Actress for *Pride of the Yankees* (1942) and Best Supporting Actress for *Mrs. Miniver* (1942). Wright was only the second actress to accomplish this feat. Who was the first?

18. Peggy jokingly introduces someone as her "son by a previous marriage." Who is this?

19. What was Fred Derry's occupation before the war?

20. In 1975, *The Best Years of Our Lives* was remade into a telefilm starring Dabney Coleman and Tom Selleck. What is the title of this remake?

21. Who is the president of the Cornbelt Trust Company?

22. What does Marie suggest Fred wear to the Blue Devil nightclub?

23. Mr. Thorpe offers Fred a job working as Mr. Merkle's assistant at Midway Drugs. How much will Fred be paid for this?

24. Homer becomes enraged by the children gawking at him through the garage window. What does he do?

25. Just after Harold Russell was presented his second Oscar for *The Best Years of Our Lives*, actor Cary Grant leaned over and made a snide comment to him. What was this?

Quiz No. 38:
Double Indemnity (1944)

Screenplay by Billy Wilder and Raymond Chandler
Directed by Billy Wilder
Starring Fred MacMurray, Barabara Stanwyck, and Edward G. Robinson
Paramount Pictures

> ***We worked well. We would discuss a situation. Once we had the broad outline, we added to and changed the original story and arrived at certain points of orientation that we needed. Then we would start scene by scene, and we started with dialogue, and then with transitions. And he was very good at that, just very, very good.*** —DIRECTOR BILLY WILDER ON COWRITER RAYMOND CHANDLER

Director Billy Wilder's classic film noir, *Double Indemnity,* is the story of an insurance salesman named Walter Neff (Fred MacMurray) who crosses paths with a beautiful woman seeking to renew her husband's insurance policy. When Neff falls for Phyllis (Barbara Stanwyck), they begin scheming to bump off her hubby and collect on the life-insurance policy. *Chicago Sun-Times*–critic Roger Ebert observes, "Standing back from the film and what it expects us to think, I see them engaged not in romance or theft, but in behavior. They're intoxicated by their personal styles; styles learned through the movies, and from radio and detective magazines. It's as if they were created by Ben Hecht through his crime dialogue. Walter and Phyllis are pulp characters with little psychological depth, and that's the way Billy Wilder wants it. His best films are sardonic comedies, and in this one, Phyllis and Walter play a bad joke on themselves."

In 1945, *Double Indemnity* received seven Academy Award nominations: Best Picture (Joseph Sistrom), Best Director (Wilder), Best Screenplay (Wilder and Raymond Chandler), Best Actress (Stanwyck), Best Sound (Loren L. Ryder), Best Black-and-White Cinematography

(John F. Seitz), and Best Original Score (Miklos Rozsa). However, the film was awarded no Oscars.

1. *Double Indemnity* was adapted from a novella penned by James M. Cain. What is the title of this novella?

2. In 1973, ABC television produced a horrible remake of *Double Indemnity*. In this telefilm, Samantha Eggar appears as Phyllis Dietrichson. What actor plays Walter Neff?

3. What is the date on Walter Neff's "confession" to Barton Keyes?

4. Before the film's release, director Billy Wilder decided to trim twenty minutes from the film by removing its final scene. What was this scene?

5. What is the name of Phyllis Dietrichson's maid?

6. Why does Walter Neff say the insurance company would not sell him life insurance?

7. Walter Neff explains that his last name has "two f's" like what?

8. What is engraved on Phyllis's anklet?

9. How many years has Keyes worked as a claims inspector?

10. What, according to Keyes, puts knots in his stomach?

11. In 1950, Pete Burness directed an Academy Award–nominated short film featuring the cartoon character Mr. Magoo, which spoofed *Double Indemnity*. What is the name of this short film?

12. Walter makes an offhand remark about wives turning unwanted husbands into quick cash. How much does he suggest he would want to help collect?

13. What is located at Third and Western?

14. Where does Phyllis say she purchased the perfume she puts on her hair?

15. What is the name of Mr. Dietrichson's daughter?

16. Who does Walter believe knows "more tricks than a carload of monkeys"?

17. How much do Walter and Phyllis plan to collect in double-indemnity insurance?

18. What does Walter say he feels "queer in the belly" about?

19. Who does Lola say she's going skating with?

20. Walter and Phyllis meet on Los Feliz. Where?

21. Walter is offered a job as Barton Keyes's assistant. How much of a pay cut would this require?

22. Who does Keyes liken to a surgeon?
23. According to her claim, how did Phyllis's husband die?
24. According to Keyes, how many volumes of actuarial tables are there dealing only with suicide?
25. Who does Lola believe conspired with Phyllis to murder Dietrichson?

Quiz No. 39:
Doctor Zhivago (1965)

Screenplay by Robert Bolt
Directed by David Lean
Starring Omar Sharif, Julie Christie, and Geraldine Chaplin
Metro-Goldwyn-Mayer

> ***I think most people will identify with the characters. They happened to be Russians in the Revolution, but I think they speak for most of us as human beings.***
> —Director David Lean

Doctor Zhivago, adapted from Nobel Prize–winner Boris Pasternak's novel, is a simple story; director David Lean sums it up when he concludes, "A man is married to one woman and in love with another." In the hands of a lesser filmmaker, this would be little more than cheesy soap opera–style melodrama, but in the hands of Lean, it becomes an epic love story. Set during World War I and the Russian Revolution, *Doctor Zhivago* follows a poet and physician named Yuri Zhivago (Omar Sharif). When Yuri is forced to leave his wife and children to aid in the war, he falls in love with an attractive young nurse named Lara (Julie Christie). After returning home, Yuri finds difficulty resuming his life and can think of nothing but Lara.

In 1966, *Doctor Zhivago* received ten Academy Award nominations: Best Picture (Carlo Ponti), Best Director (Lean), Best Adapted Screenplay (Robert Bolt), Best Supporting Actor (Tom Courtenay), Best Color Cinematography (Freddie Young), Best Art Direction–Set Decoration (John Box, Terence Marsh, and Dario Simoni), Best Color Costume Design (Phyllis Dalton), Best Substantially Original Score (Maurice Jarre), Best Film Editing (Norman Savage), and Best Sound (Franklin Milton and A. W. Watkins). The film was awarded five Oscars for its screenplay, cinematography, score, costume design, and art direction–set decoration.

1. Although Julie Christie wasn't nominated for *Doctor Zhivago,* she was awarded an Oscar for Best Actress in 1966. What film did Christie win for?

2. When Yuri wakes up from his dream about Tonya, Lara tells him she has relocated. What city has she gone to?

3. What is Komarovsky's occupation?

4. One of the performers in the film has a famous filmmaker father. Who is this?

5. What does Pasha say is the weakness of the Bolsheviks?

6. According to director David Lean, the scene in which Yuri and Lara are filmed in counterflow to the movement of the troops in the street was inspired by a scene in a film directed by King Vidor. What is this film?

7. What street does Komarovsky think it wise to avoid?

8. According to Yevgraf, what were the walls of Yuri's heart comparable to when he died?

9. Pasha asks Lara to hide something for him. What is this?

10. During filming, David Lean fired the cinematographer, hiring Freddie Young in his place. The cinematographer later became a well-known filmmaker in his own right. Who is this?

11. Between filming *Lawrence of Arabia* (1962) and *Doctor Zhivago,* David Lean performed what he called "glorified second-unit stuff" for a film directed by George Stevens. What is this film?

12. What does Komarovsky offer to Yuri as a wedding gift?

13. While filming in Spain, many extras refused to sing the song "International" for the protest scene. Why?

14. A delegate informs Yuri that the Gromeko home has ample-living space for multiple families. According to the delegate, how many families can be housed there?

15. What does Tonya say she traded for the salami she prepares for Yuri's homecoming?

16. What does Strenilkov say "killed the private life"?

17. MGM asked director David Lean to cast producer Carlo Ponti's wife. Lean told them he would cast her "providing you can convince me she can play a seventeen-year-old virgin." Who was Ponti's wife?

18. MGM wanted Paul Newman cast in the role of Zhivago. Who was David Lean's first choice for the role?

19. In school, the children are taught a course known as C.I. Arithmetic. What does the C.I. stand for?

20. After learning that he had won the Nobel Prize for his novel, *Doctor Zhivago,* what did author Boris Pasternak do at the "request" of the Kremlin?

21. Why does Lara say she's "made with joy"?

22. In 1968, a Greek film that parodies *Doctor Zhivago* was produced. What is this film?

23. Before being cast in the lead role, Omar Sharif had requested another role. What was this role?

24. Who does Komarovsky dismiss as a "murderous neurotic of no loss to anyone"?

25. Prior to *Doctor Zhivago,* David Lean had directed actor Ralph Richardson in *The Sound Barrier* (1952). However, they first met in 1934 while working together on a film when Lean was an editor. What is this film?

Quiz No. 40:
North by Northwest (1959)

Screenplay by Ernest Lehman
Directed by Alfred Hitchcock
Starring Cary Grant, Eva Marie Saint, and James Mason
Metro-Goldwyn-Mayer

> ***[The cropduster scene] became a very famous sequence. As a matter of fact, that's how I knew that Cary Grant had died. Every channel on TV was showing that shot of Cary running from the plane. It's strange, isn't it, that such a distinguished career should be remembered mostly for that one shot?***
>
> —Screenwriter Ernest Lehman

North by Northwest is an example of director Alfred Hitchcock's finest work, and is the best of his "wrong man" films. The film tells the story of a Madison Avenue ad man named Roger O. Thornhill (Cary Grant) who finds himself being attacked and hunted in a case of mistaken identity. Spies who believe he's a double agent attempt to kill him at every turn, and the police are hunting him because they believe he's a murderer. When Thornhill meets up with gorgeous Eve Kendall (Eva Marie Saint), things begin to heat up. She is the only person the desperate man can turn to, but can he trust her?

In 1960, *North by Northwest* received three Academy Award nominations: Best Original Screenplay (Ernest Lehman), Best Film Editing (George Tomasini), and Best Color Art Direction–Set Decoration (Robert F. Boyle, Henry Grace, William A. Horning, Frank R. McKelvy, and Merrill Pye). The film was awarded no Oscars.

1. What does Roger O. Thornhill's middle initial stand for?
2. To appease the censors, director Alfred Hitchcock had Eva Marie Saint overdub the line, "I never discuss love on an empty stomach." What was the original line?

3. At the end of the opening credits, a man is shown missing the bus. Who is this?

4. In 1977, Mel Brooks directed a homage to Alfred Hitchcock. The film, which spoofs *North by Northwest* and other Hitchcock films, features a character named Richard H. Thornhill. What is this film?

5. Screenwriter Ernest Lehman and Alfred Hitchcock conceived a scene in which a dead body is discovered in an automobile plant. Why wasn't this scene filmed?

6. Journalist Otis L. Guernsey, Jr., suggested a plot device to Alfred Hitchcock that he used in *North by Northwest.* What is this?

7. *North by Northwest* was the fourth collaboration between Alfred Hitchcock and Cary Grant. What were the three films they had worked together on previously?

8. Who owns the home where Vandamm first meets with Thornhill?

9. Who does Vandamm believe Thornhill is?

10. What is the name of Roger O. Thornhill's mother?

11. What room is George Kaplan staying in at the Plaza Hotel?

12. Where is Lester Townsend's wife?

13. A newspaper is shown with the headline DIPLOMAT SLAIN AT U.N. What is this newspaper?

14. When Eve asks why he's on the run, Thornhill jokingly tells her he has unpaid parking tickets. How many does he say he has?

15. What does Eve recommend for dinner?

16. Who does Thornhill tell Eve he is?

17. What three letters are on Thornhill's matchbook?

18. What number is Eve's compartment on the train?

19. As Thornhill pretends to shower, what song does he whistle?

20. What is the address where the auction is being held?

21. From where does Vandamm remark that Thornhill could use more training?

22. What are said to be "all in the same alphabet soup"?

23. What does Roger conclude that Eve's usage of sex is comparable to?

24. What does Leonard believe that neatness is "always the result of"?

25. What kind of trick does Leonard say shooting at one's own people is?

Quiz No. 41: West Side Story (1961)

Screenplay by Ernest Lehman and Arthur Laurents
Directed by Robert Wise and Jerome Robbins
Starring George Chakiris, Natalie Wood, and Rita Moreno
United Artists

> ***[My biggest challenge was] to make it acceptable for kids to be dancing in the streets. That's not a normal activity and, as a matter of fact, I was the one who insisted that we open in New York; I said that all the daytime stuff has to be done in New York. I can't fake that out here on a stage. Once you get past the daytime stuff, you're either into sunset, which you can do stage lighting for, or not and then a city street is a city street at night.***
>
> —Codirector Robert Wise

West Side Story, codirected by Robert Wise and Jerome Robbins, is a musical update of William Shakespeare's classic love story, *Romeo and Juliet*. The film finds two rival New York City street gangs engaged in a struggle for power and territory. Amid this violent backdrop, Tony (Richard Beymer), a gangster, and Maria (Natalie Wood), the sister of the rival gang leader, fall in love and in doing so must reassess their personal beliefs and loyalties.

In 1962, *West Side Story* received eleven Academy Award nominations: Best Picture (Wise), Best Director (Wise and Robbins), Best Adapted Screenplay (Ernest Lehman), Best Supporting Actor (George Chakiris), Best Supporting Actress (Rita Moreno), Best Color Cinematography (Daniel L. Fapp), Best Color Art Direction–Set Decoration (Victor A. Gangelin and Boris Leven), Best Costume Design (Irene Sharaff), Best Film Editing (Thomas Stanford), Best Scoring of a Musical Picture (Saul Chaplin, Johnny Green, Irwin Kostal, and Sid Ramin), and Best Sound (Fred Haynes and Gordon Sawyer). The film was awarded ten Oscars, losing only in its bid for Best Adapted Screenplay.

1. When Jerome Robbins and Leonard Bernstein conceived the project in 1949, it was tentatively titled, *East Side Story*. In this early

scenario, there were no gangs. What was the original familial conflict for Tony and Maria?

2. What is the significance of Robert Wise and Tony Robbins's winning the Oscar for Best Director?

3. In the original stage version of *West Side Story,* Maria sings, "I feel pretty and witty and bright/and I pity/any girl who isn't me tonight." What were the words "bright" and "tonight" changed to in the film?

4. Who dubbed Natalie Woods's singing voice?

5. Both George Chakiris, who plays Bernardo, and Tony Mordente, who plays Action, also appeared in the original London production of the play. In what roles did Chakiris and Mordente appear in the play?

6. Only two films through 2001 have been awarded more Oscars than *West Side Story*. What are these?

7. There are two rival gangs. One gang is known as the Jets. What is the name of the other gang?

8. Who dubbed Richard Beymer's singing voice?

9. What is the name of the bigoted police officer played by Simon Oakland?

10. Riff says someone has "got a rep that's bigger than the whole West Side." Whom is he referring to?

11. What is Tony's ethnicity?

12. According to the song, when are you a "top cat in town"?

13. Who dubbed Rita Moreno's singing voice?

14. What does the sign say that the Jets sing about posting, which they declare they're not kidding about?

15. To whom did Tony promise he would clean the store?

16. Who is Maria supposed to wed?

17. According to Riff, what are you without a gang?

18. Who does Bernardo refer to as a "precious jewel"?

19. Who is the "square" social worker played by John Astin?

20. At the dance, one gang wears bright colors and the other wears dark colors. Which gang's members wear dark colors?

21. What does Anita say may be thicker than Bernardo's accent?

22. According to the song, when is life all right in America?

23. Where is the "war council" to be held?

24. In the original play, Riff sang, "My mother is a bastard, my pa's an S.O.B." What is this line changed to in the film?

25. Who asks, "Fightin' over a little piece of street is so important?"

Quiz No. 42: Rear Window (1954)

Screenplay by John Michael Hayes
Directed by Alfred Hitchcock
Starring James Stewart, Grace Kelly, and Wendell Corey
Paramount Pictures

> ***I was feeling very creative at the time, the batteries were well-charged. John Michael Hayes is a radio writer and he wrote the dialogue. The killing presented something of a problem, so I used two news stories from the British press. One was the Patrick Mahon case and the other was the case of Dr. Crippen. In the Mahon case, the man killed a girl in a bungalow on the seafront of southern England. He cut up the body and threw it, piece by piece, out of a train window. But he didn't know what to do with the head, and that's where I got the idea of having them look for the victim's head in*** **Rear Window.**
>
> —Director Alfred Hitchcock

Rear Window is director Alfred Hitchcock's examination of voyeurism and human curiosity. After breaking his leg, photographer Jeff Jeffries (James Stewart) finds himself confined to a wheelchair. With little else to do, the homebound Jeffries spies on his neighbors through the rear window of his apartment. After becoming consumed by the daily lives of his neighboring tenants, he begins to suspect that a neighbor has murdered his wife.

In 1955, *Rear Window* received four Academy Award nominations: Best Director (Hitchcock), Best Screenplay (John Michael Hayes), Best Color Cinematography (Robert Burks), and Best Sound Recording (Loren L. Ryder). However, the film was awarded no Oscars.

1. *Rear Window* was remade in 1998. In that remake, actor Robert Forster appears as Charlie Moore. That same year, Forster appeared in another remake of a classic Alfred Hitchcock film. What is this?
2. Although Grace Kelly wasn't nominated for *Rear Window,* she

won an Oscar for Best Actress that year for another film. What is this film?

3. Grace Kelly already appeared in *Dial M for Murder* (1954), so this was her second film for director Alfred Hitchcock. She would later appear in a third Hitchcock film. What is this film?

4. Alfred Hitchcock was nominated by the Academy for Best Director six times. How many times did he win?

5. What does Stella say they did to Peeping Toms in the old days?

6. What does the box Lars Thorwald carries from the cleaners say?

7. According to Lisa, in "private-eye literature," who always comes to the detective's rescue?

8. One year after *Rear Window*, screenwriter John Michael Hayes worked on another Hitchcock film. What is this film?

9. Who is found lying dead with a broken neck beside Thorwald's garden?

10. One year after the release of *Rear Window*, it was remade as a comedy by a collective of Cantonese filmmakers. This film was made as a tribute to a comedian. Who is this?

11. What magazine is Lisa reading?

12. Jeff observes a man rewinding the clock in the songwriter's apartment. Who is this?

13. For thirty years, *Rear Window* was not available. It was one of the infamous five "lost Hitchcock films." What were the other four unavailable titles?

14. At the time it was built, what was significant regarding the set where *Rear Window* was filmed?

15. What is the name of Miss Torso's husband?

16. What can Stella smell "ten miles away"?

17. Whom does Jeff toast as "To See You Is to Love You" plays?

18. What is Thorwald's apartment number?

19. What does Jeff ask Lisa whether she's ever eaten with rice?

20. According to the postcard, what town is Mrs. Thorwald staying in?

21. When Jeff sarcastically asks Tom whether he needs a trail of bloody footprints to investigate Thorwald's apartment, what does Tom say he does *not* need?

22. The film is based on Cornell Woolrich's 1942 short story, "It

Had to Be Murder." Under what pseudonym did Woolrich pen the story?

23. *Rear Window* is one of four Alfred Hitchcock–directed films James Stewart appeared in. What are the other three films?

24. How many AFI Top 100 films does James Stewart appear in?

25. When Jeff says he will begin working on "love thy neighbor," who does he say he'd like to begin with?

Quiz No. 43:
KING KONG (1933)

Screenplay by Merian C. Cooper, James Creelman, Ruth Rose, and Edgar Wallace
Directed by Ernest B. Schoedsack
Starring Fay Wray, Robert Armstrong, and Bruce Cabot
Radio Pictures

> King Kong ***was never intended to be anything more than the best damned adventure picture ever made, which it is.***
>
> —PRODUCER MERIAN C. COOPER

Conceived by real-life adventurers Merian C. Cooper and Ernest B. Schoedsack, *King Kong* amazed audiences when it was released in 1933. The film was shocking in its day, and Cooper and Schoedsack were forced to trim twenty-nine scenes from it to appease the Hays Office. The film's protagonist Carl Denham (Robert Armstrong) was loosely modeled after director Schoedsack. After leading an expedition on a remote island, Denham discovers a gigantic ape. Hoping to make a quick buck, he decides to capture the beast and bring him back to the United States where he will be displayed. However, Kong has other ideas . . .

In 1934, *King Kong* received no Academy Award nominations. However, the Academy later realized its mistake and presented producer (and uncredited codirector) Merian C. Cooper an honorary Oscar in 1952.

1. Who makes an uncredited cameo appearance as an airplane machine gunner?
2. In 1933, Ernest B. Schoedsack directed three films, including *King Kong* and its sequel, *The Son of Kong*. What is the other Schoedsack-directed film released in 1933?

3. Producer Merian C. Cooper hired Willis O'Brien to bring life to Kong after viewing another film he had made. What is this film?

4. On what island is Kong's mountaintop lair located?

5. The giant wall and gate built for *King Kong* were later burnt in another film. What is this film?

6. What ship carries Ann to the South Pacific?

7. When Kong is displayed in New York, how much do tickets cost?

8. In the film's final line, what is said to have killed the ape?

9. How big were the models of Kong used in the film?

10. What does Driscoll conclude that women cannot help being?

11. Prior to *King Kong,* how many times had actress Fay Wray and director Ernest B. Schoedsack worked together?

12. What working titles were used during filming?

13. In 1949, Merian C. Cooper and Ernest B. Schoedsack collaborated on another giant-ape film. What is this film?

14. One scene that appears in the film was originally shot as a test sequence to secure funding. However, the scene was such a success that the filmmakers decided to put it into the film. What is this scene?

15. What kind of fur was used on the Kong models?

16. The jungle set used in *King Kong* was left over from another film. What is this film?

17. What legendary athlete makes an uncredited cameo appearance as a native dancer?

18. After *King Kong* went three hundred thousand dollars over budget prior to its release, RKO nearly went bankrupt. MGM offered to purchase the film, but RKO declined. How much did MGM offer for *King Kong*?

19. Why did producer Merian C. Cooper choose to cut the scene in which Kong shakes four sailors from a log bridge into a ravine, where they are eaten by large spiders?

20. Director Ernest B. Schoedsack misled actress Fay Wray by promising that she would be working with the "tallest, darkest leading man in Hollywood." According to Wray, who had she believed she would be working opposite after hearing this?

21. What horrid 1986 film reveals that Kong is not dead, but is hooked to a life-support system?

22. According to Carl Denham, what must the public have to look at in a film?

23. Who is the skipper on the crew's voyage to the South Pacific?

24. Censors claimed a scene in which five men are shown being eaten by a brontosaurus was too offensive for release. After the scene was edited, how many men were shown being eaten by the brontosaurus?

25. Carl Denham says that Kong was a "king and a god in the world he knew." What does Denham conclude Kong is in New York City?

Quiz No. 44: THE BIRTH OF A NATION (1915)

Screenplay by D.W. Griffith, Thomas F. Dixon, Jr., and Frank E. Woods
Directed by D.W. Griffith
Starring Lillian Gish, Mae Marsh, and Henry B. Walthall
David W. Griffith Corporation

> ***Mr. Griffith was incapable of prejudice against any group. Two years after the uproar over* The Birth of a Nation, *when he agreed, at the behest of British and French officials, to make propaganda films, he was obliged to portray all Germans as loathsome. This troubled him, for he never believed that there were marked differences among people. Regardless of background, he felt they were all children of God.***
>
> **—ACTRESS LILLIAN GISH**

The racist propaganda film *The Birth of a Nation* is considered—from a technical standpoint—the single most important American film ever made. With *The Birth of a Nation,* filmmaker D. W. Griffith invented much of the language of cinema, such as the close-up and the dissolve. The film also contained the first night shots. Beautifully filmed, *The Birth of a Nation* showcases Griffith's extraordinary talents as a filmmaker; unfortunately, Griffith used this considerable talent to spread racial hatred. From a historical perspective, the film is filled with inaccuracies and outright lies. Eight decades later, the film is reportedly still used as a recruiting tool for the Ku Klux Klan.

The Birth of a Nation predated the Academy Awards. However, Griffith was presented a special Oscar in 1932 for his "distinguished creative achievements as a director and producer and his invaluable initiative and lasting contributions to the progress of the motion-picture arts."

1. When the film first premiered in 1915, it had an alternate title. What was this?

2. By the introduction of the talking motion picture in 1927, how much money had *The Birth of a Nation* made?

3. What organization proclaimed the film "the meanest vilification of the Negro race" on March 6, 1915?

4. Who reportedly said of the film, "It's like writing history with lightning, and my only regret is that it is all terribly true"?

5. *The Birth of a Nation* is often inaccurately described as D. W. Griffith's first full-length film. In reality, it was his second. What was the first?

6. The film was adapted from a story penned by Thomas Dixon, Jr. What was Dixon's occupation?

7. A response film directed by John W. Noble was released in 1918. What is the name of this film?

8. Who watches approvingly as blacks are shipped to Africa in the controversial deleted scene, called "Lincoln's Solution"?

9. The character Austin Stoneman was modeled after a real-life antislavery crusader. Who was this?

10. What are the names of Stoneman's three children?

11. Thirty years after *The Birth of a Nation*, another film starring Lilian Gish would feature a shot-by-shot borrowing of the Klan's ride. What is this film?

12. Where do the Camerons reside?

13. What is Stoneman's "weakness that is to blight a nation"?

14. When Duke raises his bayonet to kill a wounded soldier, he realizes that he knows him. Who is the wounded soldier?

15. As Duke comes to this realization, what happens to him?

16. What are the starving Confederate soldiers shown eating?

17. When the Stoneman family attends a performance of Laura Keene in *Our American Cousin*, what happens?

18. Raoul Walsh, who appears in the film as John Wilkes Booth, later said, "I almost played him again once, too." Walsh added that he briefly considered assassinating a real person. Who was this?

19. Who is Stoneman's protégé?

20. In the historical facsimile showing the House of Representatives in Columbia, South Carolina, in 1871, there are 101 blacks in office. How many whites are there?

21. At the time of the film's release, Thomas F. Dixon offered a reward to any member of the National Board of Censorship or the Negroid Intermarriage Society if they could find "a single essential

error in the book or film version of *The Birth of a Nation*." How much was this reward?

22. Some scenes of Gus's punishment were excised after the premiere. What do these deleted scenes show?

23. How many times is Jeff shot?

24. What dramatic piece of music accompanied the film, which would later appear in *Apocalypse Now* (1979)?

25. What does the film declare to be the "breeder of hate"?

Quiz No. 45:
A Streetcar Named Desire (1951)

Screenplay by Tennessee Williams
Directed by Elia Kazan
Starring Vivien Leigh, Marlon Brando, and Karl Malden
Warner Bros.

> ***In many ways [Vivien Leigh] was Blanche. She was memorably beautiful, one of the great beauties of the screen, but she was also vulnerable, and her own life had been very much like that of Tennessee's wounded butterfly. . . . Like Blanche, she slept with almost everybody and was beginning to dissolve mentally and to fray at the ends physically. I might have given her a tumble if it hadn't been for Larry Olivier.***
>
> —Actor Marlon Brando

Elia Kazan's *A Streetcar Named Desire* is the story of a troubled neurotic named Blanche DuBois (Vivien Leigh), who is running from her sordid past. She comes to stay with her sister, Stella (Kim Hunter), and her violent husband, Stanley Kowalski (Marlon Brando). Stanley and Blanche clash and begin to argue from the moment she arrives, and she begins to look for an escape through a kindhearted friend of Stanley's named Mitch (Karl Malden). Mitch sees Blanche as a goddess, but soon begins to learn about her mysterious past.

In 1952, *A Streetcar Named Desire* received twelve Academy Award nominations: Best Picture (Charles K. Feldman), Best Director (Kazan), Best Screenplay (Tennessee Williams), Best Actor (Brando), Best Actress (Leigh), Best Supporting Actor (Malden), Best Supporting Actress (Hunter), Best Black-and-White Cinematography (Harry Stradling, Sr.), Best Black-and-White Art Direction–Set Decoration (Richard Day and George James Hopkins), Best Black-and-White Costume Design (Lucinda Ballard), Best Original Score (Alex North), and Best Sound (Nathan Levinson). The film was awarded four Oscars for the performances of Malden, Leigh, and Hunter, as well as for its sound.

1. In the 1984 made-for-television remake of *A Streetcar Named Desire,* what actress received an Emmy nomination for her performance as Blanche DuBois?

2. The film lost in its bid for Best Picture in 1952. What film won the Oscar?

3. Blanche says only one writer could do Stella's home justice. Who is this?

4. What is Blanche's drink of preference?

5. Blanche kisses a newspaper delivery boy. What newspaper does he work for?

6. Who killed Blanche's husband, Alan?

7. Blanche says a millionaire has invited her on a Caribbean cruise. What is his name?

8. What is the name of the code Stanley defines as meaning "what belongs to the wife belongs to the husband also"?

9. Blanche explains that the DuBois estate was lost to creditors. What was the name of this estate?

10. Blanche speaks of a certain hotel, saying she "would not be caught dead" there. What is the name of this hotel?

11. Blanche recalls dancing the Varsoviana with Alan. Where was this?

12. What was Blanche's occupation in Laurel?

13. Who did Marlon Brando lose to in his 1952 bid for Best Actor?

14. Only a few years after making *A Streetcar Named Desire,* actress Vivien Leigh suffered a mental breakdown and began to believe she was actually Blanche DuBois. In a famous remark made to a nurse in an asylum in England, Leigh stated that she was Blanche DuBois. Who did she say she was *not*?

15. What does Blanche explain as being French for "white wood"?

16. What kind of habits does Blanche say Stanley has?

17.What is the "little birthday remembrance" Stanley gives Blanche?

18. Who does Stanley quote, saying, "Every man's a king"?

19. What does Blanche see as being the "one unforgivable thing"?

20. What is depicted in the explicit final showdown between Stanley and Blanche, which was excised from the film?

21. Of whom does Blanche conclude, "This man isn't Shep Huntleigh"?

22. Stella stays with a neighbor who lives upstairs. What is her name?

23. What action does Stella admit being "sort of thrilled" by?

24. After a bad hand of poker, Stanley becomes angry and throws something out of the window. What is this?

25. Blanche admits that she was fired because she was considered "morally unfit" after having an affair with a student. How old was this student?

Quiz No. 46:
A Clockwork Orange (1971)

Screenplay by Stanley Kubrick
Directed by Stanley Kubrick
Starring Malcolm McDowell, Patrick Magee, and Michael Bates
Warner Bros.

> ***The central idea of the film has to do with the question of free will. Do we lose our humanity if we are deprived of the choice between good and evil? Do we become, as the title suggests, a clockwork orange? Recent experiments in conditioning and mind control on volunteer prisoners in America have taken this question out of the realm of science fiction.***
> —Director Stanley Kubrick

A Clockwork Orange is Stanley Kubrick's hyperviolent societal satire set in England in the not-so-distant future. Because of its violence, Kubrick's morality play was initially given an "X" rating. Like much of Kubrick's work, *A Clockwork Orange* was misunderstood and underappreciated at the time of its release. However, today the film is regarded as a remarkable achievement and is seen as one of the first great films of the 1970s, a golden age of American cinema.

In 1972, *A Clockwork Orange* received four Academy Award nominations: Best Picture (Kubrick), Best Director (Kubrick), Best Adapted Screenplay (Kubrick), and Best Film Editing (William Butler). Because of its dark nature, the controversial film was not awarded a single Oscar by the Academy's ultra-conservative voters.

1. In 1965, a rock-and-roll singer approached novelist Anthony Burgess with the idea of adapting *A Clockwork Orange* to the screen with himself in the lead role. Burgess recalls, "I admired the intelligence, if not the art, of this young man and considered that he looked the quintessence of delinquency." Who was this?
2. What is the name of the novel Frank Alexander is writing?

3. The film was nominated for four Oscars, but lost all of them to the same film. What is this film?

4. What does Alex say that milk plus drencrom will "sharpen you up" and prepare you for?

5. Novelist Anthony Burgess satirizes director Stanley Kubrick in *A Clockwork Orange: The Play,* as well as in one of his novels. In this novel, a sleazy director named Sidney Lameck is condemned for adapting a writer's work into pornography. What is this novel?

6. What is the name of the slang spoken by Alex and his droogs?

7. The Anthony Burgess novel the film was adapted from contains twenty-one chapters. According to Burgess, what is the symbolism of this?

8. What is the name of the bar that Alex and his droogs frequent?

9. Where is Alex sentenced to serve his fourteen years?

10. Although most people don't realize it, *A Clockwork Orange* is a remake. Anthony Burgess's novel had been adapted by Andy Warhol six years prior to Stanley Kubrick's film. What is the name of this obscure first adaptation?

11. What severed body part ornamentally decorates Alex's suspenders at the beginning of the film?

12. What model of automobile do Alex and his droogs steal to make their getaway?

13. Once Alex has been reprogrammed, what happens to him each time he thinks about sex or violence?

14. In his conversation with Deltoid, what does the inspector conclude "makes violence"?

15. What is Mr. Deltoid's title?

16. When Alex visits the record store, what real-life movie soundtrack is visible at the front counter?

17. As Alex has a threesome with the two girls, what music plays?

18. While Alex is away in prison, he is displaced at home by a new tenant. What is the name of the new tenant?

19. What is Alex injected with before undergoing his reprogramming?

20. It was actor Malcolm McDowell's idea to use the song "Singin' in the Rain" in the murder-rape scene. Why did McDowell choose this song?

21. What does Alex spray at the two girls before having sex with them?

22. When a police officer presses his thumb against Alex's injured nose, how does he retaliate?

23. What is the real name of the Cat Lady?

24. Where is Alex transferred for reprogramming?

25. As Alex and his droogs fight with Billyboy and his gang, what music plays over the soundtrack?

Quiz No. 47: TAXI DRIVER (1976)

Screenplay by Paul Schrader
Directed by Martin Scorsese
Starring Robert De Niro, Cybill Shepherd, and Jodie Foster
Columbia Pictures

> *I was broke. I didn't have any place to live. In this period, I started drifting and wandering about in my car. It was out of this that the metaphor for* Taxi Driver *was born. I wrote it all very quickly. I wrote it essentially as therapy.* —SCREENWRITER PAUL SCHRADER

Martin Scorsese's ultrableak film, *Taxi Driver,* is the story of Vietnam veteran Travis Bickle (Robert De Niro), who returns home and goes to work as a taxi driver. Surrounded by nothing but stoners, hookers, pimps, and filth, the lonely, isolated Bickle sinks into a world of depression and becomes obsessed with pornography and violence. Travis falls for a campaign worker named Betsy (Cybill Shepherd), but she soon becomes frightened and turns him away. Seeking an outlet to release his pent-up rage and violent tendencies, Travis zeroes in on the senator Betsy works for and begins planning to assassinate him.

In 1977, *Taxi Driver* received four Academy Award nominations: Best Picture (Julia and Michael Phillips), Best Actor (De Niro), Best Supporting Actress (Jodie Foster), and Best Original Score (Bernard Herrmann). However, the film, presumably too dark for Academy voters, was awarded no Oscars.

1. Which branch of the armed forces was Travis Bickle discharged from?
2. A theater marquee advertises a double bill, which includes *The Texas Chainsaw Massacre* (1974). What is the other film?
3. What is the name of the presidential candidate Betsy works for?
4. Actress Jodie Foster and director Martin Scorsese had already worked together on a film prior to *Taxi Driver*. What is this film?

5. Most film buffs remember the scene in which Martin Scorsese makes a cameo as a disturbed husband contemplating the murder of his wife. However, Scorsese was not supposed to appear in the scene, but the actor who had been cast was injured in an automobile accident. Who was this actor?

6. At one point, Robert Mulligan had acquired the rights to *Taxi Driver* with the intention of directing it as a vehicle for a famous actor. Who was this?

7. When Martin Scorsese initially approached composer Bernard Herrmann about scoring *Taxi Driver,* he refused. Scorsese then convinced Herrmann to read the screenplay and reconsider. Herrmann eventually agreed to score the film because he liked one scene in particular. What was this?

8. Martin Scorsese hired cinematographer Michael Chapman after screening another film he'd worked on. What is this film?

9. According to producer Julia Phillips, why did Martin Scorsese cast Cybill Shepherd?

10. How much is Travis paid to "forget" seeing Iris brutally dragged from the cab?

11. What is the name of the "X"-rated movie Travis takes Betsy to?

12. What director first handed Paul Schrader's *Taxi Driver* screenplay to Martin Scorsese?

13. When Martin Scorsese was experiencing financial difficulties with *Taxi Driver,* another director who was making a film with producer Julia Phillips offered to make the film. Who was this?

14. Composer Bernard Herrmann died only hours after completing the film's score. However, Herrmann would posthumously score another film for director Martin Scorsese. What is this film?

15. As the producers searched for financing, one studio suggested that a popular musician appear in the role of Travis Bickle. Who was this?

16. Iris's mother is visible in a photograph. Who is the woman who appears as her mother?

17. What is the nickname of the cabbie played by Peter Boyle?

18. What is the appropriate nickname Charlie gives Travis?

19. What Alfred Hitchcock film did director Martin Scorsese refer to during filming, hoping to capture its sense of paranoia?

20. After screening Martin Scorsese's *Mean Streets* (1973), producer Julia Phillips agreed to let him direct *Taxi Driver* with one condition. What was this?

21. What is the name of the man Travis purchases his guns from?

22. How much does Travis spend for the four guns?

23. How much will a brand-new Cadillac with the pink slip cost Travis?

24. Who does Travis tell the secret serviceman he is?

25. Robert De Niro first played a taxi driver in a 1971 film directed by Noel Black. What is this film?

Quiz No. 48:
Jaws (1975)

Screenplay by Peter Benchley and Carl Gottlieb
Directed by Steven Spielberg
Starring Roy Scheider, Robert Shaw, and Richard Dreyfuss
Universal Pictures

> ***You know, when I first hear the word "Jaws," I think of a period in my life when I was much younger than I am right now. And I think because I was younger, I was more courageous, or I was more stupid. I'm not sure which. So when I think about* Jaws, *I think about courage and stupidity, and I think about both of those things existing underwater.***
>
> —Director Steven Spielberg

Steven Spielberg's *Jaws* is the story of a vacation spot known as Amity Island where swimmers are attacked by a great white shark. Despite Police Chief Martin Brody's (Roy Scheider) attempts to close the beach until the shark can be captured, town officials think only of the revenue that will be lost by closing the beach. Finally, after several shark attacks, Brody is given permission to track down the shark with the aid of marine biologist Matt Hooper (Richard Dreyfuss) and grizzled sea-hunter Quint (Robert Shaw). Dubbed the first "event movie," *Jaws* broke box-office records, becoming the first film ever to gross $100 million.

In 1976, *Jaws* received four Academy Award nominations: Best Picture (David Brown and Richard D. Zanuck), Best Film Editing (Verna Fields), Best Original Score (John Williams), and Best Sound (John R. Carter, Roger Herman, Jr., Robert L. Hoyt, and Earl Mabery). The film was awarded three Oscars, losing in its bid for Best Picture.

1. What was the working title for *Jaws*?
2. What actor did Steven Spielberg first approach for the role of Quint?

3. According to screenwriter Carl Gottlieb, who wrote the Indianapolis monologue, but was not credited?

4. Who appears in a cameo as a reporter on the beach?

5. Whose voice can be heard on Quint's marine radio?

6. Who were author Peter Benchley's high-dollar choices for the roles of Brody, Hooper, and Quint?

7. In what film is a character played by Richard Dreyfuss asked a *Jaws* trivia question, which he gets wrong?

8. When Brody types up the report about the discovery of Chrissie's body, what word does he misspell?

9. What are the dates for Amity Island's Fiftieth Annual Regatta?

10. Actor Robert Shaw appears in another Peter Benchley adaptation. What is this film?

11. What three beaches does Larry Vaughn fear people will go to if Amity's is closed?

12. Noted director Bryan Singer, a huge *Jaws* fan, named his production company after a line from the film. What is the name of Singer's company?

13. What is the name of Alex's dog?

14. A bounty is offered to anyone who kills the "shark that killed Alex M. Kintner." How much is this bounty?

15. Which *Jaws* cast member also appears in *Jaws 2* (1978)and *Jaws: The Revenge* (1987)?

16. What 1997 film parodies the scene in which Hooper and Quint compare scars by having a man and a lesbian compare cunnilingus scars?

17. What does Hooper conclude the odds are that "these bozos get the exact shark"?

18. Brody has a major phobia that he overcomes in the film. What is he afraid of?

19. As Hooper is inspecting the hole in the hull of Ben Gardner's boat, what appears inside the hole?

20. What does Brody assure Vaughn that "any shark expert in the world" will inform him?

21. What does Brody say opening the beach on Independence Day is comparable to doing?

22. What is said to have happened in 1916 at Jersey Beach?

23. What is the name of the shark-related video game a boy is shown playing on Independence Day?

24. What is the name of Quint's boat?

25. The shark knocks a man played by Ted Grossman from his boat as it enters the pond. Moments later, the man's severed leg floats to the surface. In a glaring error, what is different about the man's leg when it surfaces from when it went overboard?

Quiz No. 49: SNOW WHITE AND THE SEVEN DWARFS (1937)

Screenplay by Dorothy Ann Blank, Richard Creedon, Merrill De Maris, Otto Englander, Earl Hurd, and Dick Rickard
Directed by David Hand
Starring Adriana Caselotti, Harry Stockwell, and Lucille LaVerne
Walt Disney Productions

> ***You should have heard the howls of warning when we started making a full-length cartoon. It was prophesied that nobody would sit through such a thing. But there was only one way we could do it successfully and that was to plunge ahead and go for broke—shoot the works. There could be no compromising on money, talent, or time . . . and this at a time when the whole country was in the midst of a crippling depression.***
>
> —PRODUCER WALT DISNEY

Adapted from the Grimm Brothers's fable, *Snow White and the Seven Dwarfs* is the story of an evil queen who becomes jealous because the beauty of her stepdaughter, Snow White, surpasses her own. When the queen's murder ploy fails, Snow White finds refuge with a group of dwarves living in the forest. The evil queen then disguises herself, convincing Snow White to bite into a poisoned apple that places her in a deep sleep, which can only be broken by the kiss of true love.

In 1938, *Snow White and the Seven Dwarfs* received one Academy Award nomination: Best Original Score (Frank Churchill, Leigh Harline, and Paul J. Smith). The film lost to Charles Previn's score for *One Hundred Men and a Girl* (1937). However, the film was awarded an honorary Oscar—one regular-sized statuette and seven smaller ones—and recognized as a "significant screen innovation which has charmed millions and pioneered a great new entertainment field."

1. When the film was initially proposed, a list of possible names for the seven dwarves was submitted. Which two names used in the film did *not* appear on that list?

2. Four years after the release of *Snow White and the Seven Dwarfs,* the dwarves appeared in a Disney short encouraging audiences to purchase war bonds. In the short, six of the dwarves purchase their bonds from an army recruiting station, but Dopey buys his at a bank. What is the name of this short?

3. What is "Music in Your Soup"?

4. Who sings "One Song"?

5. What song does Snow White sing at the well?

6. How does the huntsman attempt to slay Snow White?

7. When Snow White says, "Come on, perk up," to whom is she speaking?

8. The Queen commands the huntsman to bring her proof that he's murdered Snow White. What does the Queen request as sufficient proof?

9. Prior to *Snow White and the Seven Dwarfs,* producer Walt Disney had considered making two other feature-length animated films, both of which would have featured one-live performer surrounded by animated characters. The first of Disney's plans was *Alice in Wonderland,* which would have featured Mary Pickford in the lead role. Then Disney considered making *Rip Van Winkle.* What actor was to appear in the title role of this proposed film?

10. Walt Disney was inspired to make this film after he saw the 1916 live-action version, *Snow White.* In this version, what actress appears in the title role?

11. Live models were photographed for the animators to study. Dancer Marjorie Belcher stood in for Snow White. Who stood in for Prince Charming?

12. A special camera invented and developed by Walt Disney Studios was used on *Snow White and the Seven Dwarfs.* This camera, designed to give animated scenes a three-dimensional quality, was first used on the Oscar-winning short, *The Old Mill* (1937). What is the name of this camera?

13. According to the song, what do the dwarves do the "whole day through"?

14. At the beginning of the film, who does producer Walt Disney thank?

15. When the dwarves find their sink empty, what do they believe has happened?

16. What does Grumpy say all women are?

17. Who does Grumpy say is "full of black magic"?

18. What is said to lie "over seven jeweled hills and beyond the seventh fall"?

19. Grumpy complains that there is a "catch" to Snow White's cleaning and cooking for them. What is this?

20. What does the Queen use "mummy dust" for?

21. What does the Queen say will happen with one taste of the poisoned apple?

22. Which dwarf suggests that Snow White sleep in their beds?

23. After the Queen dips the apple into her cauldron, what appears on it?

24. What actor reportedly donned sunglasses at the premiere of the film in an attempt to conceal his teary eyes?

25. Who keeps vigil outside as the dwarves hold a bedside service for Snow White?

Quiz No. 50:
Butch Cassidy and the Sundance Kid (1969)

Screenplay by William Goldman
Directed by George Roy Hill
Starring Paul Newman, Robert Redford, and Katharine Ross
Twentieth Century–Fox

> ***There was a lot of, "How dare you mess around with this genre?" We were violating a whole form. You're shooting a sacred cow because you're screwing around with the Western.***
>
> —Actor Robert Redford

As the film's tagline states, "most of it's true." Director George Roy Hill's *Butch Cassidy and the Sundance Kid,* loosely based upon the exploits of the real-life train robbers, employs a lighthearted comedic tone that stands very much in contrast to Sam Peckinpah's grim Western *The Wild Bunch* (1969), which was released the same year.

In 1970, *Butch Cassidy and the Sundance Kid* received seven Academy Award nominations: Best Picture (John Foreman), Best Director (Hill), Best Original Screenplay (William Goldman), Best Cinematography (Conrad L. Hall), Best Original Score (Burt Bacharach), Best Song (Bacharach and Hal David), and Best Sound (David Dockendorf and William E. Edmondson). The film was awarded four Oscars, losing in its bids for Best Picture, Best Director, and Best Sound.

1. Four years after the release of *Butch Cassidy and the Sundance Kid,* director George Roy Hill reunited with actors Paul Newman and Robert Redford on another project. What is this film?
2. Steve McQueen was initially signed to play the role of

Sundance, but then backed out. However, Steve McQueen and Paul Newman would later appear together in another film. What is this film?

3. Ten years after the film was made, Richard Lester directed William Katt and Tom Berenger in an Oscar-nominated prequel. What is this film?

4. Warren Beatty was approached to play Sundance, but passed, opting for what he considered a better role in another film. What is this film?

5. In the film, Butch and Sundance's gang are known as the Hole-in-the-Wall Gang. What was the name of their real-life gang?

6. What character was modeled after a real-life mining superintendent named Percy Seibert?

7. After arriving in Bolivia, Butch concludes that Sundance will feel much better after doing something. What is this?

8. Mr. Macon asks Sundance what the secret to his success at playing cards is. What is Sundance's response?

9. According to screenwriter William Goldman's research, what was Etta Place's real-life profession?

10. What is the name of the Union Pacific Railroad agent who refuses to open the safe for Butch and Sundance?

11. What is the name of the Cabron County sheriff?

12. What is the name of the legendary "full-blooded" Indian tracker Butch and Sundance discuss?

13. Screenwriter William Goldman and actor Robert Redford have collaborated on five films. One of these is *Butch Cassidy and the Sundance Kid*. What are the other four films?

14. One of the real-life outlaws' siblings visited the set during filming. Who was this?

15. Both Robert Redford and Paul Newman have since named foundations after *Butch Cassidy and the Sundance Kid* references. Redford founded the Sundance Film Institute and Newman set up a camp for children afflicted with cancer. What is the name of this camp?

16. Who is described as the toughest lawman around?

17. Of Butch and Sundance, who's said to be the brains of the operation?

18. Who sings the film's theme, "Raindrops Keep Fallin' On My Head"?

19. The story of robbers Butch Cassidy and the Sundance Kid had been filmed previously in 1956. This film starred Neville Brand and Alan Hale, Jr., as the desperadoes. What is the name of this film?

20. What crime film released in 2000 pays homage to *Butch Cassidy and the Sundance Kid* through characters known only as Mr. Longbaugh and Mr. Parker?

21. What is Sundance's real name?

22. Screenwriter William Goldman wrote the screenplay with a specific actor in mind for the role of Butch Cassidy. Who was this?

23. Butch says the duo have three things going for themselves. What are these?

24. Actress Katharine Ross later reprised the role of Etta Place in a terrible made-for-television sequel which paired her with Pancho Villa. What is this film?

25. What is Carver's nickname?

Quiz No. 51:
THE PHILADELPHIA STORY (1940)

Screenplay by Donald Ogden Stewart
Directed by George Cukor
Starring Cary Grant, Katharine Hepburn, and James Stewart
Metro-Goldwyn-Mayer

> *George [Cukor] was very helpful to both Jimmy and Cary. And of course, he was always perfect for me. He was a wonderful director and this was his ideal material. It's such fun to do a really good comedy. We all got nominated, and Jimmy won the award.*
>
> —ACTRESS KATHARINE HEPBURN

Director George Cukor's *The Philadelphia Story* is a screwball comedy about a divorced couple, C. K. Dexter Haven (Cary Grant) and wealthy heiress Tracy Lord (Katharine Hepburn). Two years after their divorce, Dexter is working for a tabloid newspaper and Tracy is on the verge of remarrying. On the day of her wedding, Dexter arrives with writer Mike Connor (James Stewart) and photographer Liz Imbrie (Ruth Hussey) in the hopes of spoiling the big event.

In 1941, *The Philadelphia Story* received six Academy Award nominations: Best Picture (Joseph L. Mankiewicz), Best Director (Cukor), Best Screenplay (Donald Ogden Stewart), Best Actor (Stewart), Best Actress (Hepburn), and Best Supporting Actress (Hussey). The film was awarded two Oscars for Best Screenplay and Best Actor.

1. What actors did Katharine Hepburn suggest for the roles of Dexter and Mike?
2. Prior to *The Philadelphia Story,* director George Cukor and Katharine Hepburn had already collaborated on four films. What are these?
3. What is said to be Uncle Willie's favorite perfume?

4. When *The Philadelphia Story* ran on Broadway, who appeared in the role of C. K. Dexter Haven?

5. In 1940, two films directed by George Cukor were released. One of these is *The Philadelphia Story*. What is the other film?

6. Prior to *The Philadelphia Story,* Cary Grant and Katharine Hepburn had already appeared together in three films. What are these?

7. What is Tracy's middle name?

8. How much does an issue of *Spy* cost?

9. Tracy's father had an affair with a showgirl. What was her name?

10. An acclaimed screenwriter contributed to the screenplay, but did not receive credit. Who is this?

11. What does Tracy call Mike, saying it's the "worst kind there is"?

12. When Tracy asks Dinah if she saw a skunk in her dream, she replies, "Well, sort of." What did she see?

13. In 1956, *The Philadelphia Story* was remade as a musical starring Bing Crosby, Frank Sinatra, and Grace Kelly. What is the name of this remake?

14. Katharine Hepburn lost in her bid for Best Actress. Who defeated her?

15. The film's producer, Joseph L. Mankiewicz, would later direct a film starring Cary Grant. What is the name of this film?

16. What is Dexter's pet name for Tracy?

17. What is the name of Tracy's brother?

18. *The Philadelphia Story* was the third adaptation of a play written by Phillip Barry to be directed by George Cukor. What were the two prior adaptations?

19. In 1940, two films written or cowritten by screenwriter Donald Ogden Stewart were nominated for Best Picture. One of these is *The Philadelphia Story*. What is the other film?

20. What does Margaret Lord instruct Dinah to say only if it's "absolutely necessary"?

21. Who is the editor and publisher at Dime and Spy Incorporated?

22. What is the name of the Groucho Marx tune Dinah plays on the piano?

23. What language does Dinah say she learned before English?

24. According to Mike Connor, Kittridge respects only one thing. What is this?

25. In the 1959 made-for-television remake of *The Philadelphia Story,* what Oscar-winning actor appeared in the role of Dexter?

Quiz No. 52:
From Here to Eternity (1953)

Screenplay by Daniel Taradash and James Jones
Directed by Fred Zinneman
Starring Burt Lancaster, Montgomery Clift, and Deborah Kerr
Columbia Pictures

> ***I loved it. It was a hell of a book. And then I spoke to Harry Cohn, who was then the head of Columbia Pictures and a friend. And I said, "I'd like to play that." He said, "Well, you've never done a dramatic role. You're a guy who sings and dances with Gene Kelly."***
>
> —Actor Frank Sinatra

Adapted from James Jones's 1951 novel, Fred Zinneman's film *From Here to Eternity* depicts the lives of American soldiers and their families in 1941, which are shattered when the Japanese attack Pearl Harbor. Novelist Jones penned the first draft of the screenplay, but producers found it explicit in its depictions of sex and violence, so Oscar-winning scribe Daniel Taradash was hired to rewrite it.

In 1954, *From Here to Eternity* received thirteen Academy Award nominations: Best Picture (Buddy Adler), Best Director (Zinneman), Best Screenplay (Taradash), Best Actor (Burt Lancaster), Best Actor (Montgomery Clift), Best Actress (Deborah Kerr), Best Supporting Actor (Frank Sinatra), Best Supporting Actress (Donna Reed), Best Black-and-White Cinematography (Burnett Guffey), Best Film Editing (William A. Lyon), Best Sound (Kohn P. Livadary), Best Black-and-White Costume Design (Jean Louis), and Best Original Score (George Duning and Morris Stoloff). The film was awarded eight Oscars, losing in its bids for Best Actor, Best Actress, Best Original Score, and Best Black-and-White Costume Design. The film's eight Oscars were the most any film had garnered since *Gone with the Wind* (1939).

1. What is Prewitt's nickname?
2. How long are furloughs for division champs?

3. What actress won a Golden Globe Award for her turn as Karen Holmes in the 1979 television remake of *From Here to Eternity*?

4. Because of Prewitt's stubbornness and perceived individualism, what label does Captain Holmes give him?

5. According to Hollywood legend, who persuaded Columbia Pictures chieftain Harry Cohn to cast Frank Sinatra as Maggio?

6. What does Warden say the sergeant would do without him?

7. As a noncommissioned officer, how much time in prison does Warden face if caught sleeping with the wife of a commissioned officer?

8. How long does Prewitt plan to serve in the army?

9. Another actor was initially cast as Maggio, but later declined. Who was this?

10. When Sergeant Galovitch is demoted to private, what is he put in charge of?

11. In James Jones's novel, what was the New Congress Club known as?

12. What actor did Harry Cohn envision as Prewitt?

13. What is not permitted in the New Congress Club?

14. Standing against a railing, Karen throws something into the water. What?

15. What is Sergeant Judson's nickname?

16. Prewitt refuses to fight because of an accident that left a friend in a coma. What is the name of this friend?

17. When Prewitt hears of Maggio's torture in confinement, he is also told of Maggio's "response" to Judson. What did Maggio do?

18. What song, accompanied by Prewitt's bugle, do the soldiers sing?

19. Maggio is arrested and sentenced to be confined in the stockade. For how long is he sentenced to stay there?

20. What is the title of the novel (and film) derived from?

21. Prewitt is assigned all the worst work details. What is this known as?

22. What does Warden say Prewitt has done by turning down Captain Holmes?

23. In whose arms does Maggio die?

24. What is the name of the motel where Prewitt and Alma rendezvous?

25. Warden says he doesn't want to be an officer. Why?

Quiz No. 53:
AMADEUS (1984)

Screenplay by Peter Shaffer
Directed by Milos Forman
Starring F. Murray Abraham, Tom Hulce, and Elizabeth Barridge
The Saul Zaentz Company

> *I had a big collaborative experience with a major amount of music in* Amadeus. *That was a phenomenal adventure that included many hours a day in preparation. Because of the amount of musical work that was included in the story—and also because the brilliance of the man meant that he could do effortlessly what would be very hard for most of us to do—my job became not only to learn how to do all of those things, but learn how to do them so well that it looked like I didn't even know I was doing them.*
>
> —ACTOR TOM HULCE

Adapted from Peter Shaffer's play of the same title, Milos Forman's *Amadeus* is the story of a musician named Antonio Salieri (F. Murray Abraham) who becomes obsessed with Mozart (Tom Hulce). Although Mozart pays him little mind, Salieri perceives himself as a rival, and even becomes convinced that God has blessed Mozart with a divine talent while cursing him with mediocrity. As Salieri is slowly driven into madness by the jealousy that consumes him, he vows revenge against God and Mozart, his instrument of divinity.

In 1985, *Amadeus* received eleven Academy Award nominations: Best Picture (Saul Zaentz), Best Director (Forman), Best Adapted Screenplay (Shaffer), Best Actor (Abraham), Best Actor (Hulce), Best Cinematography (Miroslav Onducek), Best Film Editing (Michael Chandler and Nena Danevic), Best Art Direction–Set Decoration (Karel Cerny and Patrizia von Brandenstein), Best Costume Design (Theodor Pistek), Best Makeup (Paul LeBlanc and Dick Smith), and Best Sound (Mark Berger, Todd Boekelheide, Christopher Newman, and Thomas Scott). *Amadeus* was awarded eight Oscars, losing only in its bids for Best Cinematography, Best Film Editing, and Best Actor (Hulce).

1. What future *Sex and the City* regular appears as Lorl?
2. What is Salieri's first statement in the film?
3. What does Salieri call the "proudest prayer" a boy could utter?
4. Who does Salieri observe to have "no ear at all"?
5. What does Salieri burn after reading Mozart's samples?
6. When meeting Marie Antoinette, the six-year-old Mozart leaped into her arms. What did he then say to her?
7. Emperor Joseph asks Mozart to name him one German virtue. What is Mozart's response?
8. Katerina Cavalieri says that only one thing matters to a woman of taste. What is this?
9. Emperor George concludes that one thing is "wrong" with "Abduction from the Seraglio." What is this?
10. *Amadeus* was the second film Saul Zaentz produced for director Milos Forman. What was the first?
11. What, according to Leopold Mozart, does not pay?
12. After Mozart mocks him, Salieri concludes "That was not Mozart laughing at me." Who does he believe it was?
13. A member of the film's cast originated the role of Mozart in the Broadway production of *Amadeus*. Who was this?
14. What does Mozart's middle name, Amadeus, mean?
15. A secret admirer provides Mozart with a maid. Who is this admirer?
16. Mozart requests permission to adapt a French play that has been banned. What is this play?
17. With what does Salieri say his defeat became a victory?
18. Of Salieri's music, Mozart says when one "hears such sounds," only one word can be said. What is this?
19. Salieri commissions Mozart to write a requiem. Who is this requiem for?
20. In 1984, F. Murray Abraham tied with another actor for Best Actor honors at the Los Angeles Film Critics Association Awards. Who was the other actor?
21. What is the name of the chocolate confection Salieri offers Mozart's wife?

22. Milos Forman was awarded his second Oscar for Best Director for *Amadeus*. For what film did he receive his first?

23. Mozart tells Salieri that he's been foolish. Why?

24. Why does Salieri believe God kept him alive after Mozart's death?

25. Mozart admits he is a vulgar man, but what does he assure the emperor is not so vulgar?

Quiz No. 54: All Quiet on the Western Front (1930)

Screenplay by George Abbott, Del Andrews, and Maxwell Anderson
Directed by Lewis Milestone
Starring Lew Ayres, Louis Wolheim, and John Ray
Universal Pictures

> ***This book is to be neither an accusation nor a confession, and least of all an adventure, for death is not an adventure to those who stand face to face with it. It will try simply to tell of a generation of men who, even though they may have escaped the shells, were destroyed by the war.***
>
> —Author Erich Maria Remarque

All Quiet on the Western Front, an examination of war's futility, was the first significant antiwar film of the sound era. Director Lewis Milestone's grim film follows a group of fresh-faced German schoolboys who are persuaded to enlist in the military and fight in World War I by their jingoistic instructor. When the young men reach the battlefield and find themselves surrounded by the horrors of warfare, they begin to question the sense of patriotism they have been taught.

In 1931, *All Quiet on the Western Front* received four Academy Award nominations: Best Picture (Carl Laemmle, Jr.), Best Director (Milestone), Best Adapted Screenplay (George Abbott, Del Andrews, and Maxwell Anderson), and Best Cinematography (Arthur Edeson). The film was awarded two Oscars for Best Picture and Best Director.

1. What legendary filmmaker served as dialogue director?
2. In 1937, James Whale directed a sequel. In this film, Slim Summerville reprises the role of Tjaden. What is this film?
3. What is Himmelstoss's occupation?
4. During a conversation about the causes of war, one soldier concludes that "every full-grown emperor needs one war." Why is this?

5. Paul says that his classmates once believed it "beautiful and sweet" to die for one's country. What does he say "taught [them] better"?

6. What legendary filmmaker appears as an uncredited extra?

7. What is the name of the sergeant who is said to have an uncanny knack for locating food?

8. Lying in the makeshift hospital, Franz Kimmerick first realizes that his watch has been stolen. He then realizes that something else has been taken from him, causing him to ask, "Why didn't they tell me?" What is he referring to?

9. After killing him, why does Paul tell the French soldier, "You're better off than me"?

10. What does Paul say you "can't fool anybody about" for very long on the frontlines?

11. In the 1979 television remake of *All Quiet on the Western Front,* what actor was nominated for an Emmy for his performance as Stanislaus Katczinsky?

12. What nickname is Himmelstoss given?

13. What actress originally appeared as Mrs. Baumer, but was replaced in newly shot scenes when sound was added to the film?

14. A scene was added depicting the Nazis burning books in the 1939 reissued version of the film. What book is symbolically shown being burned?

15. When Paul reaches for the butterfly, the hand shown does not belong to actor Lew Ayres. Whose hand is it?

16. Katczinsky reprimands the new soldier for retrieving Behm. Why?

17. In the montage focusing on a pair of boots, what is shown?

18. After his eye-opening trip home, whom does Paul believe is the only person he has left to turn to?

19. Who was hired to authenticate the uniforms and procedures depicted in the film?

20. Lewis Milestone won the Oscar for Best Director for *All Quiet on the Western Front.* This is one of three career nominations Milestone received as a director. What are the other two films Milestone was nominated for?

21. In its prologue, the film is said to be neither an accusation nor what?

22. Why does Paul believe the dead Frenchman accuses him?

23. What does Paul's dying mother needlessly warn him about, saying, "They're no good"?

24. Before his death in 1980, what did director Lewis Milestone beg Universal to remove from the film's final sequence?

25. What does Tjaden believe is the only thing fresh soldiers know how to do?

Quiz No. 55: The Sound of Music (1965)

Screenplay by Ernest Lehman
Directed by Robert Wise
Starring Julie Andrews, Christopher Plummer, and Eleanor Parker
Twentieth Century–Fox

> *Julie Andrews had far more pressure on her.* The Sound of Music *in many ways rested on her shoulders. She wasn't a superstar yet—in fact, in March 1964, she was virtually unknown in Hollywood. Although she was a star on Broadway, Bob Wise and Saul Chaplin, the film's associate producer, had to be convinced she was photogenic enough to play the role of Maria von Trapp in their movie. They were able to view some footage of her at Disney Studios in the not-yet-released film* Mary Poppins. *After seeing just a minute of Julie, in what would be an Oscar-winning performance, Bob and Saul looked at each other and said, "Let's get out of here and hire her before someone else does!"*
>
> —Actress Charmian Carr

Adapted from Richard Rodgers and Oscar Hammerstein's 1959 Broadway musical, director Robert Wise's *The Sound of Music* tells the tale of a widower, Captain von Trapp (Christopher Plummer), who hires a new governess, Maria (Julie Andrews). While watching the captain with his new fiancée, Maria begins to fall in love with him and comes to the realization that she no longer wants to be a nun.

In 1966, *The Sound of Music* received ten Academy Award nominations: Best Picture (Saul Chaplin), Best Director (Wise), Best Actress (Andrews), Best Supporting Actress (Peggy Wood), Best Color Cinematography (Ted D. McCord), Best Film Editing (William Reynolds), Best Non-Original Score (Irwin Kostal), Best Sound (James Corcoran and Fred Hynes), Best Color Art Direction–Set Decoration (Boris Leven, Ruby R. Levitt, and Walter M. Scott), and Best Color Costume Design (Dorothy Jeakins). The film was awarded five Oscars for Best

Picture, Best Director, Best Non-Original Score, Best Film Editing, and Best Sound.

1. *The Sound of Music* is based on the autobiography of Maria von Trapp. What is the title of this book?
2. What is the name of the 1956 German film adaptation of Maria von Trapp's autobiography?
3. *The Sound of Music* was the number-one box-office hit of all time. What film did it unseat for this designation?
4. Although Marni Nixon made her screen debut in *The Sound of Music,* this was her second film working with director Robert Wise. What was their previous collaboration, and what was her involvement with this film?
5. According to the song, what will Maria's heart be blessed with?
6. What number is Maria said to be in "a long line of governesses"?
7. What is the name of the Von Trapp family butler?
8. *The Sound of Music* held the title of most successful musical film until 1978. What film then claimed this distinction?
9. What is the "first rule" of the Von Trapp household?
10. Who proclaims himself a "very charming sponge"?
11. From what does Maria fashion play clothes for the children?
12. Over what does the captain say he prefers "Austrian voices raised in song"?
13. As Maria walks through a stone archway during "I Have Confidence," she passes two women dressed in Austrian peasant garb. Who appears in a cameo as the elder of the two women?
14. What actor did Robert Wise initially consider casting for the role of Captain von Trapp?
15. Who was the first director attached to *The Sound of Music*?
16. Who sings "Climb Every Mountain" to Maria?
17. The captain says he broke off his engagement with Elsa because he realized that he was in love with another woman. Who is this?
18. What is the song the captain and his future bride sing about being rewarded for past deeds?
19. Who is the only person in the neighborhood not flying the flag of the Third Reich?
20. After fleeing the Salzburg show, where does the Von Trapp family hide?

21. When the nuns confess to having sinned, what have they done?
22. Who defends Maria, saying that the "wool of a black sheep is just as warm"?
23. How many children does Captain von Trapp have?
24. What does Maria confess that she cannot keep from doing, no matter where she goes?
25. What does Max warn Elsa must be kept in the family?

Quiz No. 56: M*A*S*H (1970)

Screenplay by Ring Lardner, Jr.
Directed by Robert Altman
Starring Donald Sutherland, Elliot Gould, and Tom Skerritt
Twentieth Century–Fox

> ***Whereas I dealt with the war and the comedy, the television series merely deals with the comedy and skims over what those men are actually there for.***
> —Director Robert Altman

Adapted from Richard Hooker's novel of the same title, *M*A*S*H* follows the Korean War exploits of the 4077th Mobile Army Surgical Hospital's two newest surgeons, Captains Hawkeye Pierce (Donald Sutherland) and Duke Forrest (Tom Skeritt). Director Robert Altman's film was a huge success and eventually spawned the long-running television series, *M*A*S*H,* which in turn spawned three more offshoots, *Trapper John, M.D., After M*A*S*H,* and *W*A*L*T*E*R.* In *Film Quarterly,* William Johnson observes that *M*A*S*H* "is not really about army life or rebellion . . . it is about the human condition, and that's why it is such an exciting comedy." Even Pauline Kael, who rarely had anything good to say about *any* film, praised it as a "marvelously unstable comedy, a tough, funny, and sophisticated burlesque of military attitudes."

In 1971, *M*A*S*H* received five Academy Award nominations: Best Picture (Ingo Preminger), Best Director (Altman), Best Adapted Screenplay (Ring Lardner, Jr.), Best Supporting Actress (Sally Kellerman), and Best Film Editing (Danford B. Greene). The film's sole Oscar was awarded to Lardner for its screenplay.

1. What does Hawkeye feel Walt needs for "therapeutic value"?
2. Walt has two nicknames. What are these?
3. What is the title of the film's theme song?

4. What uncanny *M*A*S*H*-related events transpired on February 15 and February 16, 1996?

5. Who is the "sultry bitch with the fire in her eyes"?

6. While Frank and O'Houlihan have sex, what does Radar place inside the tent?

7. What causes Hawkeye to exclaim, "Frank Burns has gone nuts"?

8. While Burns teaches Ho-Jon to read the Bible, Duke gives him something else to read. What is this?

9. Actor Robert Duvall appears in six AFI Top 100 films. One of these is *M*A*S*H*. What are the other five films?

10. When Hawkeye concludes that "you have to make certain concessions to the war," what is he referring to?

11. When O'Houlihan and Frank Burns write to report the "unwholesome" events at the 4077th, what do they say the letter is written in the interests of?

12. What does O'Houlihan say she cannot forgive?

13. Why does Henry attempt to have McIntyre arrested?

14. What does O'Houlihan believe to be "inconsistent with maximum efficiency"?

15. Who does Henry say has "all the fun"?

16. Where does O'Houlihan say she likes to call home?

17. What is said to be the "most uplifting program I've ever heard"?

18. How many women is Walt engaged to?

19. Regarding his own identity, what does Walt become convinced of?

20. What short-lived 1975 cartoon parodied *M*A*S*H* and featured characters named Coldlips, Major Sideburns, and Colonel Flake?

21. Who is said to be the best-equipped dentist in the army?

22. What type of women does Duke say he prefers?

23. What type of photographs are taken of Colonel Merrill?

24. What football star appears as Spearchucker Jones?

25. Only one actor appears in both the film *M*A*S*H* and as a regular on the television series. Who is this?

Quiz No. 57:
THE THIRD MAN (1949)

Screenplay by Graham Green
Directed by Carol Reed
Starring Joseph Cotten, Trevor Howard, and Orson Welles
Selznick Releasing Corporation

> ***Every sentence in the whole script is about Harry Lime; nobody talks about anything else for ten reels. And then there's that shot in the doorway—what a star entrance that was! In theater, you know, the old star actors never liked to come on until the end of the first act.***
>
> —ACTOR ORSON WELLES

Carol Reed's stylish thriller, *The Third Man,* is the story of American pulp writer Holly Martins (Joseph Cotten) who travels to post–World War II Vienna to see an old friend, Harry Lime (Orson Welles). However, when he arrives in Vienna, he learns that his friend has been killed. Searching for the truth, Martins becomes entangled in a web of mystery and deceit. Because of his investigation, he becomes a target of both the local authorities and the underworld figures Lime was associated with. Because of the film's breathtaking cinematography, use of framing, and the appearances of actors Cotten and Welles, *The Third Man* has been called the greatest film Orson Welles never directed.

In 1951, *The Third Man* received three Academy Award nominations: Best Director (Reed), Best Cinematography (Robert Krasker), and Best Film Editing (Oswald Hafenrichter). The film's sole Oscar was awarded to Krasker for his moody black-and-white cinematography.

1. After World War II, Vienna was divided into four zones of occupation. What were these?

2. What is the name of the 1951 radio show in which Orson Welles reprised his role as Harry Lime?

3. What are *The Lone Rider of Santa Fe* and *Death at the Double-X Ranch*?

4. What does Major Calloway say is the best thing that ever happened to Harry Lime?

5. The sergeant tells Martins that he's a fan of his books. What does he say he likes about them?

6. Orson Welles and Joseph Cotten appear in nine films together. One of these is *The Third Man*. What are the other eight?

7. Kurtz tells Martins that Harry's thoughts were of only one person when he died. Who was this?

8. When Harry's hand is seen at the end of the film, this is actually not Orson Welles's hand. Whose is it?

9. What acclaimed screenwriter contributed to the script, but did not receive credit?

10. Orson Welles used the money he earned from *The Third Man* to finance a film he was directing. What is this film?

11. Harry Lime got into trouble with the law for stealing, diluting, and selling something. What was this?

12. In what turned out to be a huge mistake on his part, Orson Welles chose to appear in the film for a hundred thousand dollars rather than receiving a percentage of the film's box office. What percentage was Welles offered?

13. What does Harry say that "no one talks in terms of"?

14. Who does Major Calloway advise Holly Martins to "leave death to"?

15. What does Dr. Winkle say his opinion is limited to?

16. What is the lecture Martins is supposed to give?

17. At the Casanova Club, who does Martins refer to as a "silly-looking bunch"?

18. According to Martins, what did Harry Lime make everything feel like?

19. What did Harry teach Martins when he was fourteen-years old?

20. In the 1997 remake, *The Third Woman,* where is the story's setting moved to?

21. How does Martins injure his hand?

22. When Popescu asks Martins about the book he's working on, what does Martins say its title is?

23. The townsfolk chase Martins because they believe him guilty of murder. Who do they think he killed?

24. A mysterious driver takes Martins, whisking him through the darkened streets of the city. Where does he take him?

25. When police officers dig up Harry's grave, whose body do they find?

Quiz No. 58:
FANTASIA (1940)

Screenplay by Joe Grant, Dick Huemer, Lee Blair, Elmer Plummer, Phil Dike, Sylvia Moberly-Holland, Norman Wright, Albert Heath, Bianca Majolie, Graham Heid, and Perce Pierce
Directed by James Algar, Samuel Armstrong, Ford Beebe, Norman Ferguson, Jim Handley, T. Hee, Wilfred Jackson, Hamilton Luske, Bill Roberts, Paul Satterfield, and Ben Sharpsteen
Starring Leopold Stokowski, Deems Taylor, and Julietta Novis
Walt Disney Productions

> ***In a profession that has been an unending voyage of discovery in the realms of color, sound, and motion,* Fantasia *represents our most exciting adventure. At last, we found a way to use in our medium the great music of all times and the flood of new ideas which it inspires. Perhaps Bach and Beethoven are strange bedfellows for Mickey Mouse, but it's all been a lot of fun.*** —PRODUCER WALT DISNEY

Fantasia is one of Walt Disney's most entertaining experiments, successfully marrying some of the most beautiful music ever written with eight perfectly choreographed animated scenes. Disney's animators reinterpret compositions written by the likes of Ludwig van Beethoven, Igor Stravinsky, Franz Schubert, and Johann Sebastian Bach. The film later spawned a lackluster sequel, *Fantasia 2000* (1999). Henry Allen of *The Washington Post* observes, "You know you are supposed to like *Fantasia* the way you are supposed to like Tom Sawyer or the Mormon Tabernacle Choir, or Bob Hope, or the recent PBS series about the Civil War—cozy icons you're obliged to enjoy as if they stand for something higher. . . . The problem being that icons tend to be disappointments, or bores, pallid homage to gentility. The point is: Don't let it worry you. *Fantasia* is still glorious."

In 1941, *Fantasia* received no Academy Award nominations.

However, it did receive a special honorary Oscar for its "unique achievement in the creation of a new form of visualized music . . . thereby widening the scope of the motion picture as entertainment and as an artform."

1. In the original version, who serves as narrator?
2. Who narrates the 1982 rerelease?
3. Who provides the voice of Mickey Mouse in *Fantasia*?
4. What controversial material was allegedly cut from *The "Pastoral Symphony* segment?
5. What is the significance of Mickey Mouse's eyes in *Fantasia*?
6. A segment created around a Claude Debussy composition was created, but cut from the film. What was the Debussy composition?
7. A wave hits a rock and spills over. A face can be seen in the curl of the wave. Whose is it?
8. As the film begins, what does the narrator welcome the audience to a "new form of"?
9. The narrator concludes that there are three types of music. What are these?
10. Who does the narrator explain that the sequences are *not* the interpretation of, which he believes is "all to the good"?
11. In *Toccata and Fugue in D Minor,* what transform into silver streaks that shoot through the heavens?
12. When the narrator says "it's funny how wrong an artist can be about his work," what musician and composition is he discussing?
13. What does the narrator tell the audience they will *not* see in *The Nutcracker Suite*?
14. During the "Dance of the Sugar Plum Fairies," what do the fireflies turn into?
15. What causes the white explosion of dewdrops that falls onto a red mushroom?
16. In "Chinese Dance," what do the red mushrooms become after shaking off the dew?
17. How old does the narrator say the story of the sorcerer's apprentice is?
18. How long is "The Sorcerer's Apprentice" segment?
19. What smacks Mickey Mouse across the backside?
20. How many buckets of water do each of the brooms carry?

21. What does the narrator inform us was Stravinsky's purpose for writing *The Rite of Spring*?
22. What do the fins of the Polypterus become?
23. What number is the symphony Beethoven called *The Pastoral*?
24. On the slopes of what mountain does *The Pastoral* take place?
25. At the bacchanal feast, what shatters the wine vat?

Quiz No. 59:
REBEL WITHOUT A CAUSE (1955)

Screenplay by Nicholas Ray, Stewart Stern, and Irving Shulman
Directed by Nicholas Ray
Starring James Dean, Natalie Wood, and Sal Mineo
Warner Bros.

> ***The drama of [James Dean's] life was the drama of desiring to belong—so was Jim Stark's. It was a conflict of violent eagerness and mistrust created very young. The intensity of his desires, his fears, could make the search at times arrogant, egocentric; but behind it was such a desperate vulnerability that one was moved, even frightened.***
>
> —DIRECTOR NICHOLAS RAY

Rebel Without a Cause, the film James Dean is most often associated with, is a study of the problems that faced middle-class teens in the 1950s, and their struggles to overcome them. While the specific situations and weapons might have changed, the film remains a poignant story in an era of high-school shootings and random acts of teen violence caused by alienation. As *San Francisco Chronicle* critic Peter Stack observes, "The crack in the pretty picture of America goes a lot deeper than we thought." Director Nicholas Ray's tale of reckless youth and aimless rebellion is also significant because it launched the careers of actors Sal Mineo, Natalie Wood, and Dennis Hopper.

In 1956, *Rebel Without a Cause* received three Academy Award nominations: Best Screenplay (Ray), Best Supporting Actor (Mineo), and Best Supporting Actress (Wood). The film was awarded no Oscars.

1. Why is Plato's mother staying in Chicago?
2. Why did Jack Warner order several scenes from *Rebel Without a Cause* reshot?
3. What future AFI Top 100 director appears in a small role as one of the goons who terrorize Jim?
4. Which cast member referred to *Rebel Without a Cause* as "Ozzie and Harriet with venom"?

5. The film was initially conceived at Warner Bros. as an adaptation of a real-life study on teen violence written by Dr. Robert Linder. What is the title of this book?

6. During preproduction, what did censors demand there be "no inference" of in the film?

7. Why is Judy arrested?

8. What is Plato's real name?

9. What nickname does Jim's father use when talking with him?

10. Shooting of the film was briefly suspended because James Dean was bedridden with sickness. What was he inflicted with?

11. What does Jim ask if Judy would like to see as he drives her home after Buzz's accident?

12. Who is Plato's screen idol?

13. What is the significance of the day Plato is arrested on?

14. What does Jim wish his father would do to his mother "just once"?

15. What do the gang members call the high-speed chase with stolen cars?

16. Before director Nicholas Ray tackled the screenplay himself, three screenwriters had tried unsuccessfully to combine Dr. Robert Linder's book and Ray's short story. Who were these screenwriters?

17. Much of the film's storyline comes from a seventeen-page short story written by director Nicholas Ray. What is the title of this story?

18. How does Plato say he got to the race?

19. Jim says his parents believe everything will be "roses and sunshine" if they do what?

20. Two years after their collaboration on *Rebel Without a Cause*, screenwriter Stewart Stern wrote a documentary about the short life of actor James Dean. This documentary was directed by Robert Altman. What is the title of this film?

21. Who does Jim say he does *not* want to be like?

22. What regarding the steps to the high school is Jim warned about?

23. What does Jim believe Plato has read too much of?

24. What do Buzz and Jim share on their walk toward the edge of the cliff?

25. Warner Bros. had signed actor Dennis Hopper after his January 5, 1955, appearance as an epileptic on a television show. What was this series?

Quiz No. 60:
Raiders of the Lost Ark (1981)

Screenplay by George Lucas, Philip Kaufman, and Lawrence Kasdan
Directed by Steven Spielberg
Starring Harrison Ford, Karen Allen, and Paul Freeman
Paramount Pictures

> ***I made it as a "B" movie. I didn't see the film as anything more than a better-made version of the Republic serials.***
>
> —Director Steven Spielberg

One of the greatest action-adventure films ever produced, *Raiders of the Lost Ark* is director Steven Spielberg's nod to the serials of the thirties and forties, as well as the Hammer Films sci-fi romp, *Quatermass and the Pit* (1967). (There are a number of references and homages to this film in *Raiders,* most notably the scene in which the spirits kill the Nazi antagonists.) *Raiders of the Lost Ark* was the first film to feature heroic archaeologist Indiana Jones (Harrison Ford)—the name itself a nod to *Nevada Smith* (1966)—who would later appear in two more feature films, as well as his own television series.

In 1982, *Raiders of the Lost Ark* received eight Academy Award nominations: Best Picture (Frank Marshall), Best Director (Spielberg), Best Cinematography (Douglas Slocombe), Best Art Direction–Set Decoration (Leslie Dilley, Michael Ford, and Norman Reynolds), Best Visual Effects (Richard Edlund, Joe Johnston, Bruce Nicholson, and Kit West), Best Film Editing (Michael Kahn), Best Sound (Roy Charman, Gregg Landaker, Steve Maslow, and Bill Varney), and Best Original Score (John Williams). The film lost in four important categories—Best Picture, Best Director, Best Cinematography, and Best Original Score—but was awarded five Oscars, including a Special Achievement Award for Sound Effects Editing (Richard L. Anderson and Ben Burtt).

1. After performing a taste test of sorts, how long does Satipo estimate the poison-tipped dart has been there?

2. When Barraca attempts to shoot him, what does Indy do?

3. The film's title was altered for a videocassette rerelease. What was the film's new title?

4. Whose remains do Indy and Satipo find inside the temple?

5. Who appears in an uncredited cameo as the German pilot Marion hits over the head?

6. Prior to Harrison Ford, another actor had been signed to play the role of Indiana Jones. However, contractual obligations led to scheduling conflicts, and the actor had to be replaced. He later said, "When I lost *Raiders*, through no fault of my own, I thought, 'Well that was my shot. From now on, I'm a TV actor.' I felt entitled to get something out of it and kept telling people 'That was *my* part.'" Who is this actor?

7. What does Satipo request in exchange for the bullwhip?

8. Just after diving under the closing door, who does Indy find impaled?

9. As Indy tells Marcus, "You know what a cautious fellow I am," what does he pack in his suitcase?

10. An attractive female student bats her eyes at Indy. What are the words written on her eyelids?

11. As Indy and Sallah remove the ark, hieroglyphics featuring characters conceived by George Lucas are visible behind them. Who are these characters?

12. What is the name of the seaplane pilot?

13. What was the Ark designed to carry?

14. According to Indy, what will the possessors of the Ark be infused with?

15. What is the name of the rod with the "elaborate headpiece" the Nazis are searching for?

16. Who was Indy's mentor at the University of Chicago?

17. What is the name of the snake on board the seaplane?

18. Who is the curator of the National Museum in Washington?

19. What letters are printed on the outside of the seaplane, and what is this a reference to?

20. A group of natives assist Belloq in stealing the idol. From what tribe are these natives?

21. How much money does Indy offer Marion for the medallion?

22. According to the markings on the headpiece, what is the height of the staff?
23. What kind of men is Indy informed will be studying the Ark?
24. What stops Toht from scarring Marion's face?
25. What happens to Toht when he grabs the medallion?

Quiz No. 61:
VERTIGO (1958)

Screenplay by Samuel A. Taylor and Alec Coppel
Directed by Alfred Hitchcock
Starring James Stewart, Kim Novak, and Barbara Bel Geddes
Paramount Pictures

> ***What I liked best is when the girl came back after having had her hair dyed blond. James Stewart is disappointed because she hasn't put her hair up in a bun. What this really means is that the girl has almost stripped, but won't take her knickers off. When he insists, she says, "All right!" and goes into the bathroom while he waits outside. What Stewart is really waiting for is for the woman to emerge totally naked this time, and ready for love.***
> —DIRECTOR ALFRED HITCHCOCK

Now viewed as director Alfred Hitchcock's most complex and multi-layered work, *Vertigo* was met with little acclaim when it was released in 1958. As a *London Observer* film critic wrote, "The last half hour is dull as ditch water, for there is no suspense, and no mystery remains except the mystery of who is supposed to care what happens." The Hitchcock noir tells the story of Scottie Ferguson (James Stewart), a man hired to watch a woman who's developed a peculiar obsession with the past.

In 1959, *Vertigo* received two Academy Award nominations: Best Art Direction–Set Decoration (Henry Bumstead, Sam Comer, Frank R. McKelvy, and Hal Pereira) and Best Sound (George Dutton). The film was awarded no Oscars.

1. According to the tagline, what will director Alfred Hitchcock engulf viewers in a whirlpool of?
2. In 1958, *Vertigo* was one of two films James Stewart and Kim Novak appeared together in. What is the other film?
3. Alfred Hitchcock optioned Pierre Boileau and Thomas Narce-

jac's novel, *D'Entre les Morts*—which he adapted into *Vertigo*—after first attempting to secure the rights to remake a French film based on another of the duo's works. What is this film?

4. Why does Scottie say he cannot go to the bar at the top of the Mark?

5. Outside the shipbuilding company, a man can be seen carrying a trumpet case. Who is this?

6. What is Scottie's real name?

7. Where does Judy Barton say she's from?

8. How much of the film's screenplay was written or conceived by cowriter Alec Coppel?

9. Who was Alfred Hitchcock's first choice for the role of Madeline?

10. Between 1958 and 1960, actress Barbara Bel Geddes and Alfred Hitchcock worked together five times. However, *Vertigo* was the only Hitchcock-directed film she ever appeared in. What are the other four projects the two worked together on?

11. Madeline accuses Scottie of being one of three things: a polltaker, a hotel resident, or what?

12. What is the name of the 1997 documentary Harrison Engle directed about the legacy of *Vertigo*?

13. In 1996, *Vertigo* received an award from the New York Film Critics Circle. What was this?

14. *Vertigo* was the third Alfred Hitchcock film that actor Tom Helmore appeared in. What are the two prior films?

15. Midge declares that she has returned to her "first love." What is this?

16. In what city does *Vertigo* take place?

17. Because of guilt and acrophobia, Scottie was forced to resign from his previous occupation. What was this?

18. Scottie asks, "What's this doohickey?" What is he referring to?

19. San Juan Batista looks quite different in the film than it does in reality. Why is this?

20. In *Vertigo,* director Alfred Hitchcock originated the famed combination of forward zoom and reverse tracking shot in an effort to give audiences a sense of vertigo. How much did this brief stairwell shot cost to film?

21. Alfred Hitchcock directed an additional scene, which was tacked onto the end of the film for its European release. Why?

22. What is the name of the book shop owned by Pop Leibel?

23. Carlotta's home was renovated after her death and later became a hotel. What is the name of this hotel?

24. According to Elster, there are four things that "spell San Francisco." What are these?

25. According to the film, what event transpired on December 3, 1831?

Quiz No. 62:
TOOTSIE (1982)

Screenplay by Larry Gelbart
Directed by Sydney Pollack
Starring Dustin Hoffman, Jessica Lange, and Teri Garr
Columbia Pictures

> ***I think some of the arguments that I had with Dustin [Hoffman] were well-publicized. Even though they were creative arguments, they were arguments just the same. We did a certain amount of fighting on that film, but a lot less than what was reported. But we still disagreed sometimes about what was funny or what wasn't or what a particular scene should or should not be about. We worked very well together once we got the arguments out of the way. . . . We'd come in the morning, maybe argue, maybe not argue, and then forget the arguments and go ahead and make the picture.***
>
> —DIRECTOR SYDNEY POLLACK

Tootsie is screenwriter Larry Gelbart's comical look at a down-on-his-luck actor named Michael Dorsey (Dustin Hoffman). Michael's problem isn't talent—the man has plenty—but he's considered such an incredible pain in the ass that no one wants to work with him. So what's a guy to do? Michael dresses like a woman, changes his name to Dorothy, and goes to work on a popular daytime soap. Soon, Dorothy becomes the talk of the town, and Michael's future looks bright until he falls in love with his costar, Julie (Jessica Lange). The problem is that Julie doesn't know he's a man!

In 1983, *Tootsie* received ten Academy Award nominations: Best Picture (Sydney Pollack and Dick Richards), Best Director (Pollack), Best Original Screenplay (Gelbart), Best Actor (Hoffman), Best Supporting Actress (Lange), Best Supporting Actress (Teri Garr), Best Cinematography (Owen Roizman), Best Film Editing (Fredric Steinkamp and William Steinkamp), Best Song (Alan Bergman, Marilyn Bergman, and Dave Grusin), and Best Sound (Richard

Alexander, Les Fresholtz, Les Larowitz, and Arthur Piantadosi). The film's sole Oscar was awarded to actress Jessica Lange.

1. Who performed the songs "Tootsie" and "It Might Be You" for the film?
2. What does a director ask Michael to walk to the center of the stage to do, annoying him?
3. What does Michael say has no effect on him as a character actor?
4. At Michael's birthday party, he is toasted because "like it or not, he makes you remember" what?
5. In 1983, Jessica Lange was awarded an Oscar for Best Supporting Actress for her turn in *Tootsie*. That same year, she was also nominated for Best Actress, but lost. For what film did Lange receive her Best Actress nomination?
6. What does Michael tell Sandy he will pick her up at 10 A.M. to do?
7. Who appears in the role of George Fields?
8. What television producer and director worked on the screenplay but did not receive credit?
9. What does George say a tomato does not have?
10. What was the film's working title?
11. Who does Dorothy call a "macho shithead"?
12. What is John Van Horn's nickname?
13. What is the name of the soap opera that features Dorothy Michaels?
14. Who does Michael say is smarter than he is?
15. A fan asks April if her character deliberately overdosed a patient in a recent episode. What is April's response?
16. After *Tootsie*, Dabney Coleman and Teri Garr worked together on two more projects. What are these?
17. What artist makes an uncredited cameo in the film, appearing on the cover of *People* with Dorothy?
18. Michael uses the "refreshing" pickup approach Julie said she would like a man to use on her. What is her response?
19. Michael says he believes in unemployment. What does he say he does *not* believe in?
20. A poster of a rock group hangs in the upstairs bedroom of Les Nichols's home. What is this group?

21. What well-known film critic appears in an uncredited cameo?

22. What are the names of Dorothy's parents?

23. Michael tells Julie that he was a better man with her, as a woman, than he ever was what?

24. In 1983, Larry Gelbart was nominated for Best Screenplay for *Tootsie.* This was his second Oscar nomination. For what screenplay did Gelbart receive his first nomination?

25. Actress Jessica Lange won her second Golden Globe Award for *Tootsie.* For what film had she won her first Golden Globe Award?

Quiz No. 63: STAGECOACH (1939)

Screenplay by Dudley Nichols
Directed by John Ford
Starring John Wayne, Claire Trevor, and Thomas Mitchell
United Artists

> *Anytime there was a chance for a reaction—which is the most important thing in a motion picture—[John Ford] always took reactions of me, so I'd be part of every scene. . . . I knew he liked that particular character as well as me, and I think this is what he would have wanted a young man to be.*
>
> —ACTOR JOHN WAYNE

Perhaps the quintessential journey film, *Stagecoach* rescued John Wayne from a forgettable string of "B" films and made him an overnight star. Dudley Nichols's screenplay follows a stagecoach traveling through the Wild West. The coach's nine passengers are faced with a number of hardships during this journey, from an Indian attack to the birth of a child. When *Stagecoach* was released, *New York Times* critic Frank S. Nugent praised, "John Ford has swept aside ten years of artifice and talkie compromise and has made a motion picture that sings a song of camera. It moves, and how beautifully it moves . . ."

In 1940, *Stagecoach* received seven Academy Award nominations: Best Picture (Walter Wanger), Best Director (Ford), Best Supporting Actor (Thomas Mitchell), Best Original Score (Richard Hageman, W. Franke Harling, John Leipold, and Leo Shuken), Best Art Direction (Alexander Toluboff), Best Black-and-White Cinematography (Bert Glennon), and Best Film Editing (Otho Lovering and Dorothy Spencer). The film's two Oscars were awarded for Best Supporting Actor and Best Original Score.

1. Tim Holt appears very briefly in the film. For this appearance, he was paid five thousand dollars. How much was John Wayne, the lead, paid for his work in the film?
2. What is the "disease" Josiah Boone and Dallas are the victims of?
3. If "talk was credit," who does Jerry say would be his best customer?
4. How does Curly know that Gatewood did not receive a telegraph?
5. What was producer Martin Rackin's nonsensical reason for remaking *Stagecoach* in 1966?
6. What is Ringo's real name?
7. What happened to Ringo's brother and father?
8. Where is Peacock from?
9. Who are both Curly and Ringo after in Lordsburg?
10. What kind of man, according to Gatewood, does the United States need for a president?
11. Who does Hatfield call a "drunken beast"?
12. In 1986, a horrid made-for-television remake of *Stagecoach* was produced that featured Country-Western singers in all the roles. In this version, who appears as Ringo?
13. What does Chris conclude is the good thing about having an Apache wife?
14. Where were Dallas's parents killed?
15. Chris says finding another wife will be easy. What does he say will *not* be so easy to replace?
16. Before John Wayne was cast, director John Ford asked Wayne whether he had any suggestions for the role of Ringo. Wayne gave him the name of one actor. Who was this?
17. After Ringo proposes, Dallas asks someone for advice. Who?
18. How many children does Peacock have?
19. At what age did Ringo go to prison?
20. Ringo tells Curly to look at the hills. What does he see?
21. Hatfield attempts to save Mrs. Mallory from the Apaches. How?
22. As the stagecoach pulls into town, we see Luke Plummer playing poker. What does his final hand consist of?
23. When asked why the Indians didn't simply shoot the horses to stop the stagecoach, what was John Ford's reply?

24. Tim Holt appears in two AFI Top 100 films. One of these is *Stagecoach*. What is the other film?

25. In 1940, Bert Glennon received two Oscar nominations for Best Cinematography. One of these was for *Stagecoach*. What was the other film Glennon was nominated for?

Quiz No. 64:
Close Encounters of the Third Kind (1977)

Screenplay by Steven Spielberg
Directed by Steven Spielberg
Starring Richard Dreyfuss, Teri Garr, and Melinda Dillon
Columbia Pictures

> ***We all felt that this particular project was a noble agenda. This was a big idea Steven [Spielberg] was talking about. It wasn't just a sci-fi movie, and it wasn't just about monsters from the Id. It was that we are not only not alone, but that we have relatively little to fear. People don't realize, or it's hard for people to remember that Close*** **Encounters** ***was truly the first cultural iconic moment that said, "Calm down, we're okay. They can be our friends." That was a huge statement, and I, along with lots of other people, wanted to participate in that.***
>
> —Actor Richard Dreyfuss

Rather than resting on his laurels after the success of *Jaws* (1975), Steven Spielberg helmed this taut examination of humans who make contact with extraterrestrials (a subject he would revisit in *E.T. The Extra-Terrestrial,* 1982). Coupled with his pal George Lucas's *Star Wars* (1977), Spielberg's film changed the way Hollywood saw special effects. *Ain't It Cool News* critic Harry Knowles praises, "This film, for me, is unassailable. It's this gleaming, gorgeous better-than-CG film, made of magic lights and lens flares. The look in [Richard] Dreyfuss's eyes—he's seeing these things; I believe it. There is a fervor to him, an honesty to his consuming thirst to understand what it is he has seen."

In 1978, *Close Encounters of the Third Kind* received eight Academy Award nominations: Best Director (Spielberg), Best Supporting Actress (Melinda Dillon), Best Cinematography (Vilmos Zsigmond), Best Art Direction–Set Decoration (Phil Abramson, Joe Alves, and

Daniel A. Lomino), Best Visual Effects (Roy Arbogast, Gregory Jein, Douglas Trumbull, Mathew Yuricich, and Richard Yuricich), Best Film Editing (Michael Kahn), Best Original Score (John Williams), and Best Sound (Gene S. Cantamessa, Robert J. Glass, Robert Knudson, and Don MacDougall). The film was awarded one Oscar for its cinematography, as well as an honorary Oscar for its sound effects editing (Frank Warner).

1. What famed filmmaker appears in the film as Claude Lacombe?

2. The first draft of *Close Encounters of the Third Kind* was written by a very distinguished screenwriter. However, he does not receive credit. Who is this?

3. Before Richard Dreyfuss was cast, several actors were approached to play Roy Neary. Which of the following actors was not approached: Jack Nicholson, Robert De Niro, Al Pacino, James Caan, or Gene Hackman?

4. During filming, one of the actors told a *New York Times* reporter that the film was badly organized and called producer Julia Phillips "incompetent" and "unprofessional." Who was this?

5. What was the working title of the film?

6. *Close Encounters of the Third Kind* was very loosely based upon a book written by Dr. J. Allen Hynek. What is the title of this book?

7. There are three levels of alien encounters. What are these?

8. What news anchor agreed to meet with Steven Spielberg in a bar to discuss appearing in the film's news reports?

9. The elderly Mexican tells the scientists that the "sun came out at night." What does he say it then did?

10. Roy's recurring vision of Devil's Tower was conceived by a filmmaker friend of director Steven Spielberg. Who was this?

11. As Roy plays with the train set, what epic film is visible on the television behind him?

12. During filming, Richard Dreyfuss passed out. Although a doctor was then persuaded to blame the incident on "heat prostration," producer Julia Phillips says that something else caused Dreyfuss to pass out. What was this?

13. Richard Dreyfuss has appeared in three Steven Spielberg–directed films. One of these is *Close Encounters of the Third Kind*. What are the other two films?

14. Conversations were held with two different musicians regard-

ing a possible *Close Encounters of the Third Kind* pop song. One of them is a former Beatle and the other is the former frontman for the funk band Parliament. Who are these musicians?

15. What acronym was used for *Close Encounters of the Third Kind* during filming?

16. Roy describes the UFO as looking like an ice-cream cone, causing Ronnie to ask him what flavor. What is his response?

17. From what newspaper does Ronnie cut articles regarding the UFO sightings?

18. Thirteen years before making *Close Encounters of the Third Kind,* Steven Spielberg directed a similar film about aliens visiting the earth. The film stars Carol Stromme and Andrew Owen. What is the title of this film?

19. What well-known actor played a national guardsman in *Close Encounters of the Third Kind* only to see his scenes completely cut from the final film?

20. According to Lacombe, who is Zoltan Kodaly?

21. At Station Fourteen, what is received in response to the transmitted musical notes?

22. Who appears in the film as Toby Neary?

23. As Jillian holds Barry, the record player roars to life. What song does it play?

24. What is the significance of Major Benchley's name?

25. The government concocts a cover story to evacuate the area and keep people away from Devil's Tower. What is this story?

Quiz No. 65:
THE SILENCE OF THE LAMBS (1991)

Screenplay by Ted Tally
Directed by Jonathan Demme
Starring Anthony Hopkins, Jodie Foster, and Ted Levine
Orion Pictures

> ***Lecter has sort of a weird charm in the book and we were very conscious of that. He had a smiling face and was very witty and bright. We found in Anthony [Hopkins] an actor who can play any role, like Hitler, and we knew he could handle language better than most actors can. Lecter speaks in such a classical and grammatical way that the American actors would be stumbling over the dialogue.***
>
> —SCREENWRITER TED TALLY

The Silence of the Lambs follows the cat-and-mouse game between a young FBI agent, Clarice Starling (Jodie Foster), and cannibalistic serial killer Hannibal Lecter (Anthony Hopkins). The developing relationship between Starling and Lecter is deeply disturbing and is the golden fiber that holds *The Silence of the Lambs* together. Already considered a modern classic, the film's stature should continue to increase in the years to come provided executive producer Dino DeLaurentiis can overcome the temptation to produce more shoddy sequels.

In 1992, *The Silence of the Lambs* received seven Academy Award nominations: Best Picture (Ronald M. Bozman, Edward Saxon, and Kenneth Utt), Best Director (Jonathan Demme), Best Adapted Screenplay (Ted Tally), Best Actor (Hopkins), Best Actress (Foster), Best Film Editing (Craig McKay), and Best Sound (Tom Fleischman and Christopher Newman). *The Silence of the Lambs* swept the five major categories—Best Picture, Best Director, Best Screenplay, Best Actor, and Best Actress.

1. What filmmaker appears as FBI Director Hayden Burke?

2. Anthony Hopkins says he patterned Hannibal Lecter's speech pattern after that of a character in a Stanley Kubrick movie. What is this?

3. *The Silence of the Lambs* was only the third film ever to sweep the Academy Awards, winning Oscars in each of the five major categories. What are the other two films to accomplish this feat?

4. Only two actors appear in both *The Silence of the Lambs* and its predecessor, *Manhunter* (1986). Who are they?

5. Clarice was a double major in college. What were her majors?

6. Jack Crawford has a huge *National Inquisitor* headline hanging on his office wall. What does it say?

7. *The Silence of the Lambs* was released on the eve of a holiday in 1991. What was the holiday?

8. Prior to his first meeting with Clarice, Hannibal has not seen a woman in a number of years. How many?

9. In a scene cut from the film, Mr. Brigham gives Clarice something before she leaves West Virginia. What is this?

10. What is found inside Benjamin Raspail's throat?

11. Why didn't Buffalo Bill's first victim drift as his later victims would?

12. What does Lecter call "unspeakably ugly"?

13. When recalling her stay at the ranch, what haunting sound does Clarice say awakened her?

14. How long does Buffalo Bill allow his victims to remain alive?

15. What actor originated the role of Hannibal Lecter in *Manhunter*?

16. After listening to Clarice's teary-eyed tale of her discovery on the ranch, what meal does Hannibal request?

17. Why does Clarice say she does not fear that the escaped Hannibal will come after her?

18. Before she is captured, Senator Martin's daughter is singing along to a Tom Petty tune. What is this song?

19. Who referred Buffalo Bill to Hannibal Lecter?

20. Jodie Foster does not appear in the film's sequel, *Hannibal* (2001). What actress was hired to replace her?

21. What is the name of Senator Martin's captured daughter?

22. What does Clarice say is her worst memory from childhood?
23. What are Lecter's final words to Senator Martin?
24. Buffalo Bill owns a dog. What breed of dog is it?
25. Anthony Hopkins played another brilliant but crazed, murdering doctor in a 1999 film directed by Jon Turteltaub. What is this film?

Quiz No. 66: **Network (1976)**

Screenplay by Paddy Chayefsky
Directed by Sidney Lumet
Starring Peter Finch, Faye Dunaway, and William Holden
Metro-Goldwyn-Mayer

> ***Nobody could resist doing a satire on television, especially with a Paddy Chayefsky script. Chayefsky is one of the finest American writers that has ever worked in movies. . . . Paddy had a sense of the ridiculous and could write about it and write about it with humor. He also had great compassion and a fine sense of drama, so it's one of the best scripts that ever came across my desk.***
>
> —DIRECTOR SIDNEY LUMET

Network is a blackly comic satirical indictment of yellow journalism and the shock tactics employed by the network news. Paddy Chayefsky's brilliant script asks how far networks will go to achieve higher ratings and when the tabloidistic news becomes pure entertainment. *Chicago Sun-Times* critic Roger Ebert laments, "When Chayefsky created Howard Beale, could he have imagined Jerry Springer, Howard Stern, and the World Wrestling Federation?"

In 1977, *Network* received ten Academy Award nominations: Best Picture (Howard Gottfried), Best Director (Sidney Lumet), Best Original Screenplay (Chayefsky), Best Actor (Peter Finch), Best Actor (William Holden), Best Actress (Faye Dunaway), Best Supporting Actor (Ned Beatty), Best Supporting Actress (Beatrice Straight), Best Cinematography (Owen Roizman), and Best Film Editing (Alan Heim). The film was awarded four Oscars for Dunaway, Straight, and Finch's acting, and screenwriter Chayefsky won his third Best Screenplay statuette.

1. *Network* was the second film ever awarded three of the four acting Oscars. What was the first film to accomplish this feat?

2. Screenwriter Paddy Chayefsky received his third Oscar for *Network*. For what films had he received his two previous Oscars?

3. What college did Diane attend?

4. What veteran actor turned down the role of Howard Beale because he thought the film's concept was ridiculous?

5. What is the name of the network Howard Beale works for?

6. Peter Finch was not present at the Academy Awards to accept his Best Actor Oscar. Why?

7. What show does Max say would "wipe fuckin' Disney right off the air"?

8. When Howard announces his intent to commit suicide on live television, what ratings share does he predict the network will easily obtain?

9. Hackett says the station he runs is not a respectable one. What kind of network does he believe it is?

10. Who does Diane dub a "latter-day prophet"?

11. Diane calls her affair with Max "a many-splendored thing." What is the significance of this line?

12. What does Howard define as the "reasons we give for living"?

13. What, according to Hackett, is the annual deficit caused by the network's news division?

14. What does Max observe that women believe to be the "most savage thing" she can do to a man?

15. What is the only thing Diane says she wants from life?

16. Great Ahmed Khan is eating as Laureen discusses the network's offer to him. What is he eating?

17. How long have Max and his wife been married?

18. When Mary Ann Gifford and Laureen begin arguing over production costs, Great Ahmed Khan breaks up the squabble. How does he do this?

19. What percentage of his viewers does Howard Beale conclude read books?

20. By mid-November, Howard Beale's show is a huge success. Only three shows are said to have higher ratings. What are these?

21. What is the name of Max's seventeen-year-old daughter?

22. From whom does Max conclude that Diane learned about life?

23. Laureen says that one day Great Ahmed Khan will be a television star "just like" whom?

24. Diane envisions a "homosexual soap opera." What title does she propose?

25. When Howard Beale describes the "faceless voice" that came to him in the night, whom does Max ask him to talk with?

Quiz No. 67:
The Manchurian Candidate (1962)

Screenplay by George Axelrod
Directed by John Frankenheimer
Starring Frank Sinatra, Laurence Harvey, and Janet Leigh
United Artists

> ***I think it's the best screenplay I ever wrote; certainly it's [John] Frankenheimer's best picture, and it's one of Sinatra's top three performances. And of course, Angela Lansbury very deservingly got a nomination for what she did. The poor thing, you know, went from failure to classic without ever passing through success.***
>
> —Screenwriter George Axelrod

The Manchurian Candidate, a Cold War thriller about training assassins through brainwashing, is director John Frankenheimer's finest film. The film's at times unbelievable storyline comes from the 1959 Richard Condon novel of the same title. "This picture plays some wonderful, crazy games about the Right and the Left," observes film critic Pauline Kael. "Although it's a thriller, it might be the most sophisticated political satire ever made in Hollywood."

In 1963, *The Manchurian Candidate* received two Academy Award nominations: Best Supporting Actress (Angela Lansbury) and Best Film Editing (Ferris Webster). The film was awarded no Oscars.

1. United Artists initially didn't want to produce *The Manchurian Candidate* because they felt it could be perceived as being un-American. Who convinced United Artists chief Arthur Krim to greenlight the film?
2. How many months did Marco spend in Korea?
3. Who was the real-life owner of the plane belonging to Senator Iselin in the film?

4. How much older than Laurence Harvey is Angela Lansbury, the actress who plays his mother?

5. Who did novelist Richard Condon name the members of Marco's platoon after?

6. When John Iselin asks his wife to give him a number of card-carrying Communists, she tells him fifty-seven. How does she come up with this number?

7. After the assassination of President John F. Kennedy, *The Manchurian Candidate* was promptly pulled from theaters and shelved for more than twenty-five years. According to screenwriter George Axelrod whose idea was it to pull the film?

8. Ironically, someone closely involved with the production of *The Manchurian Candidate* drove Bobby Kennedy to his hotel the night he was assassinated. Who was this?

9. What type of plants are discussed in Marco's recurring dreams?

10. What garb does Raymond don for his mission at the convention?

11. Who tells Raymond that the programming links no longer work?

12. Who does Marco suggest to lead the "Stupidity Division"?

13. What does Raymond put on only seconds before committing suicide?

14. Who does Marco say he remembers "that Chinese cat" smiling like?

15. According to Senator Thomas Jordan, what is Mrs. Iselin's criterion for deciding who is a Communist?

16. After winning his suit against Mrs. Iselin, what did Thomas Jordan do with the money he received?

17. John Iselin is obsessed with a former United States president. Who is this?

18. Marco says that Shaw is not difficult to like. What does he say he is?

19. Raymond believes the world is made up of two irreconcilable groups. Who are these?

20. What politician has controversial talk-show host William Cooper dubbed the "real-life Manchurian candidate"?

21. From what organization are the doctors who brainwash Raymond?

22. When Raymond arrives at four A.M. to murder Gaines, he finds him awake. What is he doing?

23. What two things are described as being "uniquely American symptoms"?

24. How does Marco describe the odor of his Korean captor?

25. How many members of Raymond's platoon did not return home from Korea?

Quiz No. 68: An American in Paris (1951)

Screenplay by Alan Jay Lerner
Directed by Vincente Minnelli
Starring Gene Kelly, Leslie Caron, and Oscar Levant
Metro-Goldwyn-Mayer

> ***In the** American in Paris **ballet, Gene Kelly plays an artist. He's loved the people that painted Paris, he loves Paris, and he loves this girl. And you have to say that when he loses the girl, Paris will lose its flavor, it will become a cold city, it will become an unfriendly city. At times there will be euphoria and happiness and at times there will be the realization that it's—it's ashes, you know.***
>
> —DIRECTOR VINCENTE MINNELLI

An American in Paris tells the story of a mediocre painter and expatriate American soldier named Jerry Mulligan (Gene Kelly) who is now living in Paris. Struggling financially, he allows himself to be kept by a wealthy heiress. He then falls for a beautiful young woman named Lise (Leslie Caron), who is engaged to a carousel singer named Henri Baurel (Georges Guetary). Constructed around the catalogue of composer George Gershwin—the film's title was derived from a Gershwin tone poem—the film features a lavish seventeen-minute ballet sequence, "An American in Paris," which is the high point of the film. *Apollo Movie Guide* critic Brian Webster observes, "The Gershwin score may be the big star of the show, but Gene Kelly's performance is certainly the glue that holds it together. Kelly's remarkable ability to be both strong and subtle on the dance floor works to great effect here, and his charisma makes it easy to believe that Lise would fall for him."

In 1952, *An American in Paris* received eight Academy Award nominations: Best Picture (Arthur Freed), Best Director (Vincente Minnelli), Best Screenplay (Alan Jay Lerner), Best Non-Original Score (Saul Chaplin and Johnny Green), Best Film Editing (Adrienne Fazan), Best

Color Art Direction–Set Decoration (E. Preston Ames, Cedric Gibbons, F. Keough Gleason, and Edwin B. Willis), Best Cinematography (John Alton and Alfred Gilks), and Best Color Costume Design (Orry-Kelly, Walter Plunkett, and Irene Sharaff). The film was awarded six Oscars, losing only in the categories of Best Director and Best Film Editing.

1. After experimenting with brief ballet sequences in *Yolanda and the Thief* (1945) and *Ziegfield Follies* (1946), Vincente Minnelli was inspired to direct a lengthy ballet sequence after the success of a 1948 British film. What is this film?
2. Who choreographed *An American in Paris*?
3. What is the name of the MGM collective that included Gene Kelly, Vincente Minnelli, Arthur Freed, Betty Comden, and Saul Chaplin, among others, who produced such musicals as *Singin' in the Rain* (1952) and *An American in Paris*?
4. What 1997 Anthony Waller–directed horror film's title references *An American in Paris*?
5. Actress Cyd Charisse was replaced by Leslie Caron prior to shooting. Why?
6. The dream sequence in which Adam envisions himself as the piano player and each of the audience members was loosely adapted from a Buster Keaton routine in another film. What is this film?
7. Like many of producer Arthur Freed's musicals, *An American in Paris* was constructed around the catalogue of a single composer. Freed's first musical of this mold was a 1946 film featuring the catalogue of Jerome Kern. What is this film?
8. How many female singing roles are there in *An American in Paris*?
9. What is the name of the successful musician for whom Jerry worked as an accompanist fifteen years earlier?
10. Producer Arthur Freed had first envisioned making a George Gershwin biopic. Why didn't he?
11. What is the recurring symbol that connects each of the six sequences in the dream ballet, "An American in Paris"?
12. Where did producer Arthur Freed come up with the idea to make Jerry Mulligan an expatriate GI who stayed in Europe after World War II?

13. Gene Kelly appears in four films directed by Vincente Minnelli. One of these is *An American in Paris*. What are the other three films?

14. When producer Arthur Freed first approached screenwriter Alan Jay Lerner about *An American in Paris,* the writer was signed by MGM to write another musical. What was this film?

15. The "American in Paris Ballet" was performed by the Metro-Goldwyn-Mayer Symphony Orchestra. How many musicians assembled to perform this arrangement: fifty, sixty-three, seventy-two, or eighty?

16. Who directed the "Embraceable You" sequence?

17. What does Adam offer as a "pretentious way of saying" that he's unemployed?

18. Who does Adam call a "shocking degenerate"?

19. The character Adam Cook was loosely modeled after a real-life expatriate-musician who was a close friend of George Gershwin. Who was this?

20. What is the name of the nightclub in which Milo explains her art-world connections?

21. How much did the seventeen-minute dream ballet cost to produce?

22. What does Lise observe as having ways of making people forget?

23. When Jerry asks Milo what holds her gown up, what is her response?

24. Although Georges Guetary appears in the film as Henri Baurel, screenwriter Alan Jay Lerner had written the part specifically for another actor. Who was this?

25. Vincent Van Gogh is one of the artists represented in the dream ballet. Five years after *An American in Paris,* Vincente Minelli would direct a Van Gogh biopic starring Kirk Douglas. What is this film?

Quiz No. 69: Shane (1953)

Screenplay by Jack Schaefer, A. B. Guthrie, Jr., and Jack Sher
Directed by George Stevens
Starring Alan Ladd, Jean Arthur, and Van Heflin
Paramount Pictures

> ***[Alan Ladd's size] was an interesting thing for the picture because he didn't tower above the others—the mountains did. We kept him as high off the ground as possible so he wouldn't be dwarfed by people.***
>
> —Director George Stevens

Some call George Stevens's richly textured Technicolor masterpiece, *Shane,* the quintessential Western. Others disagree. Regardless, *Shane* remains a highly respected film and, as its appearance here would indicate, it is recognized as one of the finest films ever produced. Based on Jack Schaefer's 1949 novel, *Shane* is the story of a wandering gunfighter who comes to the defense of settlers who are being preyed upon by a merciless cattle baron. The film's closing scene, in which young Joey Starrett (Brandon De Wilde) calls after the badly wounded gunfighter, is easily one of the most memorable in the history of American cinema.

In 1954, *Shane* received six Academy Award nominations: Best Picture (Stevens), Best Director (Stevens), Best Screenplay (A. B. Guthrie, Jr.), Best Supporting Actor (De Wilde), Best Supporting Actor (Jack Palance), and Best Color Cinematography (Loyal Griggs). The film's sole Oscar was awarded for its cinematography.

1. *Shane* is part of director George Stevens's *American Trilogy.* What are the other two films that make up this trilogy?
2. As Shane approaches the Starrett farm, Marion is singing inside the house. What song is she singing?
3. What does Marion insist will "not be [her] boy's life"?

4. Having just arrived at the farm, where does Shane tell Joe Starrett he's heading?
5. What is the title of the film's theme song?
6. What tune is played as Shane dances with Marion?
7. What country is Shipstead originally from?
8. When Shane explains that "most of them have tricks of their own," whom is he referring to?
9. Wilson arrives on a holiday. Which one?
10. What kind of catalogue does Joe peruse in the film?
11. The music that plays during Shane's ride to the showdown was recycled from an earlier film. What is this film?
12. What does Shane believe of "a man who watches things"?
13. What does Shane jokingly say he would do if he caught Ryker's men cutting the fence?
14. When Shane travels to town to purchase soda for Joey, what three flavors are available?
15. When Shane first arrives, Joe Starrett is suspicious of him. Who does he believe Shane is?
16. Who does Shane introduce himself as to Rufus Ryker?
17. Where is Wilson from?
18. What actor appears in the film as Frank Torrey?
19. What does Joey beg Shane to teach him?
20. When does Rufus Ryker insist the squatters must be gone by?
21. Who does Joey say he loves Shane "almost as much as"?
22. What type of pistol does Torrey carry?
23. Who assists Shane when he brawls with Ryker's men?
24. Ernie complains that he's tired of being insulted by Ryker's men. What is the insulting name they call him?
25. What nickname does Calloway give Shane?

Quiz No. 70:
THE FRENCH CONNECTION (1971)

Screenplay by Ernest Tidyman
Directed by William Friedkin
Starring Gene Hackman, Fernando Rey, and Roy Scheider
Twentieth Century–Fox

> ***Gene [Hackman] was a genuine liberal, and he didn't really like Eddie Egan and he didn't want to bring out that side of himself which was buried deep within him but which he had managed to cover for many years. So I constantly prodded him to become more and more evil, because the film is about that thin line between the policeman and the criminal. And the policeman in that film is just as evil and demented—if not more so—than the narcotics smuggler.***
>
> —DIRECTOR WILLIAM FRIEDKIN

Based on journalist Robin Moore's book about real-life detectives Eddie Egan and Sonny Grosso, director William Friedkin's gritty thriller follows two Manhattan cops attempting to intercept a $32-million heroin shipment from France. A *Box-Office Magazine* reviewer praises, "A thriller in every sense of the word, *The French Connection* has what most pictures that deal with drugs lack, namely, action."

In 1972, *The French Connection* received eight Academy Award nominations: Best Picture (Philip D'Antoni), Best Director (Friedkin), Best Adapted Screenplay (Ernest Tidyman), Best Actor (Gene Hackman), Best Supporting Actor (Roy Scheider), Best Cinematography (Owen Roizman), Best Film Editing (Gerald B. Greenberg), and Best Sound (Christopher Newman). The film was awarded five Oscars, losing in its bids for Best Supporting Actor, Best Sound, and Best Cinematography.

1. Four years after this film, *The French Connection II* (1975) was made. Eleven years later, a third installment, *Popeye Doyle* (1986) was

produced. What unlikely actor takes over in the title role for Gene Hackman in this made-for-television disaster?

2. During the real-life heroin bust that the film is based upon, Eddie Egan turned to his partner, Sonny Grosso, and told him that they would be the subjects of a film someday. Who did Egan say would portray them?

3. Who appear in *The French Connection* as Simonson and Klein?

4. When this film was made, it had what was widely considered the best car-chase scene ever filmed. In 1985, director William Friedkin attempted to outdo himself in this respect in another film. What is this film?

5. During the chase scene, what is significant regarding the woman pushing a stroller who is nearly run down?

6. Who are the actors who appear as the drug users in the bar scene?

7. What noted filmmaker directed the sequel, *The French Connection II*?

8. Producer Philip D'Antoni gave the film's crew a mandate. What was this?

9. Sal Boca was captured after attempting to rob Tiffany's in broad daylight. However, he did not go to jail. Why?

10. Sal Boca operates a deli. What is the name of this deli?

11. What do Doyle and Russo lead the department in each year?

12. The character Sal Boca was modeled after a man named Patsy Fucca. When he heard *The French Connection* would be filmed, Fucca approached Eddie Egan with a demand. According to Egan, Fucca told him he was "in for trouble" if this demand was not met. What was this?

13. After the success of *The French Connection,* its subjects, Eddie Egan and Sonny Grosso, both embarked on careers in the film industry. What were these?

14. In 1973, producer Philip D'Antoni made his directorial debut with an unofficial sequel in which Roy Scheider reprises his role. What is this film?

15. Joel Weinstock says he's learned one thing. What is this?

16. What is Popeye's real name?

17. What is the significance of William Friedkin's Oscar for Best Director?

18. Before becoming a police officer, Eddie Egan was a centerfielder for a triple-A baseball team. What major-league organization's farm club did Egan play for?

19. Actor Gene Hackman objected to one scene in the film and, as a result, took fifteen takes to get it right. William Friedkin has since called this the "most difficult performance" he's ever had to work with. What is this scene?

20. As Doyle and Russo watch the brown Lincoln, the neighborhood children are playing in the street. What game are they playing?

21. What is 18LU13?

22. What is Henri Devereaux's occupation?

23. When the police block the road, what mocking gesture does Doyle make to Alain Charnier?

24. Who does Doyle refer to as Frog One?

25. Eddie Egan explains that artistic liberties were taken with the scene in which Popeye Doyle is shot. In what way?

Quiz No. 71:
Forrest Gump (1994)

Screenplay by Eric Roth
Directed by Robert Zemeckis
Starring Tom Hanks, Robin Wright, and Gary Sinise
Paramount Pictures

> ***Other than the fact that it's a wonderful life-reaffirming love story, on the surface, I think it's been embraced because every single person in the audience can project his or her own feelings on the era. That's what I felt when I read it and that's why I felt I had to make it. I said, "Here's an opportunity that I have where I'm not a filmmaker imposing his beliefs about something." I'm being neutral, which allows the [viewers] to feel what they themselves wish to feel.***
>
> —Director Robert Zemeckis

Director Robert Zemeckis's *Forrest Gump* is the picaresque story of a likeable half-wit (Tom Hanks) who becomes a college football star, a war hero, a world champion Ping-Pong player, a shrimp-boat captain, and a multi-millionaire gardener. Forrest falls in love with n'er-do-well Jenny Curran (Robin Wright) along the way, and spends two years of his life running across the United States. Much of the film's appeal comes from Special Effects Supervisor Ken Ralston's masterful integration of new footage with archival material, giving the effect that Forrest is actually shaking hands and rubbing elbows with the likes of Richard Nixon, Jack Kennedy, and slain-rocker John Lennon.

In 1995, *Forrest Gump* received thirteen Academy Award nominations: Best Picture (Wendy Finerman, Steve Starkey, and Steve Tisch), Best Director (Zemeckis), Best Adapted Screenplay (Eric Roth), Best Actor (Hanks), Best Supporting Actor (Gary Sinise), Best Visual Effects (Allen Hall, George Murphy, Stephen Rosenbaum, and Ralston), Best Film Editing (Arthur Schmidt), Best Art Direction–Set Decoration (Rick Carter and Nancy Haigh), Best Cinematography

(Don Burgess), Best Sound-Effects Editing (Gloria S. Borders and Randy Thom), Best Makeup (Judith A. Cory, Hallie D'Amore, and Daniel C. Striepeke), Best Original Score (Alan Silvestri), and Best Sound (Tom Johnson, William B. Kaplan, Dennis S. Sands, and Thom). The film was awarded six Oscars for Best Picture, Best Director, Best Adapted Screenplay, Best Actor, Best Film Editing, and Best Sound-Effects Editing.

1. What is Forrest Gump's IQ?

2. Who appears in a brief cameo as the first boy on the bus who refuses to allow Forrest to sit beside him?

3. What is the name of the Payton Reed–directed documentary about the making of *Forrest Gump*?

4. Gary Sinise's Lieutenant Dan says the day Forrest is a shrimp-boat captain is the day he'll be an astronaut. The year after *Forrest Gump* was made, both Sinise and Tom Hanks played astronauts in a film directed by Ron Howard. What is this film?

5. *Forrest Gump* was the second novel written by Winston Groom to be adapted into a film. The first Groom adaptation was made for Home Box Office and stars Scott Glenn, Jamie Lee Curtis, and Bette Davis. What is this film?

6. Who doubled for Tom Hanks during many of the running sequences?

7. What are the names of the two women Lieutenant Dan invites back to his apartment on New Year's Eve?

8. What is the name of Lieutenant Dan's fiancée?

9. When Jenny sings naked, what stage name does she use?

10. What day of the week does Forrest say Jenny died on?

11. Forrest and Bubba are given two standing orders from Lieutenant Dan. What are these?

12. Why would it have been impossible for Forrest to have inspired John Lennon's song "Imagine" during his appearance on *The Dick Cavett Show*?

13. Forrest and Bubba are assigned to the Ninth Infantry in Vietnam. What company are they in?

14. What actor made his screen debut as Forrest Junior?

15. It would have been impossible for Forrest to spend New Year's Eve with Lieutenant Dan in 1971 after having just appeared on *The*

Dick Cavett Show to discuss his trip to China with the United States Ping-Pong team. Why?

16. The rosary Lieutenant Dan wears was actually worn by a soldier in Vietnam. Who was this?

17. How many wounded soldiers does Forrest carry out of the jungle?

18. In Hollywood, when Jenny is asked to go to San Francisco, a theater marquee is visible in the background. What film is advertised on it?

19. The scene in which Lieutenant Dan yells, "I'm walkin' here!" to a cab is a nod to another AFI Top 100 film. What is this?

20. What is the name of Winston Groom's sequelization of *Forrest Gump*?

21. Six years after making *Forrest Gump,* director Robert Zemeckis and Tom Hanks reteamed for their second film together. What is this film?

22. What is the name of the hurricane that destroys the shrimp boats?

23. Who makes a brief cameo as the red-headed girl on the school bus?

24. Sally Fields and Tom Hanks appeared together in another film prior to *Forrest Gump*. What is this film?

25. What is Lieutenant Dan's last name?

Quiz No. 72:
Ben-Hur (1959)

Screenplay by Karl Tunberg
Directed by William Wyler
Starring Charlton Heston, Jack Hawkins, and Stephen Boyd
Metro-Goldwyn-Mayer

> ***From the beginning, we knew it was going to be a tough shoot. So it by God was; I think the toughest I've ever done.***
>
> —Actor Charlton Heston

Director William Wyler's epic *Ben-Hur* is the story of two friends, Judah Ben-Hur (Charlton Heston) and Messala (Stephen Boyd), who become separated by their political beliefs. When Messala becomes the commander of the Roman army, he uses his newly elevated position to persecute Judah and his family. The wrongly imprisoned Judah vows that one day he will have revenge against his old friend.

In 1960, *Ben-Hur* received twelve Academy Award nominations: Best Picture (Sam Zimbalist), Best Director (Wyler), Best Adapted Screenplay (Karl Tunberg), Best Actor (Heston), Best Supporting Actor (Hugh Griffith), Best Color Art Direction–Set Decoration (Edward C. Carafagno, William A. Horning, and Hugh Hunt), Best Color Cinematography (Robert Surtees), Best Color Costume Design (Elizabeth Haffenden), Best Special Effects (A. Arnold Gillespie, Milo B. Lory, and Robert MacDonald), Best Film Editing (John D. Dunning and Ralph E. Winters), Best Original Score (Miklos Rozsa), and Best Sound (Franklin Milton). The film was awarded eleven Oscars—the most any film had received at that time—and lost only in its bid for Best Adapted Screenplay.

1. What is the film's subtitle?
2. *Ben-Hur* won eleven Oscars and is only one of two films (to date) that have accomplished this feat. What is the other film?

3. Three years prior to *Ben-Hur,* Charlton Heston appeared in another successful Biblical adaptation, which was directed by Cecil B. DeMille. What is this film?

4. The film opens showing Michelangelo's famed painting on the ceiling of the Sistine Chapel. Six years after making *Ben-Hur,* Charlton Heston would portray Michelangelo in another film. What is this film?

5. Messala mentions John the Baptist. In 1965, Charlton Heston would portray John the Baptist in another film. What is this film?

6. One year prior to *Ben-Hur*'s release, Charlton Heston and William Wyler had collaborated on another film. What is this film?

7. *Ben-Hur* is a remake. How many versions of *Ben-Hur* had been filmed prior to this most famous one?

8. When Messala warns Judah to "be wise," what type of world does he conclude they are living in?

9. What, according to Quintus Arrius, "keeps a man alive"?

10. Actor Charlton Heston would later recall, "[It] is a hard-won and largely useless skill, but I can't help taking pride in it." What was he referring to?

11. Who is called Simonides's "other half"?

12. Who dubs himself the hand of Caesar, proclaiming himself ready to "crush all those who challenge his authority"?

13. Strangely enough, the four white horses that appear in the film were flown in on a passenger plane. From where were they flown?

14. How many weeks did it take Miklos Rozsa to write the film's score: four, six, eight, or ten?

15. What actor was initially offered the role of Judah Ben-Hur?

16. According to uncredited screenwriter Gore Vidal, Judah had a homosexual affair in his past with another character from the film. Who is this?

17. After receiving contradictory reports from historical consultants regarding the architecture of the stadium in Jerusalem, what did the producers study to help them determine the design they would ultimately use?

18. At the 1960 Academy Awards, *Ben-Hur* cleaned up. Backstage, director William Wyler reconciled with an actor he had been feuding with for two years. Who was this?

19. After being freed, Miriam and Tirzah are exiled. Where are they sent?

20. What two people combined are said to make one considerable man?

21. A primary member of the film's crew had worked as an assistant director on the 1925 version of *Ben-Hur*. Who was this?

22. Who choreographed the famed chariot race?

23. How many stuntmen where killed during the filming of the chariot-race sequence?

24. What does the sheik say will "blind the eyes of Rome"?

25. According to Esther, who shall receive mercy?

Quiz No. 73:
Wuthering Heights (1939)

Screenplay by Charles MacArthur and Ben Hecht
Directed by William Wyler
Starring Merle Oberon, Laurence Olivier, and Geraldine Fitzgerald
United Artists

> ***If any film actor is having trouble with his career, can't master the medium and wonders whether it's worth it, let him pray to meet a man like William Wyler. Wyler was a marvelous sneerer, debunker; and he brought me down. I knew nothing of film acting or that I had to learn its technique; it took a long time and several unhandsome degrees of the torture of his sarcasm before I realized it.***
>
> —Actor Laurence Olivier

Adapted from Emily Bronte's classic novel, director William Wyler's *Wuthering Heights* centers around a young man named Heathcliff (Laurence Olivier) who falls in love with his beautiful stepsister, Cathy (Merle Oberon). After losing her to the gentlemanly Edgar Linton (David Niven), Heathcliff bitterly vows to destroy him, as well as his stepbrother Hindley (Hugh Williams) for mistreating him. Film critic David Mermelstein raves, "Sam Goldwyn's favorite film is among the true classics of Hollywood's Golden Age. A richly textured romantic melodrama, this William Wyler picture has it all."

In 1940, *Wuthering Heights* received eight Academy Award nominations: Best Picture (Samuel Goldwyn), Best Director (Wyler), Best Adapted Screenplay (Ben Hecht and Charles MacArthur), Best Actor (Olivier), Best Supporting Actress (Geraldine Fitzgerald), Best Black-and-White Cinematography (Gregg Toland), Best Art Direction (James Basevi), and Best Original Score (Alfred Newman). The film's sole Oscar was awarded for its score.

1. In what room of the house is Mr. Lockwood told that no one has slept in for many years?

2. What does Cathy envision in a "pretty world"?

3. Who does Hindley call "Gypsy scum"?

4. Prior to *Wuthering Heights,* director William Wyler and David Niven had worked together on another film. What was their previous collaboration?

5. In 1940, acclaimed cinematographer Gregg Toland was nominated by the Academy for his work on two films. One of these was *Wuthering Heights*. What was the other film?

6. What is the name of Wuthering Heights's gossiping housekeeper?

7. What is said to be a "gift of God, although it's as dark as if it came from the devil"?

8. Who hits Heathcliff in the head with a rock, knocking him unconscious?

9. Cathy proposes a contest to Heathcliff in which the loser must "be the other's slave." What is this contest?

10. In the 1920 adaptation of *Wuthering Heights,* what actor appeared as Heathcliff?

11. During production of the film, producer Samuel Goldwyn repeatedly mispronounced its title. What did he call *Wuthering Heights*?

12. Who was Laurence Olivier engaged to while filming *Wuthering Heights*?

13. Which of these was not a title producer Samuel Goldwyn suggested for the film: *Pretty World*, *The Wild Heart*, or *Bring Me the World*?

14. Whose "milk-white" face does Cathy say she hates the look of?

15. Who does Ellen call a "harem-scarem child with dirty hands and a willful heart"?

16. What is the only thing Cathy says must remain in the world for her life to be full?

17. What scene did producer Samuel Goldwyn have shot by H. C. Potter with stand-in doubles after William Wyler had completed the film?

18. Who directed the 1992 remake starring Juliette Binoche and Ralph Fiennes?

19. How does Heathcliff die?

20. Who owns the dogs that attack Cathy and Heathcliff?

21. What was the destination of the brigantine Heathcliff jumped from?

22. What is the name of the Yorkshire widower who found Heathcliff in the streets and took him in as his own son?

23. When Lockwood asks Ellen who Cathy is, what is her memorable response?

24. Thirteen years after making *Wuthering Heights,* Laurence Olivier and William Wyler worked together on another film. What is this film?

25. The final scene in which Cathy and Heathcliff unite was conceived by producer Samuel Goldwyn, who had been inspired by a 1938 film with a similar scene. What is this film?

Quiz No. 74:
THE GOLD RUSH (1925)

Screenplay by Charles Chaplin
Directed by Charles Chaplin
Starring Charles Chaplin, Mack Swain, and Tom Murray
United Artists

> *For six months, I developed a series of comedy sequences and began shooting without a script, feeling that a story would evolve from comedy routine and business. Of course, I was led up many a blind alley, and many amusing sequences were discarded. One was a love scene with an Eskimo girl who teaches the Tramp to kiss in Eskimo fashion by rubbing noses together. When he departs in a quest for gold, he passionately rubs his nose against hers in a fond farewell. . . . But the Eskimo part was cut out because it conflicted with the more important story of the dance-hall girl.*
>
> —DIRECTOR CHARLES CHAPLIN

The Gold Rush is one of the finest films Charles Chaplin ever made, which is really saying something considering the man's filmography is filled with classic laugh-a-minute examinations of American society. While Chaplin's work is sometimes dismissed by today's general audience—certainly not by critics or academicians—as being simplistic showcases of physical comedy, they are much more than that. In each of his films, Chaplin had something to say about the world around him. Certainly, Chaplin's films are humorous, but they also provided messages that remain poignant today, even if their storylines and settings don't always. That *The Gold Rush,* a silent film made two years before the first talking film, remains appreciated today is truly a testament to the genius behind it.

The initial release of *The Gold Rush* predated the Academy Awards. In 1943, the rereleased film received two Academy Award nominations: Best Original Score (Max Terr) and Best Sound (Chaplin). However, the film was awarded no Oscars.

1. In a 1993 film directed by Jeremiah Chechik, actor Johnny Depp recreates the famed "Dance of the Dinner Rolls" sequence from *The Gold Rush*. What is this film?

2. The Thanksgiving dinner scene was inspired by a historically themed book Chaplin read that was written by Charles Fayette McGlashan. What is the title or subject of this book?

3. Who narrates the 1942 rereleased version of the film?

4. Who were the twenty-five hundred men Charles Chaplin hired to play the prospectors?

5. How many takes did Chaplin shoot of the scene in which the two men eat a boot?

6. What was the boot that Big Jim and the Tramp eat actually made of?

7. Whom is the film dedicated to?

8. When we first see the Tramp, he is being followed. Who is following him?

9. A friend of Chaplin's purchased one quarter of the film for "a sum exceeding many times the cost." Who was this?

10. What is Black Larsen burning the first time he's shown in the film?

11. When Larsen catches the Tramp eating in his cabin, he orders him to leave. The Tramp tries to obey, but cannot. Why?

12. As Big Jim and Larsen fight over the rifle, the Tramp runs frantically around the cabin. Why?

13. When Larsen accuses the Tramp of having eaten a candle, the Tramp denies this. However, something gives him away. What?

14. When the three men draw cards, what card does Larsen draw?

15. What happens to the two sleeping policemen Larsen stumbles across?

16. As the Tramp eats his Thanksgiving dinner, what does he carefully remove, discarding onto another plate?

17. What does the deliriously hungry Big Jim begin to envision that the Tramp is?

18. Charles Chaplin first conceived the basic idea for *The Gold Rush* after seeing a photograph of prospectors at a friend's home. Who was this friend?

19. As the Tramp attempts to defend himself with the rifle, what menacing weapon does Big Jim wield?

20. In the narrated reissue, what is Larsen said to have the soul of?

21. Where is Georgia employed?
22. The Tramp discovers a ripped photograph. What is the photograph of?
23. To spite Jack, Georgia decides to dance with another man. Who does she dance with?
24. What's wrong with the rope the Tramp tries to use for a belt?
25. Who was the first actress cast as Georgia?

Quiz No. 75:
Dances with Wolves (1990)

Screenplay by Michael Blake
Directed by Kevin Costner
Starring Kevin Costner, Mary McDonnell, and Graham Greene
Orion Pictures Corporation

> ***I read a lot of history, and I just became fascinated with the history of the Plains Indians. I couldn't stop reading about them. Eventually it filled up inside me, and it had to come out.***
>
> —Screenwriter Michael Blake

Kevin Costner's revisionist Western, *Dances With Wolves,* is the story of a Civil War Union lieutenant named John Dunbar. After being decorated for an act of presumed bravery, he is given his choice of assignments. When he requests to see the dying American frontier, he is assigned to a deserted, run-down camp in the middle of nowhere. While awaiting reinforcements, Dunbar establishes contact with a nearby tribe of Sioux Indians. *Dances With Wolves,* which Costner directed, produced, and stars in, is one of only two films longer than three hours that earned more than $100 million in the nineties.

In 1991, *Dances With Wolves* received twelve Academy Award nominations: Best Picture (Costner and Jim Wilson), Best Director (Costner), Best Adapted Screenplay (Michael Blake), Best Actor (Costner), Best Supporting Actor (Graham Greene), Best Supporting Actress (Mary McDonnell), Best Cinematography (Dean Semler), Best Film Editing (Neil Travis), Best Original Score (John Barry), Best Sound (Bill W. Benton, Jeffrey Perkins, Gregory H. Watkins, and Russell Williams), Best Art Direction–Set Decoration (Jeffrey Beecroft and Lisa Dean), and Best Costume Design (Elsa Zamparelli). The film was awarded seven Oscars, losing in its bids for costume design, art direction–set decoration, and all three acting nominations.

1. Who would later declare on *The Red Green Show* that actor Graham Greene should have won an Oscar for *Dances With Wolves*?

2. Prior to *Dances With Wolves,* screenwriter Michael Blake's sole produced writing credit was a 1982 film that also starred Kevin Costner. What is this film?

3. Dunbar is given a horse for his valor. What is the name of this horse?

4. What is the name of Dunbar's escort to Fort Sedgwick?

5. What does Dunbar name the wolf that visits him daily?

6. Whom does a naked Dunbar catch attempting to steal his horse?

7. What was Stands with a Fist's name before she was adopted by the Sioux?

8. What incident causes Dunbar to conclude, "The gap between us was greater than I ever could have imagined"?

9. What does the Sioux word *tatonka* mean?

10. How many suicides are attempted in the film?

11. Who must decide how long Stands with a Fist will mourn?

12. The morning after his first night at Fort Sedgwick, Dunbar is awakened by the sound of footsteps. He quickly grabs his gun and jumps to his feet. Who does he find outside?

13. What is Kicking Bird's position within the tribe?

14. Two primary crew members appear in a cameo as the doctors examining Dunbar's leg at the beginning of the film. Who are these?

15. When Dunbar attempts to say "grass grows on the prairie" in Sioux, what does he mistakenly say, causing Stands with a Fist to laugh?

16. Who does Dunbar take back to the fort with him to get rifles?

17. Who stages nightly gambling in the Sioux camp?

18. Who was Wind in His Hair's best friend?

19. What is the name of Kicking Bird's wife?

20. What is the "great honor" Kicking Bird asks of Dunbar?

21. According to Kicking Bird, what is the one trail that matters most?

22. How many white men does Dunbar tell Kicking Bird will be coming?

23. The day following Dunbar's revelation regarding the white men, the Sioux move. Where do they move to?

24. What does Dunbar travel back to the fort to retrieve, causing him to be captured by soldiers?

25. Who does Dunbar call a "great loss" after the second battle against the Pawnee?

Quiz No. 76: City Lights (1931)

Screenplay by Charles Chaplin
Directed by Charles Chaplin
Starring Charles Chaplin, Virginia Cherrill, and Florence Lee
United Artists

> ***It evolved from a story of a clown who, through an accident at the circus, has lost his sight. He has a little daughter, a sick nervous child, and when he returns from the hospital the doctor warns him that he must hide his blindness from her until she is well and strong enough to understand, as the shock might be too much for her. His stumblings and bumpings into things make the little girl laugh joyously. But that was too "icky." However, the blindness of the clown was transferred to the flower girl in* City Lights.**
>
> —Director Charles Chaplin

No other film in Charles Chaplin's catalogue so completely displays his genius as does *City Lights,* which he wrote, produced, directed, scored, and also acted in. While most film academicians consider Orson Welles's *Citizen Kane* (1941) the greatest film ever made, Welles himself called *City Lights* the closest thing to perfection that Hollywood ever produced. Chaplin's Tramp falls for a blind girl (Virginia Cherrill) and tries to assist her. The Tramp finds himself in a series of misadventures along the way, appearing in a boxing match and going to jail when he's mistaken for a mugger.

In 1932, *City Lights* received no Academy Award nominations.

1. What is the subtitle of the film?
2. When the dust sheet is removed from the Greco-Roman statue, what do the assembled crowd find on the figure's lap?
3. When the Tramp decides to help the Blind Girl, what job does he take?
4. In "That Afternoon," what does the Tramp swallow?

5. In "The Fight," who is originally scheduled to fight the Tramp?

6. During *City Lights*'s February 1931 premiere, what prompted Charles Chaplin to storm up the aisle screaming, "Where's that stupid son-of-a-bitch manager? I'll kill him!"?

7. A noted scientist attended the *City Lights* premiere as a guest of Charles Chaplin's. At the end of the film, the scientist wept, causing Chaplin to conclude, "This is further evidence that scientists are incurable sentimentalists." Who was this scientist?

8. True or false: *City Lights* has no sound.

9. What is the title of the film's first segment?

10. An essay by Charles Chaplin on pantomime was published in a prominent publication just before the release of *City Lights*. What was this publication?

11. Charles Chaplin replaced actor Henry Clive before his scenes were completed. Why?

12. Taunting him, what do the newspaper boys take from the Tramp?

13. After purchasing a flower, the Tramp watches the Blind Girl, who believes he's gone. Unbeknownst to her, what does she then do to him?

14. When the Tramp tries to stop the Millionaire during his first suicide attempt, what happens to him?

15. When the Millionaire and the Tramp toast, where does most of the champagne wind up?

16. The second time the Millionaire attempts to commit suicide, what method does he use?

17. Three different composers were hired to score *City Lights,* but either quit or were fired during production. Who were they?

18. What type of automobile does the Blind Girl believe the Tramp owns?

19. The Millionaire gives the Tramp an extravagant gift after dinner, saying, "Keep it, it's yours." What is this gift?

20. A flowerpot falls from a window and lands on the Tramps' head. Who knocks it from the ledge?

21. The Tramp follows a smoking man down the street, waiting for his cigarette butt. While this is a usual activity for vagrants, the Tramp's method is quite unusual. Why is this?

22. Halfway through the shoot, Charles Chaplin decided actress

Virginia Cherrill was unsuitable. He considered replacing her with an actress who had appeared in another of his films. Who was this?

23. The Blind Girl and her grandmother face eviction. How much rent do they owe?

24. In the cafe scene, one of the extras was a then-struggling actress named Jean Pope. Who is Jean Pope better known as today?

25. In the Tramp's boxing match, how much is the purse?

Quiz No. 77:
American Graffiti (1973)

Screenplay by George Lucas, Gloria Katz, and Willard Hyuck
Directed by George Lucas
Starring Richard Dreyfuss, Ron Howard, and Harrison Ford
Universal Pictures

> ***We had an amazing amount of freedom writing that script since the only person we had to deal with was George [Lucas]. Nowadays you sit around in rooms with eighty studio people, but back then, it was just us and George thinking out loud, "Hey, I remember one of my friends doing this," and so on. We even started naming our characters after friends we'd gone to high school with. It was great fun. George especially liked all the weird stuff—the Goat Killer, for example, or Toad vomiting.***
>
> —SCREENWRITER WILLARD HYUCK

George Lucas's first studio film, *American Graffiti,* follows two buddies, Curt (Richard Dreyfuss) and Steve (Ron Howard), the night before they must leave for college. In a night that none of them will forget, Steve breaks up with his girlfriend, their nerdy friend Toad (Charles Martin Smith) picks up a sexy blonde, and John Milner (Paul Le Mat) gets stuck with a thirteen-year-old girl he can't shake. Meanwhile Curt spends the entire night chasing a mysterious woman in a white T-Bird. Other misadventures include Toad losing Milner's car and Curt angering a street gang known as the Pharaohs.

In 1974, *American Graffiti* received five Academy Award nominations: Best Picture (Francis Ford Coppola and Gary Kurtz), Best Director (Lucas), Best Original Screenplay (Lucas, Gloria Katz, and Willard Huyck), Best Supporting Actress (Candy Clark), and Best Film Editing (Verna Fields and Marcia Lucas). However, the film was awarded no Oscars.

1. What future pop singer choreographed *American Graffiti*?

2. What is the number on John Milner's license plate, and what is its significance?

3. Who directed the inferior sequel, *More American Graffiti* (1979)?

4. According to the film's postscript, what happened to John Fields in December 1964?

5. Actress Mackenzie Phillips made her big-screen debut in *American Graffiti*. In keeping with the film's sixties-rock theme, Phillips's father was a well-known sixties-rock musician. Who is Mackenzie Phillips's father?

6. John asks Carol to file a ticket in his glove compartment. What does he ask her to file it under?

7. Where did screenwriter Willard Hyuck, director George Lucas, and producer Francis Ford Coppola meet?

8. According to John Milner, when did rock-and-roll begin going downhill?

9. A 1963 film is advertised on a theater marquee. This is a continuity mistake as the film takes place in 1962. What is the film advertised?

10. What *American Graffiti* character appears, uncredited, as a policeman in the sequel, *More American Graffiti*?

11. Who is the owner of Hepcat Jewelers?

12. Why does Carol say her mother won't allow her to listen to Wolfman Jack?

13. What is the name of the appliance store where Curt watches *Ozzie and Harriet*?

14. What Chuck Berry tune plays over the soundtrack when John and Carol are attacked with a water balloon?

15. What make of automobile does Laurie drive?

16. In Debbie's story, what does the killer leave lying beside each of his victims?

17. In what year was a slightly longer version of American Graffiti reissued?

18. What character was Cindy Williams initially interested in playing?

19. What actor appears as Joe, the hood who intimidates Curt?

20. According to the film's postscript, what is Steve Bolander's occupation in Modesto, California?

21. What question did theatrical trailers ask audiences?
22. How much is Curt's Moose Lodge scholarship?
23. What is Terry Fields's nickname?
24. Who does Eddie believe "really put out"?
25. Where do Terry and Debbie order a "Double Chubby Chuck"?

Quiz No. 78:
ROCKY (1976)

Screenplay by Sylvester Stallone
Directed by John G. Avildsen
Starring Sylvester Stallone, Talia Shire, and Burgess Meredith
United Artists

> ***That's what* Rocky *is all about: pride, reputation, and not being another bum in the neighborhood.***
> —ACTOR SYLVESTER STALLONE

Rocky Balboa (Sylvester Stallone) is a struggling boxer who works at a Philadelphia meat plant and makes extra money working as a collector for a small-time loan shark. When heavyweight champion Apollo Creed (Carl Weathers) searches for an unknown Caucasian opponent, Balboa receives a once-in-a-lifetime opportunity. The film was a tremendous success and later spawned four sequels, all of which lacked the heart of the original.

In 1977, *Rocky* received ten Academy Award nominations: Best Picture (Robert Chartoff and Irwin Winkler), Best Director (John G. Avildsen), Best Original Screenplay (Stallone), Best Actor (Stallone), Best Actress (Talia Shire), Best Supporting Actor (Burgess Meredith), Best Supporting Actor (Burt Young), Best Film Editing (Scott Conrad and Richard Halsey), Best Song (Carol Connors, Bill Conti, and Ayn Robbins), and Best Sound (Bud Alper, Lyle J. Burbridge, William L. McCaughey, and Harry W. Tetrick). The film was awarded three Oscars for Best Picture, Best Director, and Best Film Editing.

1. Sylvester Stallone would later say, "I truly feel without [his/her] participation in the film it would never have had an emotional core." Who was Stallone referring to?
2. Apollo Creed was loosely modeled after a real-life boxer. Who was this?

3. Fourteen years after *Rocky,* John G. Avildsen would direct Sylvester Stallone in another film. What is this film?

4. Producer Irwin Winkler's son, Charles, directed a film about another boxer named Rocky in 1999. What is the name of this film?

5. According to the film's tagline, what was a million-to-one shot?

6. What does Sylvester Stallone say is the single most important scene in *Rocky*?

7. What real-life boxer makes an appearance in the film just before Rocky's bout with Apollo?

8. What is the name of Rocky's goldfish?

9. How much money does Gazzo give Rocky for his date with Adrian?

10. What two things does Apollo say sports make you do?

11. Mickey promises that Rocky will eat lightning and do what?

12. Rocky keeps his locker combination written down so he won't forget it. Where does he keep it?

13. Of his sixty-five-dollar "winner's share" from his fight with Spider Rico, how much does Rocky clear?

14. What is the name of the bar where Rocky and Paulie hang out?

15. When Adrian asks Rocky why he wants to fight, what is his response?

16. United Artists agreed to cast Sylvester Stallone in the lead role as long as the film's budget remained under one million dollars. What was the film's final budget?

17. Whose head does Apollo Creed vow to crack like the Liberty Bell at the Bicentennial Super Battle?

18. What does Apollo Creed say "sounds like a damned monster movie"?

19. What are the names of Rocky's pet turtles?

20. Sylvester Stallone was inspired to write *Rocky* after watching a real-life boxing match. What was this match?

21. The film's ending was changed after test screenings. How did the film originally end?

22. In 1970, fledgling actor Sylvester Stallone appeared in an adult film, *The Party at Kitty and Studs*. The film was heavily edited and rereleased under another title after the success of *Rocky*. What is this new title?

23. Sylvester Stallone had cowritten another film before *Rocky* was made. What is this film?

24. What is the name of Adrian's boss at the pet shop?

25. The producers offered Sylvester Stallone $150,000 to step aside so they could cast a more "bankable" actor in the title role. Who was this actor?

Quiz No. 79: The Deer Hunter (1978)

Screenplay by Deric Washburn, Michael Cimino, Louis Garfinkle, and Quinn K. Redeker
Directed by Michael Cimino
Starring Robert De Niro, Christopher Walken, and John Cazale
Universal Pictures

> *I thought the war was wrong, but what bothered me [most] was that people who went to war became victims of it; they were used for the whims of others. I don't think the policymakers had the smarts. I didn't respect their decisions, or what they were doing. And it was a right of many people to feel, "Why should I go and get involved with something that's unclear—and pay for it with my life?" It takes people like that to make changes.*
>
> —Actor Robert De Niro

Michael Cimino's *The Deer Hunter* follows three Pennsylvania factory workers, Michael (Robert De Niro), Steven (John Savage), and Nick (Christopher Walken) who enlist in the army to fight in Vietnam. After the three are captured by the Vietcong, they are forced to play Russian roulette against each other. *The Deer Hunter* is a study of war and its effect on the lives and psyche of its participants. After the war, each of the scarred soldiers buries himself in delusion, but cannot escape the painful memories of war.

In 1979, *The Deer Hunter* received nine Academy Award nominations: Best Picture (Cimino, Michael Deeley, John Peverall, and Barry Spikings), Best Director (Cimino), Best Original Screenplay (Cimino, Louis Garfinkle, Quinn K. Redeker, and Deric Washburn), Best Actor (De Niro), Best Supporting Actor (Walken), Best Supporting Actress (Meryl Streep), Best Cinematography (Vilmos Zsigmond), Best Film Editing (Peter Zinner), and Best Sound (C. Darin Knight, William L. McCaughey, Richard Portman, and Aaron Rochin). The film was awarded five Oscars for Best Film, Best Director, Best Sound, Best Film

Editing, and Best Supporting Actor for Walken's unforgettable performance.

1. While filming *The Deer Hunter*, who was actor John Cazale engaged to?
2. In the first draft of the screenplay, which character dies at the Russian-roulette table?
3. What useless item does Steven complain that Angela often sends him?
4. In the Russian-roulette game against Nick at the POW camp, how many bullets does Michael request to play with?
5. Director Michael Cimino's follow-up to *The Deer Hunter* also featured actor Christopher Walken. What is this film?
6. In 1979, screenwriter Quinn K. Redeker began an eight-year stint as Alex Marshall on *Days of Our Lives*. In 1987, he began a seven-year stint appearing on another soap opera. What is this soap?
7. In a 1998 Terrence Malick film, John Savage plays another soldier sent over the edge by the horrors of war. What is this film?
8. What is the name of the bar owned by John Welsh?
9. What condiment does Axel put on his Twinkie?
10. Fourteen years after *The Deer Hunter*, actors Christopher Walken and Robert De Niro would appear together in another film. What is this film?
11. Eleven years after *The Deer Hunter*, actors Robert De Niro and John Savage would work together on another Vietnam-themed project. What is this?
12. When Axel says, "You can dress him up, but you can't take him anywhere," who is he referring to?
13. What does Nick do to "keep the fear up"?
14. John Welsh says he would be going to Vietnam if not for what?
15. What is Nick's last name?
16. Beginning with *The Deer Hunter* in the seventies, Robert De Niro and Meryl Streep have appeared together in one film in each decade through the nineties. What are the other two films the two actors appear together in?
17. Steven and Angela marry because she's pregnant. Prior to the wedding, how many times have they had sex?
18. What does Michael explain as a "blessing on the hunter sent by the great wolf to his children"?

19. When presenting director Michael Cimino his Oscar for Best Picture at the 1979 Academy Awards, John Wayne mispronounced Cimino's name. What did he call him?

20. What happened on March 12, 1978?

21. What does Michael proclaim is "what it's all about"?

22. In what 1994 film does Christopher Walken parody his role in *The Deer Hunter*?

23. While watching a football game at the bar, Nick bets twenty dollars that the Steelers will win by twenty points or more. Stan then bets another twenty dollars. What is Stan's bet?

24. What Frankie Valli song do the guys sing to Steven's mother?

25. Actor John Cazale appeared in only five films before his death. How many of these films appear on the AFI Top 100 list?

Quiz No. 80:
The Wild Bunch (1969)

Screenplay by Walon Green, Sam Peckinpah, and Roy N. Sickner
Directed by Sam Peckinpah
Starring William Holden, Ernest Borgnine, and Robert Ryan
Warner Bros.

I wanted to show them for the bastards that they really were.
—Director Sam Peckinpah

As film critic Stephen J. Brennan explains, *The Wild Bunch* is a Western "set in a period when codes of honor and gunfighting are being superseded by mechanization and the machine gun. Money buys honor, and the main characters feel increasingly ill-suited to living in this era of changing technology." Led by Pike Bishop (William Holden), the aging outlaws set out to make one last score before retirement. However, things don't go as planned, and the gang is chased to Mexico by a posse led by Bishop's former partner, Deke Thornton (Robert Ryan).

In 1970, *The Wild Bunch* received two Academy Award nominations: Best Original Screenplay (Walon Green, Sam Peckinpah, and, Roy N. Sickner) and Best Original Score (Jerry Fielding). However, the film was awarded no Oscars.

1. What is significant regarding *The Wild Bunch*'s 3,643 editorial cuts?
2. *The Wild Bunch* was heavily influenced by a 1967 Spaghetti Western directed by Sergio Corbucci. What is this film?
3. What town does the Wild Bunch ride into as the film opens: San Rafael, San Juan, San Jose, or San Diego?
4. According to Mayor Wainscoat, what is the price in town for a drink?

5. When a woman calls Crazy Lee "trash," how does he respond?

6. On what river was the Rio Grande bridge explosion actually filmed?

7. Where was Deke Thornton imprisoned?

8. Warren Oates and Ben Johnson appear as brothers Lyle and Tector Gorch. Four years prior to *The Wild Bunch,* the two actors had appeared together in another Sam Peckinpah film. What is this film?

9. According to legend, more rounds were fired during the production of *The Wild Bunch* than were fired in what war?

10. After the bank robbery, the robbers empty their sacks. What are they filled with?

11. Ernest Borgnine limps throughout *The Wild Bunch.* This real-life injury was caused by an accident on the set of another film. What was this film?

12. Who is Syke's grandson?

13. Thornton asks what's in Agua Verde. What is Coffer's response?

14. At the end of the film, Sykes asks Thornton about his plans. Thornton says he plans to "drift around," and do what?

15. In the mid-sixties, Sam Peckinpah had directed a film which was cut to shreds by another editor. After the success of the *The Wild Bunch,* Columbia invited Peckinpah to return and reedit this film, but Peckinpah declined. What is this film?

16. Who is the self-appointed Mexican warlord played by Emilio Fernandez?

17. What kind of person, according to Don Jose speculates the most about being a child again?

18. How many cases of rifles do Lieutenant Zamorra say are in the shipment?

19. What does Pike say the gold cuts "an awfully lot of"?

20. Pike had once been caught making love to a married woman. Her husband shot and killed her. What did he do to Pike?

21. Just before the dynamite explodes, Pike salutes someone. Who?

22. Pike says, "What I don't know about, I sure as hell am gonna learn." What is he referring to?

23. How much money does Lieutenant Zamorra promise to pay the Wild Bunch for stealing the shipment of weapons?

24. On May 5, 1968, actor Albert Dekker was found dead in his apartment. Inside the bathroom, which was chained from the outside,

his body was bound and handcuffed, hanging from a rope, with obscenities scrawled on it. What did the coroner conclude to be the cause of Dekker's death?

25. Who fires the first shot into Pike's back: Lieutenant Zamorra, an elderly man wearing a sombrero, Deke Thornton, or a small child in an army uniform?

Quiz No. 81:
Modern Times (1936)

Screenplay by Charles Chaplin
Directed by Charles Chaplin
Starring Charles Chaplin, Paulette Goddard, and Henry Bergman
United Artists

> ***Paulette struck me as being somewhat of a gamine. This would be a wonderful quality for me to get on the screen. I could imagine us meeting in a crowded patrol wagon, the Tramp and the Gamine, and the Tramp being very gallant and offering her his seat. This was the basis on which I could build plot and sundry gags.***
>
> —Director Charles Chaplin

A brilliant piece of social criticism, *Modern Times* is Charles Chaplin's satire of modern industry, where factory workers are little more than intricate cogs inside a giant machine. After being dehumanized working in a steel mill, the Tramp (Chaplin) suffers a nervous breakdown. He then meets up with an orphan girl (Paulette Goddard), but soon finds himself in jail for a crime he did not commit. After he is freed, the Tramp finds employment as a night watchman in a department store. However, things soon go awry and the Tramp finds himself behind bars again. *Modern Times* is also significant because it allowed audiences to hear Chaplin's voice for the first time. In true Chaplin fashion, the Tramp speaks only garbled gibberish.

In 1937, *Modern Times* received no Academy Award nominations.

1. What composer scored *Modern Times*?
2. Which of the following was *Modern Times*'s working title: *The Masses, The Industrial Age, Mechanization Melancholy,* or *The Working Man*?
3. The film opens with a symbolic shot of animals running. What kind of animals are these?

4. When the Tramp suffers a breakdown at the factory, what does he spray in the faces of his coworkers?

5. Actors Charles Chaplin and Chester Conklin appear in nineteen films together. They made only one film together after *Modern Times*. What was this?

6. On *Modern Times*, Charles Chaplin shot only 215,000 feet of film, as opposed to *City Lights* (1931), on which he shot 800,000 feet of film. What was the main reason for this?

7. When the Tramp is leaving the hospital after being "cured" of his breakdown, what does the doctor warn him to avoid?

8. Who do the police believe the Tramp is the first time he goes to jail?

9. In jail, what does the Tramp inadvertently pour on his food?

10. Who was Charles Chaplin married to when he made *Modern Times*?

11. When his employer tells him to get back to work, what is the Tramp doing in the restroom?

12. One of the Gamine's sisters is played by the daughter of a prominent crew member. Who is this?

13. Who does the Gamine find murdered in the midst of the riot?

14. When the Tramp is pardoned from jail, what does he request?

15. Who is J. Widdecombe Billows?

16. In 1937, Charles Chaplin was sued by a pair of French producers alleging that he had lifted elements of a film they had made. The lawsuit was later dropped. What is the film Chaplin was accused of ripping off?

17. The Tramp's foreman at the shipyard asks him to find a large wedge. What's wrong with the wedge the Tramp retrieves?

18. While being arrested for ordering a meal he cannot pay for, the Tramp steals something else outside the restaurant. What is this?

19. One of the robbers, Big Bill, recognizes the Tramp. How does he know him?

20. What is the name of the steel mill where the Tramp works?

21. Two years after her death, archival footage of actress Paulette Goddard appeared in a Charles Chaplin biopic. What is the title of this film?

22. When the feeding machine goes haywire on the Tramp, what does it shove into his mouth in place of food?

23. The Tramp finds employment at a shipyard after displaying a letter of recommendation. Who is the letter from?

24. What is the Gamine arrested for stealing?

25. Actress Paulette Goddard appeared in two films in 1936. One of these is *Modern Times*. The other was a Laurel and Hardy comedy. What is this film?

Quiz No. 82: GIANT (1956)

Screenplay by Fred Guiol and Ivan Moffat
Directed by George Stevens
Starring Rock Hudson, Elizabeth Taylor, and James Dean
Warner Bros.

> ***[James] Dean was always late and really very unprofessional, [behaving like] the Broadway actor who comes to California and deigns to make a motion picture—that attitude . . . I didn't like him. Dean was hard to be around. He hated George Stevens, didn't think he was a good director, and was always angry and full of contempt. He never smiled, was sulky, and had no manners.***
>
> —ACTOR ROCK HUDSON

Preceded by *A Place in the Sun* (1951) and *Shane* (1953), *Giant* is the final installment in director George Stevens's *American Trilogy.* Adapted from Edna Ferber's novel of the same title, *Giant* follows the lives of Texas rancher Bick Benedict (Rock Hudson) and his wife, Leslie (Elizabeth Taylor), and their rivalry with cowhand Jett Rink (James Dean). A sermon on the evils of materialism, racial prejudice, and sexual discrimination, the film unfolds across two generations of the Benedict family. Small-time cowboy Rink becomes a wealthy oil tycoon, which further fuels the fires of their rivalry, and young Jordan Benedict marries a Hispanic woman, which was taboo in Texas at the time in which the story takes place.

In 1957, *Giant* received ten Academy Award nominations: Best Picture (Henry Ginsberg and George Stevens, Jr.), Best Director (Stevens), Best Adapted Screenplay (Fred Guiol and Ivan Moffat), Best Actor (Hudson), Best Actor (Dean), Best Supporting Actress (Mercedes McCambridge), Best Film Editing (Philip W. Anderson, Fred Bohanan, and William Hornbeck), Best Color Costume Design (Marjorie Best and Moss Mabry), Best Color Art Direction–Set Decoration

(Ralph S. Hurst and Boris Leven), and Best Original Score (Dimitri Tiomkin). The film's sole Oscar was awarded for Best Director.

1. Twenty-four years after *Giant* was released, Rock Hudson and Elizabeth Taylor would appear together in another film. What is this film?
2. While shooting on June 3, 1955, James Dean froze up and found himself unable to speak his lines. In an effort to loosen himself up, what did Dean then do in front of an estimated twenty-five-hundred onlookers?
3. What is Bick's real name?
4. Before his death, James Dean was scheduled to appear in a film for MGM after *Giant*. In the film, Dean was cast as boxer Rocky Graziano. What is this film?
5. For some scenes, James Dean's voice had to be overdubbed. Whose voice was used for this?
6. Director George Stevens and James Dean got into an argument over a scene after Dean made a suggestion that was not used. However, Stevens later admitted that he had been wrong. "What Jimmy wanted to do would have been the cutest bit in the movie," Stevens said. "His point was that it had to do with pride." What had Dean suggested?
7. What is the name of Jett Rink's oil company?
8. What is the name of Jordy's wife?
9. What does Uncle Bawley predict Jett Rink would do if given enough rope?
10. Director George Stevens initially considered casting an actor he had worked with on *Shane* (1953) in the role of Jett Rink. Who was this?
11. Rock Hudson would later describe a scene from the film featuring himself and Elizabeth Taylor. "We were both so hung over we couldn't speak," Hudson said. "That's what made the scene." What scene was this?
12. Just before shooting *Giant,* one of the film's stars appeared in a road-safety publicity film, saying, "Drive carefully. It's perhaps my life that you will save." Who was this?
13. Director George Stevens gave Rock Hudson his choice of two actresses to appear opposite. One of them was Elizabeth Taylor. Who was the other?

14. What subject does Bick say "takes a heap of readin' " to cover?

15. Jett Rink was modeled after a real-life Texas oilman. Who is this?

16. How many days beyond the planned shooting schedule did the filming of *Giant* last?

17. In what small Texas town was *Giant* filmed?

18. To avoid clichés in *Giant,* director George Stevens set out to cast actors who had never done what?

19. Despite Bick's plans for Jordy to follow in his footsteps, he has other plans. What occupation does Jordy aspire to enter?

20. Elizabeth Taylor was paid $175,000 for appearing in *Giant.* Rock Hudson received $100,000. How much did James Dean earn?

21. The film's shooting schedule had to be shifted, allowing James Dean to make *Rebel Without a Cause* (1955) before filming began. What caused this delay?

22. Director George Stevens's first choice for the role of Leslie was unavailable because she was appearing on Broadway in *Ondine.* Who is this?

23. Bick gets into a brawl with the racist owner of a diner. What is the name of the diner?

24. During the *Giant* shoot, Elizabeth Taylor gave James Dean a Siamese cat as a gift. What was the cat's name?

25. Which of the following actors was *not* considered for the role of Jett Rink: Marlon Brando, Robert Mitchum, Jack Palance, Richard Burton, or Dennis Hopper?

Quiz No. 83:
PLATOON (1986)

Screenplay by Oliver Stone
Directed by Oliver Stone
Starring Tom Berenger, Willem Dafoe, and Charlie Sheen
Orion Pictures

> *The essential conflict between Elias and Barnes grew in my mind. Two gods. Two different views of the war. The angry Achilles versus the conscience-stricken Hector fighting for a lost cause on the dusty plains of Troy. It mirrored the very civil war that I'd witnessed in all the units I was in—on the one hand, the lifers, the juicers, and the moron white-element (part Southern, part rural) against, on the other, the hippie, dope smoking, black, and progressive white-element . . . Right versus Left.*
>
> —DIRECTOR OLIVER STONE

Based on his own experiences as a Twenty-fifth Infantryman in Vietnam, Oliver Stone's *Platoon* is quite simply one of the finest war films ever made. In the film, Stone is represented through PFC Chris Taylor (Charlie Sheen). A nineteen-year-old college dropout, the still-green Taylor finds himself in hell, where a soldier could die at any given moment—at the hands of the enemy or one of his comrades. *Washington Post* critic Paul Attanasio observes, "This is not the Vietnam of op-ed writers, rabble-rousers, or esthetic visionaries, not Vietnam-as-a-metaphor or Vietnam-the-way-it-should-have-been. It is a movie about Vietnam as it was, alive with authenticity, seen through the eyes of a master filmmaker who lost his innocence there."

In 1987, *Platoon* received eight Academy Award nominations: Best Picture (Arnold Kopelson), Best Director (Stone), Best Original Screenplay (Stone), Best Supporting Actor (Tom Berenger), Best Supporting Actor (Willem Dafoe), Best Cinematography (Robert Richardson), Best Film Editing (Claire Simpson), and Best Sound (Charles Grenzbach, Simon Kaye, Richard D. Rogers, and John Wilkinson). The film was awarded four Oscars for Best Picture, Best Director, Best Film Editing, and Best Sound.

1. Oliver Stone's *Platoon* script was optioned in 1976 by Marty Bregman. Who was slated to direct then?

2. According to the film's tagline, what is the first casualty of war?

3. What is said to be the improbability of reason?

4. What future filmmaker appears as Big Harold?

5. One year after making *Platoon,* Oliver Stone directed another film featuring actors Charlie Sheen and John C. McGinley. What is this film?

6. In 1987, screenwriter Oliver Stone was nominated twice by the Academy for Best Original Screenplay. Stone received one of the nominations for *Platoon*. What is the other film Stone was nominated for?

7. The platoon splits into two factions. Who are their leaders?

8. Who does King refer to as "a crusader"?

9. How many times does Barnes shoot Elias?

10. A member of the film crew makes a cameo appearance in the film as a soldier with a mohawk. Who is this?

11. *Platoon* is the first film in Oliver Stone's Vietnam trilogy. What are the two films that follow it?

12. Actors Tom Berenger and Willem Dafoe appear together in two other Vietnam-related films. What are these?

13. According to Junior, what does a Christian *not* do?

14. Of whom does Barnes say, "I personally am gonna take an interest in seeing them suffer"?

15. A company commander is shown talking over the radio in a bunker when a suicide runner attacks. Who makes a cameo appearance in the film as the commanding officer?

16. Charlie Sheen's father, Martin Sheen, appears in a similar narrative leading role in another AFI Top 100 film about the Vietnam war. What is this film?

17. According to King, what will happen if you "keep your pecker hard and your powder dry"?

18. What does Barnes conclude to be reality?

19. What actor makes an early appearance as Lerner?

20. Before Charlie Sheen was cast, the role of Chris was offered to another actor who turned it down. Who was this?

21. Manny disappears in the film. What happens to him?

22. What is the "unwritten rule"?

23. Barnes invites the six soldiers who are talking about him to try to kill him. He is attacked by only one soldier. Who is this?

24. How does Francis sustain the injury to his leg?

25. When *Platoon* aired on network television, many expletives had to be overdubbed. In this version, what replaces the sentence, "He thinks he's Jesus Fuckin' Christ"?

Quiz No. 84:
Fargo (1996)

Screenplay by Joel Coen and Ethan Coen
Directed by Joel Coen
Starring William H. Macy, Frances McDormand, Steve Buscemi, and Peter Stormare
Gramercy Pictures

> ***The story that follows is about Minnesota. It evokes the abstract landscape of our childhood—a bleak, windswept tundra, resembling Siberia except for its Ford dealerships and Hardees restaurants. It aims to be both homey and exotic; and pretends to be true.***
>
> —Screenwriter Ethan Coen

Fargo finds Minnesota car salesman Jerry Lundegaard (William H. Macy) in desperate need of money. Seeing no other way to raise the cash, Jerry hires two bumbling hoods to kidnap his wife and demand a ransom from his wealthy father-in-law. Then, once the ransom is paid, Jerry and the kidnappers will split the money fifty-fifty. Believing he has devised the perfect crime, Jerry sees no way it can go wrong. And then everything does . . .

In 1997, *Fargo* received seven Academy Award nominations: Best Picture (Ethan Coen), Best Director (Joel Coen), Best Original Screenplay (Coen and Coen), Best Actress (Frances McDormand), Best Supporting Actor (William H. Macy), Best Cinematography (Roger Deakins), and Best Film Editing (Roderick Jaynes). The film was awarded two Oscars for Best Original Screenplay and Best Actress.

1. Who was actress Frances McDormand married to when she appeared in *Fargo*?
2. After he's shot, Carl says, "You fuckin' shot me!" Actor Steve Buscemi uses this same line in another film. What is this film?
3. What is the name of the Indian mechanic who introduces Jerry to the kidnappers?

4. When Margie is called to work early in the morning, what does Norm insist that she's "gotta" do?

5. Actors Steve Buscemi and Peter Stormare would reunite in 1998, appearing together in two films. What are these?

6. While writing the screenplay for *Fargo,* Joel and Ethan Coen referred to a book written by Howard Mohr. What is the title of this book?

7. What singer makes a cameo appearance in the film as himself?

8. After the kidnappers have sex with the two prostitutes, they watch a late-night talk show. Which one?

9. According to Wade, what do kids *not* do at McDonalds?

10. The film's editor used a pseudonym, Roderick Jaynes. Who is this?

11. Filming of the outdoor scenes had to be moved around various parts of Minnesota, North Dakota, and Canada. Why?

12. What is Gaear's favorite restaurant?

13. Roger Deakins received his second Oscar nomination for Best Cinematography for *Fargo*. What film did he receive his previous nomination for?

14. *Fargo* was the fourth Coen Brothers film that Frances McDormand appeared in. What was the first?

15. A friend of the Coen Brothers makes a brief cameo appearance as the actor on the soap opera Gaear watches. Who is this?

16. According to director Joel Coen, *Fargo* was inspired by a Japanese film directed by Akira Kurosawa. Coen calls this "probably the best kidnapping film ever made." What is this film?

17. The Coen Brothers were nominated for the prestigious *Palme d'Or* at the Cannes Film Festival. This was the third time they received a nomination for this award. What are the two Coen Brothers's films previously nominated?

18. How much money does Jerry receive from General Motors to finance the nonexistent automobiles?

19. What is the name of Wade's assistant?

20. A bartender tells the police that Carl asked where he could get some "action." What is the name of the bar where this happened?

21.*Fargo* proclaims itself "based on a true story." Whose story is this?

22. Actress Larissa Kokernot worked with Frances McDormand on her Minnesota accent for the film. What role does Kokernot appear in?

23. In Margie's joke, what did the "guy who couldn't afford personalized tags" change his name to?

24. Who is the loan agent Wade refers Jerry to at Midwest Federal?

25. Carl says he's in town for "just a little of the ol' in-and-out." This is a reference to another film. What is this?

Quiz No. 85:
DUCK SOUP (1933)

Screenplay by Bert Kalmar, Nat Perrin, Harry Ruby, and Arthur Sheekman
Directed by Leo McCarey
Starring Groucho Marx, Harpo Marx, and Chico Marx
Paramount Pictures

> ***I never wanted to make the film, but the Marx Brothers asked for me. I refused. Then they got angry with the studio, broke their contract and left. Feeling secure, I now accepted the renewal of my own contract with the studio. But soon they were reconciled with Paramount and I found myself directing the Marx Brothers. The amazing thing about that movie was that I succeeded in not going crazy. They were completely mad.***
>
> —DIRECTOR LEO MCCAREY

A brilliant farce, *Duck Soup* satirizes dictatorship, Cold War politics, and the absurdity of war. When Rufus T. Firefly (Groucho Marx) is appointed the leader of a small nation, wackiness ensues. Neighboring country Sylvania sends two spies, Chicolini (Chico Marx) and Pinky (Harpo Marx), to observe Firefly, who's busy enacting nonsensical new laws. Firefly unknowingly hires the two spies to assist him. In one of the film's most humorous scenes, both Chicolini and Pinky disguise themselves as Firefly, which adds to the confusion. Soon, the two nations go to war, during which time Firefly kills the wrong soldiers and Chicolini decides to "switch sides."

In 1934, *Duck Soup* received no Academy Award nominations. However, in 1974, Groucho Marx was presented with an honorary Oscar recognizing his "brilliant creativity and the unequaled achievements of the Marx Brothers in the art of motion-picture comedy."

1. What country banned *Duck Soup* because it pokes fun at dictators?
2. Who becomes Firefly's secretary of war?

3. Why does Chicolini reason that Pinkie tore up the telegram?

4. Who becomes the presidential chauffeur?

5. Who conceived the film's title?

6. The name of the rival country Sylvania is a reference to a 1929 Ernst Lubitsch film. What is this film?

7. When informed that the workers are demanding shorter hours, Firefly agrees to cut one hour. Which is this?

8. Why does Firefly say it's too late to prevent the war?

9. Before the film opened, officials from Fredonia, New York, asked the filmmakers to change the name of the country, Freedonia, as they felt it hurt the image of their town. What was Groucho Marx's response?

10. After leaving the Marx Brothers act, Zeppo Marx became an inventor and a manufacturer. In keeping with *Duck Soup*'s theme of war, Zeppo's Marman Products manufactured a product that proved significant in World War II. What was this?

11. *Duck Soup* was part of a five-picture deal the Marx Brothers had with Paramount. After *Duck Soup,* how many films did they have left to make to fulfill their obligation to Paramount?

12. How many "gals" does Firefly joke about being enough for him?

13. How did Chicolini and Pinky "fool" Firefly at the baseball game on Wednesday?

14. Who is the character Vera Marcal meant to parody?

15. How many Marx Brothers films did Zeppo appear in after *Duck Soup*?

16. During the battle scene, Firefly dons five different historical uniforms. What are these?

17. Why does Chicolini propose a "standing army"?

18. Firefly tells Mrs. Teasdale he can see her bending over a hot stove. What does he say he *cannot* see?

19. What happens when Mrs. Teasdale attempts to sing the national anthem?

20. Although he was long gone when they made *Duck Soup,* there was originally a fifth member of the Marx Brothers. Who was this?

21. Who does Chicolini claim accompanied "Admiral Byrd to the Pole"?

22. Rufus T. Firefly explains that his family traveled on the upper deck of the Mayflower. Where does Firefly say the horseflies were?

23. What is the name of the "mythical kingdom" that has gone bankrupt?

24. While Sylvania decides whether to lend $20 million, Firefly asks for a loan "until payday." How much is this?

25. Actress Margaret Dumont would ultimately appear in seven of the Marx Brothers's films. *Duck Soup* was her third. What were the two previous Marx Brothers–Margaret Dumont collaborations?

Quiz No. 86:
MUTINY ON THE BOUNTY (1935)

Screenplay by Talbot Jennings, Jules Furthman, and Carey Wilson
Directed by Frank Lloyd
Starring Charles Laughton, Clark Gable, and Franchot Tone
Metro-Goldwyn-Mayer

> ***Most of the time we had to stand on the deck of the vessel, and the only seats were guns, anchors, chain cables, and such-like restful things. Before I took the part of Captain Bligh, I considered myself to be one of the world's worst sailors. But after rolling around in a small wooden ship for seven weeks, I think I could stand anything now.***
>
> —ACTOR CHARLES LAUGHTON

Mutiny on the Bounty is the true story of a crew's uprising against its tyrannical leader, Captain William Bligh (Charles Laughton). After being set adrift in a tiny boat, Bligh commandeers it an amazing thirty-six hundred miles to civilization. When the mutiny is reported, the ship's crewmen are taken to trial. After explaining Bligh's unreasonable methods, midshipman Roger Byam (Franchot Tone) is freed to return to work. The film's implication that this incident ushered in British naval reform is historically inaccurate.

In 1936, *Mutiny on the Bounty* received eight Academy Award nominations: Best Picture (Irving Thalberg), Best Director (Frank Lloyd), Best Adapted Screenplay (Jules Furthman, Talbot Jennings, and Carey Wilson), Best Actor (Clark Gable), Best Actor (Laughton), Best Actor (Tone), Best Film Editing (Margaret Booth), and Best Original Score (Nat W. Finston and Herbert Stothart). The film's sole Oscar was awarded for Best Picture.

1. Before Franchot Tone was cast as Roger Byam, MGM tried to land another actor who was under contract with Paramount. However, Paramount refused to release him. Who was this actor?
2. The uniform Charles Laughton wears in the film is exactly like

the uniform worn by the real-life Captain Bligh. Where did the uniform come from?

3. At the end of the film, Roger Byam is assigned to a new ship. This is historically inaccurate. What happened to the real-life Roger Byam?

4. Bligh reminds his crewmen that he is three things. What are these?

5. During the seven-week shoot, second-unit cameraman Glenn Strong died. How did Strong die?

6. In 1950, a Looney Toons parody of *Mutiny on the Bounty* was made featuring Yosemite Sam as Captain Bligh and Bugs Bunny as Fletcher Christian. What is the title of this cartoon?

7. Bligh says the sailors respect only one law. What is this law?

8. When called to testify, Roger Byam suggests an alternative method of treatment. Rather than flaying the backs of the sailors, what does he suggest be lifted by their leaders?

9. What punishment does Bligh inflict when a sailor requests water?

10. What is significant regarding Clark Gable's physical appearance in *Mutiny on the Bounty*?

11. Another version of this story featuring Errol Flynn as Captain Bligh had been filmed two years earlier. What is the title of this version?

12. Clark Gable, Charles Laughton, and Franchot Tone were all nominated by the Academy for Best Actor in 1936. However, all of them lost. Who beat them?

13. Bligh orders that a sick elderly doctor be brought to the deck to observe the flogging of five sailors. What is the name of this doctor?

14. What is the name of the woman Roger Byam falls in love with?

15. A vacationing actor sailing in the vicinity where *Mutiny on the Bounty* was being filmed asked director Frank Lloyd if he could work on the film as an extra. The well-known actor was dressed as a sailor and given a fake mustache. Who is this actor?

16. What does accused mutineer Fletcher Christian predict future generations will "spell mutiny with"?

17. After the mutiny, Bligh takes command of another ship. What is the name of this ship?

18. In 1962, *Mutiny on the Bounty* was remade by Lewis Milestone. In this remake, who appears in the role of Fletcher Christian?

19. Fletcher Christian says he's never known a better seaman than Bligh. What does he say the captain is "as a man"?

20. Charles Laughton was sick during most of the film's shoot. What was wrong with him?

21. What is the name of the island in the Dutch West Indies where Bligh eventually turns up?

22. According to Captain Bligh, what is the "lowest form of animal life" in the British Navy?

23. How many mutinies did the real-life William Bligh survive?

24. What actor appears as Captain Bligh in Roger Donaldson's 1984 remake, *Bounty*?

25. Eight years after *Mutiny on the Bounty* was released, Charles Laughton appeared in another film directed by Frank Lloyd. What is this film?

Quiz No. 87:
Frankenstein (1931)

Screenplay by Francis Edward Faragoh and Garrett Fort
Directed by James Whale
Starring Colin Clive, Mae Clark, and Boris Karloff
Universal Pictures

> ***I spent three and a half hours in the makeup chair getting ready for the day's work. The makeup itself was quite painful, particularly the putty on my eyes. There were days when I thought I would never be able to hold out until the end of the day.*** —Actor Boris Karloff

Following closely on the heels of *Dracula* (1930), Universal Pictures released *Frankenstein* in 1931. Although the film took artistic liberties with the plotline of Mary Shelley's classic novel, it left audiences with an enduring image of a monster that has since become an icon of American popular culture. In *Frankenstein,* the maniacal Dr. Henry Frankenstein (Colin Clive) discovers the key to creating life. From the stolen corpses of the freshly dead, he constructs a new body, which he then brings to life. After accidentally giving the Monster (Boris Karloff) a defective brain, Frankenstein's creation becomes violent. Noted film critic Leonard Maltin calls *Frankenstein* the "definitive monster movie, with Clive as the ultimate mad scientist . . . It's creaky at times, and cries for a musical score, but it's still impressive, as is Karloff's performance in the role that made him a star."

In 1932, *Frankenstein* received no Academy Award nominations.

1. *Frankenstein* reappeared in six Universal sequels. However, only one of these was directed by James Whale, the filmmaker who made *Frankenstein*. What is the name of this film?
2. What sentence was removed from the film before its release?
3. What does Dr. Frankenstein say the storm holds "the electrical secrets" of?

4. Throughout the years, the Frankenstein monster has appeared in many films. Which of the following actors has *not* appeared in a film as the Frankenstein monster: Robert De Niro, Vincent Price, Randy Quaid, Bo Svenson, or Christopher Lee?

5. The first adaptation of Mary Shelley's novel was produced by Thomas Edison in 1910. In this version, what actor plays Frankenstein's monster?

6. Whose face does Dr. Frankenstein shovel dirt into?

7. What does Waldman believe to be Dr. Frankenstein's "insane ambition"?

8. What does Waldman see as the only thing "that can come of" Frankenstein's work?

9. Why was an epilogue added to the film?

10. In 1958, Boris Karloff appeared in a non-Universal Frankenstein film. This time, however, he played the role of Dr. Frankenstein rather than the monster. What is the name of this film?

11. In his "friendly warning," Edward van Sloan concludes that Dr. Frankenstein created his monster without taking whom into account?

12. Who commissions the group of peasants that hunts for the monster?

13. What does Dr. Frankenstein liken to spending time with Mary?

14. Dr. Frankenstein declares that "there can be no wedding as long as" what?

15. Bela Lugosi was first offered the role of the monster, but passed. However, Lugosi would later play the Frankenstein monster in a 1943 film. What is this film?

16. How is Fritz killed?

17. What does the monster fear?

18. What does Waldman promise to preserve for Dr. Frankenstein?

19. Who was the first director hired to develop *Frankenstein* in 1930?

20. In 1974, Mel Brooks directed a parody of *Frankenstein* starring Gene Wilder, Marty Feldman, and Peter Boyle. What is this film?

21. The label on the jar reads DYSFUNCTIO CEREBRI. What does this mean?

22. On the day of his engagement, what did Dr. Frankenstein say he'd begun to doubt due to his being on "the verge of a discovery"?

23. What is Dr. Frankenstein's first name?

24. What is the name of the medical school from which Fritz steals the brain?

25. Throughout the years, the Frankenstein monster would meet up with Dracula numerous times. What is the first film the two appear together in?

Quiz No. 88:
EASY RIDER (1969)

Screenplay by Dennis Hopper, Peter Fonda, and Terry Southern
Directed by Dennis Hopper
Starring Peter Fonda, Dennis Hopper, and Jack Nicholson
Columbia Pictures

> ***The first thing I put down on paper was the image of the motorcycle. I wanted to make it attractive to people . . . like a red, white, and blue cock.***
> —SCREENWRITER PETER FONDA

For many viewers, *Easy Rider* represents a bygone era when society frowned upon those who chose to wear their hair long or live life on the road. However, upon closer inspection you will find that its messages are as poignant today as they were in 1969. *Easy Rider* follows bikers Wyatt (Peter Fonda) and Billy (Dennis Hopper) on a cross-country trek to New Orleans. Along the way, they find themselves in a number of predicaments and meet up with a variety of offbeat characters, including George Hansen (Jack Nicholson). As *Ain't It Cool News* critic Harry Knowles raves, "[The film] reminds you why Jack Nicholson is a god, why Peter Fonda is a god, and why Dennis Hopper is a god. The scenes of them upon that Captain America motorcycle and the flaming Billy-Cycle are the perfect iconoclastic images."

In 1970, *Easy Rider* received two Academy Award nominations: Best Original Screenplay (Dennis Hopper, Peter Fonda, and Terry Southern) and Best Supporting Actor (Jack Nicholson). The film was awarded no Oscars.

1. The tank of Captain America's bike would later appear as a lamp in a 1994 film starring Peter Fonda. What is this film?
2. Two years after *Easy Rider* was released, Dennis Hopper directed his second film. This story of a film shoot in Peru also features Peter Fonda. What is this film?

3. What Steppenwolf tune plays as Billy and Wyatt complete the drug transaction with Connection?

4. What adorns Billy's necklace?

5. Two years before making *Easy Rider,* Dennis Hopper, Jack Nicholson, and Peter Fonda all worked together on a film directed by Roger Corman. Hopper served as second-unit director, Nicholson wrote the screenplay, and Fonda appeared in it. What is this film?

6. In 1982, Michael O'Donahue wrote a screenplay for a sequel to *Easy Rider* that takes place in the afterlife. However, the film was never made. What is the title of this script?

7. The tagline for *Easy Rider* begins with "A man went looking for America . . ." Where does it say he found it?

8. At the parade, Billy and Wyatt are arrested. What are they charged with?

9. What is Wyatt's astrological sign?

10. In 1999, Peter Fonda narrated a documentary about motorcycles. What is the title of this documentary?

11. According to Dennis Hopper, why didn't he cast Rip Torn in the role of George?

12. As Billy claims that he cannot be hit because he's invisible, what strikes him in the chest?

13. When Wyatt asks the Stranger if he would like to be someone else, who does he say he'd "like to try"?

14. *Easy Rider* stars Dennis Hopper and Jack Nicholson appear together in a 1968 film with the Monkees. Nicholson also cowrote the screenplay. What is this film?

15. Who appears in a cameo as Connection, the drug dealer?

16. What is George Hansen's occupation?

17. What does George call the rednecks' rude comments at the diner?

18. How many UFOs does George claim to have seen in a formation?

19. Who does George conclude that the "scissor-happy people" want everyone to look like?

20. What future pop star makes a brief appearance as a New Orleans prostitute named Mary?

21. Dennis Hopper appears in four AFI Top 100 films. What are these films?

22. George believes aliens have landed on Earth. What planet does he believe they're from?

23. What type of cell does the deputy at the diner jokingly suggest Billy and Wyatt be locked in?

24. What does Billy sing about finding at the Mardi Gras?

25. In 1969, two films were released that were cowritten by Terry Southern. One of these is *Easy Rider*. The other film stars Peter Sellers, Ringo Starr, and John Cleese. What is this film?

Quiz No. 89:
PATTON (1970)

Screenplay by Francis Ford Coppola and Edmund H. North
Directed by Franklin J. Schaffner
Starring George C. Scott, Karl Malden, and Michael Bates
Twentieth Century–Fox

> ***There was considerable concern at the corporate level at Twentieth Century–Fox that the studio was making a film about General Patton. This was at the height of antiwar feeling in America. What were we doing honoring somebody who was the very epitome of militarism?***
>
> —PRODUCER RICHARD ZANUCK

While Franklin J. Schaffner's biopic, *Patton,* is in many ways historically inaccurate, those who knew General George S. Patton credit the film with capturing the spirit of its subject. Film critic James Berardinelli observes, "With its larger-than-life, yet at the same time singularly human, portrayal of George S. Patton, Jr., Franklin Schaffner's picture is an example of filmmaking at its finest. From production design and battle choreography to simple one-on-one dramatic acting, *Patton* has it all. There is no scene in all 170 minutes that doesn't work on some level."

In 1971, *Patton* received ten Academy Award nominations: Best Picture (Frank McCarthy), Best Director (Schaffner), Best Adapted Screenplay (Francis Ford Coppola and Edmund H. North), Best Actor (Scott), Best Cinematography (Fred J. Koenekamp), Best Film Editing (Hugh S. Fowler), Best Art Direction–Set Decoration (Antonio Mateos, Urie McCleary, Gil Parrondo, and Pierre-Louis Thevenet), Best Sound (Don J. Bassman and Douglas O. Williams), Best Special Visual Effects (Alex Weldon), and Best Original Score (Jerry Goldsmith). The film was awarded seven Oscars, losing only in its bids for Best Cinematography, Best Special Visual Effects, and Best Original Score.

1. According to General Patton's grandson, Twentieth Century–Fox could not make an authorized biopic based on Patton's own memoirs because they inquired at the wrong time. According to him, when did the producers contact Patton's wife?

2. Omar Bradley says he does his job because he was trained to do it. Why does he conclude that Patton does his job?

3. What are the two books *Patton* was adapted from?

4. What general worked on the film as a military consultant?

5. Prior to *Patton,* Karl Malden and George C. Scott had appeared together in only one film. What is this?

6. When Patton says, "Look at this nasty-faced son-of-a-bitch," to whom is he referring?

7. In 1971, George C. Scott won the Oscar for Best Actor for his turn in *Patton.* However, he refused to accept the award. Why?

8. In 1986, George C. Scott would reprise his role in a made-for-television sequel. What is the title of this film?

9. After being attacked by Luftwaffe, what does Patton say he would do if he could find the "Nazi son-of-a-bitches" flying them?

10. Approximately twenty minutes was trimmed from the version of *Patton* that was released in Italy. What were these scenes?

11. Patton orders two soldiers to be removed from the field hospital. What do they suffer from?

12. What does the German officer conclude of British officers and American soldiers?

13. What was the film's working title?

14. When tearing a pinup from the wall, Patton states, "This is a barracks . . ." What does he say it is *not*?

15. When a minister asks Patton if he reads the Bible, what is his memorable response?

16. Patton was first conceived by Darryl F. Zanuck and Frank McCarthy in 1951. However, the project was shelved in 1956. Why?

17. In what country was *Patton* filmed?

18. Patton describes Morocco as being a combination of two things. What are these?

19. What does Patton call the "most-conquered city in history"?

20. Who does Patton believe is the only person who would carry a pearl-handled revolver?

21. Who did the film's producers refer to as "doves"?

22. Why was the film's introduction filmed last?

23. Patton says he wouldn't give a "hoot in hell" for any man who lost and did what?

24. What does Patton say that no "bastard" has ever won a war by doing?

25. Patton believes there is only one proper way for a professional soldier to die. What is this?

Quiz No. 90: THE JAZZ SINGER (1927)

Screenplay by Alfred A. Cohn
Directed by Alan Crosland
Starring Al Jolson, May McAvoy, and Warner Oland
Warner Bros.

> ***Everything was new and strange to me. I would do a scene five times with tears in my eyes and then Alan Crosland would say, "Do it again—and put some feeling into it."*** —ACTOR AL JOLSON

Often credited as the first full-length talking film, *The Jazz Singer* is actually a silent film—complete with dialogue cards—featuring recorded musical sequences and minor dialogue. In *The Jazz Singer,* a young Jewish boy named Jakie Rabinowitz forsakes his family heritage to become a professional jazz singer. This causes his father to declare, "I have no son." After Jakie becomes a big success, he leaves the bright lights of Broadway to assume his father's position as the synagogue cantor.

In 1929, *The Jazz Singer* received one Academy Award nomination: Best Adapted Screenplay (Alfred A. Cohn). The film lost in its bid for this Oscar. However, Warner Brothers was awarded an honorary Oscar "for producing *The Jazz Singer,* the pioneering outstanding talking picture, which has revolutionized the industry."

1. Nineteen years after *The Jazz Singer,* actor Al Jolson auditioned twice for a role, but lost it to Larry Parks because the producers didn't feel he was bankable. What was this role?
2. In 1952, *The Jazz Singer* was remade by director Michael Curtiz. Who appeared in the lead role in this version?
3. *The Jazz Singer* was adapted from a play written by Samson Raphaelson. What is the title of this play?

4. Jakie's father is the fifth generation of Rabinowitz men to become what?

5. Three years after *The Jazz Singer*, Al Jolson sang "Mammy" in another film. What is this film?

6. Where does Jakie tell Mary Dale he first "caught her act"?

7. In the 1980 remake of *The Jazz Singer*, what is Jakie Rabinowitz's name changed to?

8. *The Jazz Singer* was easily the most important film Warner Bros. had ever made. However, the Warner brothers were conspicuously absent from the film's premiere. Why?

9. How much money does Jakie earn per week at the State Theatre?

10. In 1928, Al Jolson followed up *The Jazz Singer* with a film that was an even bigger success. What is this film?

11. What is the name of the sound device that made *The Jazz Singer* "talk"?

12. What does thirteen-year-old Jakie promise to do if his father whips him again?

13. In Chicago, Jakie attends a matinee performance by a Jewish singer who reminds him of his father. What is the name of this singer?

14. What two actors were first approached for the lead role in *The Jazz Singer*?

15. Two successful films were made about singer Al Jolson in the late forties. A third film about Jolson's life in the military was planned, but never made. What was the title of this unproduced film?

16. What is the first song Jakie sings in the film?

17. What does Jakie change his name to as an adult?

18. What pop singer appears in the lead role in the 1980 remake of *The Jazz Singer*?

19. What does Mary Dale say Jakie has in his voice that sets him apart from the other jazz singers?

20. What future Academy Award–winning actress makes a cameo as a chorus girl?

21. According to the opening title card, what does "a spirit in every living soul" cry for?

22. Inside Muller's Bar and Cafe, who is young Jakie introduced as?

23. What is the name of Jakie's mother?

24. What is the first song in the film actually sung by Al Jolson?

25. Four films directed by Alan Crosland were released in 1927. One of these is *The Jazz Singer*. What are the other three films?

Quiz No. 91: My Fair Lady (1964)

Screenplay by Alan Jay Lerner
Directed by George Cukor
Starring Audrey Hepburn, Rex Harrison, and Stanley Holloway
Warner Bros.

> ***Originally I had a block about appearing in a musical. I went to a voice teacher for a while, but that did no good. My range is about one and a half notes. I ended up talking the musical numbers, which was revolutionary at the time.***
> —Actor Rex Harrison

Based on the George Bernard Shaw play *Pygmalion,* George Cukor's *My Fair Lady* is one of the most-beloved musicals ever produced. In the film, arrogant phonetics-instructor Henry Higgins (Rex Harrison) makes a wager that he can transform an unrefined "commoner" into a proper young lady. After convincing Eliza Doolittle (Audrey Hepburn), a cockney-bred flower girl, to train under his instruction, he finds himself growing "accustomed to her face" and unable to live without her.

In 1965, *My Fair Lady* received twelve Academy Award nominations: Best Picture (Jack L. Warner), Best Director (Cukor), Best Adapted Screenplay (Alan Jay Lerner), Best Actor (Harrison), Best Supporting Actor (Stanley Holloway), Best Supporting Actress (Gladys Cooper), Best Color Cinematography (Harry Stradling, Jr.), Best Film Editing (William H. Ziegler), Best Color Art Direction–Set Decoration (Gene Allen, Cecil Beaton, and George James Hopkins), Best Color Costume Design (Beaton), Best Adapted Score (Andre Previn), and Best Sound (George Groves). The film was awarded eight Oscars, losing in its bids for Best Adapted Screenplay, Best Supporting Actor, Best Supporting Actress, and Best Film Editing.

1. Who provided the singing voice for Eliza Doolittle?

2. The musicals *West Side Story* (1961), *My Fair Lady*, and *The Sound of Music* (1965) all appear on the AFI Top 100 list. Which actress do the three films share?

3. What does Higgins remind Eliza that English "is the language of"?

4. What is located at 27A Wimpole Street?

5. George Bernard Shaw's play *Pygmalion* had previously been adapted to film in 1938. In this version of the film, directed by Anthony Asquith and Leslie Howard, what actress appeared in the role of Eliza Doolittle?

6. Why does Alfred Doolittle claim he has no morals?

7. According to the song, where is "that soggy plain"?

8. Higgins concludes that the French "don't care what they do" as long as what happens?

9. While staying with Higgins, Eliza sends for only two possessions from her father's home. What are these?

10. Which cast member died during filming on October 31, 1963?

11. What were the cast and crew of *My Fair Lady* informed of during the filming of the garden scene?

12. What does Eliza do on the corner of Tottenham Court Road?

13. According to Eliza's father, what did the Lord create liquor to be?

14. What sickness claimed Eliza's aunt?

15. In 1964, Audrey Hepburn appeared in two films. One of these was *My Fair Lady*. The other film reunited Hepburn with William Holden, her costar in *Sabrina* (1954. What is this film?

16. In the song "An Ordinary Man," what two authors does Higgins say he would like to talk about when a woman talks of love?

17. In Eliza's song "Just You Wait," what fate befalls Higgins?

18. What does Higgins say he'd prefer a new edition of to allowing a woman into his life?

19. Who is jokingly called "one of the most original moralists in England"?

20. Screenwriter Alan Jay Lerner cowrote two AFI Top 100 musicals. One of these is *My Fair Lady*. What is the other film?

21. Who provided the singing voice for Freddie Eynsford-Hill?

22. Higgins says that the moment a woman becomes friends with him she becomes "jealous, exacting, suspicious," and what?

23. In what song does Higgins sing about "verbal class distinction"?

24. Where was Eliza born?

25. Actor Rex Harrison lobbied for another actress to be cast as Eliza Doolittle. However, Jack Warner didn't think an unknown should be cast, so he instead cast Audrey Hepburn. The following year, the actress Warner passed on was awarded the Oscar for Best Actress for her turn in another musical. Who is this?

Quiz No. 92:
A PLACE IN THE SUN (1951)

Screenplay by Harry Brown and Michael Wilson
Directed by George Stevens
Starring Montgomery Clift, Elizabeth Taylor, and Shelley Winters
Paramount Pictures

> *All I did was just sort of whistle and hum my way through the films, powdering my nose and getting a great kick out of wearing pretty clothes—dying to wear more makeup, higher heels, lower-cut dresses. The first time I ever considered* acting *when I was young was in* A Place in the Sun. *I was seventeen and just thrilled to be in the film because it was my first kind of adult role. It was a tricky part because this girl is so rich and spoiled that it would have been easy to play her as absolutely vacuous. But, I think she was a girl who could care a great deal.*
>
> —ACTRESS ELIZABETH TAYLOR

After meeting a wealthy uncle he never even knew existed, George Eastman (Montgomery Clift) finds himself employed at his uncle's factory. Despite a strict rule that he cannot date any of his coworkers, George begins dating Alice Tripp (Shelley Winters), who promises not to tell. However, George's life changes when he meets beautiful high-society girl Angela Vickers (Elizabeth Taylor). Upon seeing Angela, George is at once infatuated, and he soon learns that the feeling is mutual. The only problem now is that Alice refuses to step aside, and the situation becomes worse when she discovers that she's pregnant.

In 1952, *A Place in the Sun* received nine Academy Award nominations: Best Picture (George Stevens, Jr.), Best Director (George Stevens), Best Adapted Screenplay (Harry Brown and Michael Wilson), Best Actor (Clift), Best Actress (Winters), Best Black-and-White Cinematography (William C. Mellor), Best Film Editing (William Hornbeck), Best Black-and-White Costume Design (Edith Head), and Best Original Score (Franz Waxman). The film was awarded six Oscars, but lost in three important categories: Best Picture, Best Actor, and Best Actress.

1. Theodore Dreiser's novel, *An American Tragedy,* which *A Place in the Sun* is based upon, was previously adapted by Joseph von Sternberg in 1931. Before this, another director was slated to adapt the novel for Paramount Pictures, but he wound up walking away because he felt the studio "aspired to make this scandalous novel a run-of-the mill . . . tale of 'boy meets girl.' " Who was this filmmaker?

2. The first time George visits Eastman Industries he is not allowed to enter until he produces something. What is this?

3. Why does Alice say she does not wear swimsuits?

4. What is the name of Alice's "fierce" landlady?

5. What *Giant* (1956) screenwriter served as associate producer on both *A Place in the Sun* and *Shane* (1953)?

6. Who sarcastically remarks, "I always wanted to look like a bellhop"?

7. When George tells Angela that he is the "happiest person in the world," what is her response?

8. When Alice goes to the doctor, she does so under a pseudonym. What is this?

9. What is the date George circles on his calendar?

10. In 1956, Elizabeth Taylor saved the life of one of her *A Place in the Sun* costars. Who was this?

11. What does Eastman Industries manufacture?

12. What does Earl warn George that he must "be aware [of] every minute"?

13. Of whom does Angela remark, "I've known them intimately for some years and they're quite nice"?

14. How does Alice learn that George spent the afternoon at the lake with Angela and her family?

15. Three years prior to *A Place in the Sun,* Shelley Winters and Montgomery Clift appeared together in another film. What is this film?

16. George runs into Alice at the theater. What is the film they are viewing?

17. The blinking neon sign outside George's apartment reminds him of Angela. What does it say?

18. Why is the word "abortion" never used in the film?

19. When George takes Alice to have an abortion, what is the name of the doctor she sees?

20. In 1952, Shelly Winters was nominated for an Academy Award for Best Actress, but lost. However, eight years later she would win her first Oscar for another film directed by George Stevens. What is this film?

21. Inside his uncle's office, George sees a check made out for one hundred thousand dollars. Who is the check written to?

22. As George talks on the telephone with his mother, an appropriate sign is visible on the wall behind her. What does it read?

23. George purchases a tweed suit he sees in a shop window. How much does the suit cost?

24. As the film opens, what is George Eastman doing?

25. Director George Stevens's final film was released in 1970. In this film, Elizabeth Taylor appears as a Las Vegas chorus girl. What is this film?

Quiz No. 93:
THE APARTMENT (1960)

Screenplay by I.A.L. Diamond and Billy Wilder
Directed by Billy Wilder
Starring Jack Lemmon, Shirley MacLaine, and Fred MacMurray
United Artists

> ***Even today, decades after winning three Oscars for the film, Wilder is still tweaking the story of* The Apartment. *He sometimes wonders if he should have given Jack Lemmon "a limp, or some physical deformity" to increase sympathy for the character. And he expresses surprise that audiences would root for [Shirley] MacLaine and Lemmon as lovers. But, it is their very lack of traditional smoldering qualities that make the union of Baxter and Kubelik a celebration of romantic misfits everywhere.***
>
> —AUTHOR-DIRECTOR CAMERON CROWE

Director-screenwriter Billy Wilder's *The Apartment* is a razor-sharp satire of life in the American workplace and just what it takes to climb the ladder of success. A struggling insurance clerk named C. C. "Bud" Baxter (Jack Lemmon) finds himself on the fast track to success after loaning out his apartment to his slimy superior Mr. Sheldrake (Fred MacMurray) for extramarital affairs. The only problem is that Baxter isn't happy anymore; despite his advancement at work, he's never able to relax in his own home and, what's worse, he finds himself falling in love with his boss's mistress, Fran Kubelik (Shirley MacLaine).

In 1961, *The Apartment* received ten Academy Award nominations: Best Picture (Wilder), Best Director (Wilder), Best Original Screenplay (I.A.L. Diamond and Wilder), Best Actor (Lemmon), Best Actress (MacLaine), Best Supporting Actor (Jack Kruschen), Best Black-and-White Cinematography (Joseph LaShelle), Best Film Editing (Daniel Mandell), Best Black-and-White Art Direction–Set Decoration (Edward G. Boyle and Alexander Trauner), and Best Sound (Gordon Sawyer). The film was awarded five Oscars—three of which went to Wilder—for Best Picture, Best Director, Best Original Screenplay, Best Film Editing, and Best Black-and-White Art Direction–Set Decoration.

1. What does Doctor Dreyfuss advise Bud to be?

2. What is the name of the insurance company where Bud is employed?

3. What is the only night of the week Mr. Vanderhof "can get away"?

4. Bud says he once tried to commit suicide after a failed romance in Cincinnati. Where did he shoot himself?

5. Jack Lemmon appeared in seven films directed by Billy Wilder. One of these is *The Apartment*. What are the other six films?

6. Mr. Sheldrake says it "takes years to work your way up to the twenty-seventh floor." How long does he conclude that it takes to "be out on the street again"?

7. Bud stops Fran from writing a letter to Mrs. Sheldrake, giving her two reasons why she shouldn't do it. What are these?

8. Bud prides himself in being a good cook, but what does he admit being "lousy" at?

9. Who does Mr. Sheldrake fire for giving a "pep talk" to Fran at the Christmas party?

10. While filming *The Apartment,* screenwriters I.A.L. Diamond and Billy Wilder wrote a forty-page treatment for a comedy about a gang of jewel thieves, which would have starred a famous comedy team. However, funding for the film fell apart when one of the would-be stars suffered a heart attack. What was this famous comedy team?

11. When Fran concludes that "some poor slob must have five colds a year," what is Bud's response?

12. Bud concludes that the 31,259 people employed at the home office of the insurance company outnumber the population of a town in Mississippi. What is this town?

13. What is Bud's weekly take-home pay?

14. Dobisch leaves the wrong key under Bud's mat. What is this key for?

15. According to Billy Wilder *The Apartment* was inspired by a film directed by David Lean. What is this film?

16. The famous shot showing the many rows of desks is a nod to a similar scene in a 1928 film directed by King Vidor. What is this film?

17. Which of Bud's coworkers telephones from a pay phone on Sixty-first Street with a blonde that "looks like Marilyn Monroe"?

18. Why does Bud say his landlady raised his rent?

19. At the beginning of the film, on what floor of the insurance building does Bud work?

20. Three years after collaborating on *The Apartment,* Shirley MacLaine and Jack Lemmon appeared together in another film directed by Billy Wilder. What is this film?

21. What does Fran conclude a woman should not wear when seeing a married man?

22. In what department of the insurance company does Bud work in at the opening of the film?

23. Bud leaves a note on the record player. What does it say?

24. When Fran says, "It makes me look the way I feel," what is she referring to?

25. In 1961, *The Apartment* was awarded the Academy Award for Best Picture. Since then, only one other black-and-white film has received this honor. What is this film?

Quiz No. 94:
GoodFellas (1990)

Screenplay by Martin Scorsese and Nicholas Pileggi
Directed by Martin Scorsese
Starring Robert De Niro, Ray Liotta, and Joe Pesci
Warner Bros.

> ***I got to the office one day, and there was a message: "Call Martin Scorsese." I thought someone was playing a joke on me. So I didn't return the call. But, later in the week, the phone rang at home late at night, and a voice said, "My name is Martin Scorsese. I'm a film director. I've been looking for this book for years." And I said, "I've been waiting for this phone call all my life."***
>
> —Author Nicholas Pileggi

Director Martin Scorsese's *GoodFellas* follows the rise and fall of gangster Henry Hill (Ray Liotta), from his early introduction to the Mafia to his dropping dime in exchange for enrollment in the Witness Protection Program three decades later. In *MacLeans,* film critic Brad D. Johnson concludes, "Charting Hill's progress from the 1950s to the 1980s, from innocence to corruption, Scorsese mirrors the larger evolution of American culture. His movie is a slice of life—and death—from a criminal culture that seems an exaggerated version of the world outside. Funny and frightening, unpredictable and provocative, *GoodFellas* may be the most authentic Mafia picture ever made."

In 1991, *GoodFellas* received six Academy Award nominations: Best Picture (Irwin Winkler), Best Director (Scorsese), Best Adapted Screenplay (Scorsese and Nicholas Pileggi), Best Supporting Actor (Joe Pesci), Best Supporting Actress (Lorraine Bracco), and Best Film Editing (Thelma Schoonmaker). The film's sole Oscar was awarded for Joe Pesci's scene-stealing performance.

1. *GoodFellas* is based upon a best-selling book written by Nicholas Pileggi. What is the title of this book?

2. In real life, what well-known Mobster came to the club with Billy Batts the night he was murdered?

3. When Martin Scorsese and Nicholas Pileggi began working on this project, it shared the title of the book it was adapted from. Why did Scorsese decide to change its title to *GoodFellas*?

4. Which part of himself does Henry tell Karen's mother is Jewish?

5. Jimmy Conway's nickname is a reference to a 1934 film starring James Cagney. What is his nickname?

6. What Francois Truffaut film did director Martin Scorsese screen for writer Nicholas Pileggi to give him an idea of what he "was aiming for"?

7. When producer Michael Powell read the screenplay for *GoodFellas,* he called it "a masterpiece." What two AFI Top 100 films did Powell compare it to?

8. What is the name of the getaway driver played by Samuel L. Jackson?

9. Who is the "whore" living in apartment 2-R?

10. Who does Tommy remark that the old fisherman in his mother's painting resembles?

11. Who is the African-American singer Tommy's girlfriend compliments at the Copa, irritating Tommy?

12. According to Tommy, what does Spider's family consist of?

13. What is the name of the club Henry and Tommy torch?

14. After Henry gets "pinched" for the first time, what does Jimmy give him?

15. According to Jimmy, what are the "two greatest things in life"?

16. In May 1980, what does Henry deliver to Jimmy only to say he no longer wants them?

17. How many people lived in Henry's house as he was growing up?

18. What does Henry do at the pizzeria, causing Tuddy to call him "a real jerk"?

19. According to Henry, why did Jimmy tip the bartender a hundred dollars?

20. While cooking in prison, Vinnie is in charge of the tomato sauce. Henry says he likes the sauce, but has one complaint. What is this?

21. After he is warned not to spend too much of the heist money, what lavish item does Frankie Carbone purchase?

22. In an attempt to justify his purchasing a new Cadillac, Johnny "Roastbeef" says he purchased it in someone else's name. Whose name did he use?

23. What does Lois do after being told not to?

24. When Bobby Vinton sends champagne to Henry and Karen's table, what song is he singing?

25. What regular from *The Sopranos* appears as Spider?

Quiz No. 95: PULP FICTION (1994)

Screenplay by Quentin Tarantino and Roger Avary
Directed by Quentin Tarantino
Starring John Travolta, Samuel L. Jackson, and Uma Thurman
Miramax Films

> *What I wanted to do with the three stories was to start with the three oldest chestnuts in the world. You've seen them a zillion times. You don't need to be caught up with the story because you already know it. The guy takes out the Mob guy's wife—"but don't touch her." And what happens if they touch? You've seen that triangle a zillion times. Or the boxer who's supposed to throw the fight and doesn't—you've seen that a zillion times, too.* —DIRECTOR QUENTIN TARANTINO

Screenwriter-director Quentin Tarantino's *Pulp Fiction* masterfully intertwines three seemingly unrelated storylines. Two hitmen, Vincent Vega (John Travolta) and Jules Winfield (Samuel L. Jackson), spend an afternoon murdering a group of men who doublecrossed their boss, cleaning up the brains of a man they've accidentally killed, and discussing the finer points of religion and television sitcoms. In the second story, aging boxer Butch Coolidge (Bruce Willis) accepts money to take a dive, but changes his mind at the twelfth hour. In the third story, hitman Vincent is asked to take the wife of his out-of-town crime-boss to dinner. Having heard rumors concerning coworkers who have met untimely ends for flirting with Mia Wallace (Uma Thurman), Vincent knows that she is strictly off-limits. However, after a night of discussing popular culture and dancing, he starts to analyze what he sees as a connection between himself and Mia.

In 1995, *Pulp Fiction* received seven Academy Award nominations: Best Picture (Lawrence Bender), Best Director (Tarantino), Best Original Screenplay (Tarantino and Roger Avary), Best Actor (Travolta), Best Supporting Actor (Jackson), Best Supporting Actress

(Thurman), and Best Film Editing (Sally Menke). The film's sole Oscar was awarded for Best Original Screenplay.

1. "The Gold Watch" segment was originally part of an unproduced screenplay written by Roger Avary. What is the title of this screenplay?

2. The scene in which Butch meets up with Marsellus at the intersection was borrowed from a film directed by Alfred Hitchcock. What is this film?

3. What fictitious brand of cigarettes does Butch smoke?

4. The "Ezekial 25:17" monologue originally appeared in an earlier screenplay written by Quentin Tarantino. What is this screenplay?

5. What is the combination to the briefcase?

6. One of director Quentin Tarantino's cinematic heroes, Sonny Chiba, visited the set during the filming of Samuel L. Jackson's "Ezekial 25:17" monologue. What is the significance of this visit?

7. When the Fourth Man's bullets miss Jules and Vincent, what does Jules call this?

8. According to screenwriter-director Quentin Tarantino, what is the relationship between the characters played by Michael Madsen in *Reservoir Dogs* (1992) and John Travolta's character Vincent Vega?

9. What future filmmaker served as a production assistant on both *Pulp Fiction* and Roger Avary's *Killing Zoe* in 1994?

10. What Peter O'Donnell novel is Vincent shown reading on the toilet and throughout the film?

11. What was the original title Quentin Tarantino envisioned for *Pulp Fiction*?

12. According to Esmerelda Villalobos, what does her name mean?

13. When *Pulp Fiction* was first released, some fans speculated that Marsellus Wallace wears a Band-Aid on the back of his head to conceal the number 666. However, this is not true. Why does Marsellus Wallace wear a Band-Aid in *Pulp Fiction*?

14. What does Lance search frantically for before Vincent gives Mia the adrenaline shot?

15. How much does Mia's milkshake at Jack Rabbit Slim's cost?

16. What actor makes a cameo as Buddy Holly?

17. What fifties icon does Vincent conclude must have the night off at Jack Rabbit Slim's?

18. A character named Winston Wolf previously appeared in an

unfilmed treatment written by Quentin Tarantino. What is the title of this treatment?

19. What weapon was Raven McCoy's specialty on *Fox Force Five*?

20. In the original screenplay for *Pulp Fiction*, where is Marvin accidentally shot?

21. From what Quentin Tarantino screenplay did the scene in which Marvin is accidentally shot originate?

22. What kind of pancakes does Fabienne crave?

23. From what fictitious restaurant did Brett purchase his cheeseburger?

24. What slogan is imprinted on Jules's wallet?

25. Whom does Jules plan to "walk the Earth" like?

Quiz No. 96:
The Searchers (1956)

Screenplay by Frank S. Nugent
Directed by John Ford
Starring John Wayne, Jeffrey Hunter, and Vera Miles
Warner Bros.

> ***We watched some of the rushes together. Duke was special in the film, and he knew it. Remember the scene when Ethan's looking at the white women who have spent years with the Indians? You could see sympathy and hate in his eyes at the same time. He was never better.***
>
> —Actress Mary St. John

How ironic is it that John Wayne, the personification of the classic cinematic hero, is most revered for his turn in *The Searchers,* a film in which he plays a dark, brooding character driven by racial hatred? Civil War veteran Ethan Edwards (Wayne) embarks on a mission to rescue a niece who has been kidnapped by Indians. The search lasts many years and Ethan becomes fueled by obsession and his hatred of Indians. Filmmaker Steven Spielberg raves, "[The film] has so many superlatives. It's John Wayne's best performance. . . . It's a study in dramatic framing and composition. It contains the single most harrowing moment in any film I've ever seen."

In 1957, *The Searchers* received no Academy Award nominations.

1. Who appears in the film as Lieutenant Greenhill?
2. In what year does the story begin?
3. How does Mrs. Jorgensen define a "Texican"?
4. Ethan tells Brad that it was not Lucy he saw in the Indian camp. How can he be sure?
5. What does Clayton tell the wounded man to hold because "it will make you feel good"?
6. Samuel Johnson has two occupations. One is being a minister. What is his other occupation?

7. Ethan loses Martha twice. How so?

8. At the Edwards's funeral service, what song do the mourners sing around the graves?

9. Why does Ethan shoot the Indian corpse in the eyes?

10. When Ethan is asked whether he wants to stop searching for Lucy and Debbie, he gives a memorable four-word response. What is this?

11. *The Searchers* is based upon a novel penned by Alan Le May. Six years before *The Searchers,* Le May directed a Western film himself. What is this film?

12. When actor Ward Bond died in 1960, he left *Searchers* costar John Wayne his hunting rifle. Why?

13. One year after *The Searchers* was released, actor Ward Bond played director John Ford in a film under the pseudonym John Dodge. What is this film?

14. How many years does Ethan's search last?

15. What *Gunsmoke* regular appears as Charlie?

16. Why does Ethan kill the buffalo?

17. John Wayne's youngest son was named after a character in *The Searchers*. What is his name?

18. After agreeing to take Ethan to Scar's camp, Emilio says he cannot accept his money. Why?

19. What name does Marty inadvertently give to the Indian squaw?

20. *The Searchers* was adapted from a novel by Alan Le May. Fourteen years prior to *The Searchers,* Le May cowrote a Cecil B. DeMille film starring John Wayne. What is this film?

21. Futterman demands a reward for providing information about Debbie. How much does he want?

22. Marty complains that he has no kin, money, or horses. What does he proclaim to be "all I got"?

23. John Wayne holds the record for appearing in the most leading roles. How many leading roles did Wayne appear in: 117, 134, 142, 198, or 207?

24. Actors Ward Bond and John Wayne became close friends while playing football in college. What college did the two attend?

25. *The Searchers* was one of two films starring John Wayne that were released in 1956. The other film features Wayne horribly miscast as Genghis Khan. What is this film?

Quiz No. 97: Bringing Up Baby (1938)

Screenplay by Dudley Nichols and Hagar Wilde
Directed by Howard Hawks
Starring Katharine Hepburn, Cary Grant, and Charles Ruggles
RKO Pictures

> ***Cary [Grant] was so funny on this picture. He was fatter, and at this point his boiling energy was at its peak. We would laugh from morning to night. [Howard] Hawks was fun, too. He usually got to work late. Cary and I were always there early. Everyone contributed anything and everything they could think of to that script.***
>
> —Actress Katharine Hepburn

Howard Hawks's *Bringing Up Baby* is considered the definitive screwball comedy. It also features Katharine Hepburn's only appearance in a slapstick comedy. When Susan (Hepburn) begins to pursue absent-minded zoologist David Huxley (Cary Grant), David's life takes a turn for the worse and the two find themselves in a series of misadventures. After locating a rare bone following a long, arduous search, David is horrified when Susan's dog gets his paws on it and hides it. Things become even sillier when a pet leopard named Baby is switched with a killer leopard who has just escaped from a traveling zoo.

In 1939, *Bringing Up Baby* received no Academy Award nominations.

1. In 1972, Peter Bogdanovich directed a homage to *Bringing Up Baby*. What is the name of this film?
2. What hole is Susan on when she mistakes David's golf ball for her own?
3. David was loosely modeled after a comedian. Who was this comedian?

4. Susan tells the police that David is "Jerry the Nipper." David explains, "Officer, she's making it up from motion pictures she's seen." From what 1937 film might Susan have seen a character known as Jerry the Nipper?

5. How old is Baby?

6. What word does Dr. Lehman caution Susan not to use?

7. What does Alice tell David will be their baby?

8. A year before reuniting on *Bringing Up Baby,* Cary Grant and Skippy the terrier appeared together in a comedy directed by Leo McCarey. What is this film?

9. When David receives the package containing the intercostal clavicle bone, what does the delivery man advise?

10. Because Katharine Hepburn had never done screwball comedy before, director Howard Hawks hired a comedian to work with her. This comedian also appears in the film. Who is this performer?

11. What line of dialogue with a double meaning was Hawks proud to have slipped past the censors?

12. According to director Howard Hawks, he had to remove one line from the screenplay because Katharine Hepburn and Cary Grant would laugh every time they tried to film it. "They were just putting dirty connotations on it, and then they'd go off into peals of laughter," Hawks recalled. What was the line?

13. What "mistake" did Howard Hawks say he made with this film that he never made again?

14. According to Dr. Lehman, the love impulse in men frequently reveals itself in terms of what?

15. What is Susan's pet name for Alexander Peabody?

16. What is the name of David's fiancée?

17. Susan's brother, Mark, sends a telegram. From where does he send it?

18. David concludes that there are only two things he *must* do. What are these things?

19. As David digs in search of the clavicle bone, what does Susan cheerfully observe of the hunt?

20. As Baby cries out in the night, what does Applegate dismiss the sound as?

21. What is Baby's favorite song?

22. What does Susan accidentally strike Alexander Peabody with?

23. Howard Hawks was once asked what message he was trying to convey with *Bringing Up Baby*. What was his response?

24. What noted actor makes an uncredited cameo as a policeman?

25. *Bringing Up Baby* was one of two films cowritten by Hagar Wilde and Dudley Nichols released in 1938. The other film features Fred Astaire and Ginger Rogers. What is this film?

Quiz No. 98:
UNFORGIVEN (1992)

Screenplay by David Webb Peoples
Directed by Clint Eastwood
Starring Clint Eastwood, Morgan Freeman, and Gene Hackman
Warner Bros.

> ***As for what makes this Western different from the others, it seems to me that the film deals with violence and its consequences a lot more than those I've done before. In the past, there were a lot of people killed gratuitously in my pictures, and what I liked about this story was that people aren't killed, and acts of violence aren't perpetrated, without there being certain consequences. That's a problem I thought it was important to talk about today.***
>
> —DIRECTOR CLINT EASTWOOD

Director Clint Eastwood's revisionist Western, *Unforgiven,* follows a pair of aged, time-worn outlaws hoping to collect on a bounty offered for the murder of two cowboys who assaulted a prostitute. Unlike any Western that preceded it, *Unforgiven* shows the gunfighter in a less-than-heroic light. Rather than glorifying the gunfighters, the film shows them for what they likely were: cold-hearted, bitter, alcoholic murderers. A beautifully constructed film, *Unforgiven* serves as the perfect bookend for the many Westerns in which Eastwood has appeared throughout his career.

In 1993, *Unforgiven* received nine Academy Award nominations: Best Picture (Eastwood), Best Director (Eastwood), Best Original Screenplay (David Webb Peoples), Best Actor (Eastwood), Best Supporting Actor (Gene Hackman), Best Cinematography (Jack N. Green), Best Film Editing (Joel Cox), Best Art Direction–Set Decoration (Janice Blackie-Goodine and Henry Bumstead), and Best Sound (Richard Alexander, Les Fresholtz, Vern Poore, and Rob Young). The film was awarded four Oscars for Best Picture, Best Director, Best Supporting Actor, and Best Film Editing.

1. *Unforgiven* was dedicated to two filmmakers Clint Eastwood had worked with numerous times. Who were these filmmakers?

2. What is the name of Will Munny's deceased wife?

3. Who is the madam at the brothel?

4. After Ned is murdered, he is propped up outside the saloon with a sign hanging on him. What does the sign say?

5. When Will Munny arrives at Greely's seeking revenge, what does he advise "any man [who] don't want to get killed" to do?

6. What city is Delilah Fitzgerald from?

7. When Little Bill fines the cowboys, what does he say they must bring to Skinny in the fall?

8. Who is the Schofield Kid's uncle?

9. At the beginning of the film, what is wrong with Will Munny's hogs?

10. Five years after collaborating on *Unforgiven,* Gene Hackman and director Clint Eastwood worked together on another film. What is this film?

11. In 1993, Clint Eastwood was awarded the Oscar for Best Director for this film. Two years before, another actor, Kevin Costner, received the award for directing the Western *Dances With Wolves* (1990). In 1993, Eastwood and Costner made a film together. What is this film?

12. How did the Schofield Kid receive his nickname?

13. When Little Bill says, "I'll see you in Hell, William Munny," what is Will's response?

14. When Little Bill's deputies cock their rifles, what is Beauchamp's reaction?

15. On what ranch does Quick Mike work?

16. Since he carried only one gun, how did Two-Gun Corcoran receive his nickname?

17. What does Little Bill incorrectly call English Bob's biography, *The Duke of Death*?

18. As Quick Mike heads for the outhouse, what does he jokingly say he will do if he's ambushed?

19. Who is the murderer who shoots Chinese people for fun?

20. When the Kid confesses that he's never killed anyone before, what does he say he did to the "Mexican with the knife"?

21. Who does Clyde say is the "worst damned carpenter"?

22. What does Big Whiskey Ordinance Fourteen prohibit?
23. What is the name of Ned's wife?
24. What does Will say he's "always been lucky" about?
25. *Unforgiven* was intended as a bookend to Clint Eastwood's long career of Western films. Eastwood has indicated that it's unlikely he will appear in another Western. What was the first Western film Eastwood appeared in?

Quiz No. 99:
GUESS WHO'S COMING TO DINNER (1967)

Screenplay by William Rose
Directed by Stanley Kramer
Starring Spencer Tracy, Katharine Hepburn, and Sidney Poitier
Columbia Pictures

> ***Having done* A Patch of Blue, *I had already crossed this societal boundary, but the culture at large, even the liberal and enlightened subculture, had not. Spencer Tracy and Katharine Hepburn were exceedingly decent people, and I think their politics were sound, but I still think asking them to be any more "liberated" in the America that we knew at that time would have been expecting a hell of a lot too much.***
>
> —ACTOR SIDNEY POITIER

Guess Who's Coming to Dinner is director Stanley Kramer's examination of interracial relationships in America and the effects they can have on the family system. When Joey Drayton (Katharine Houghton) returns home with her new boyfriend, John Prentice (Sidney Poitier), a wealthy, well-educated young doctor who happens to be a black man, her liberal parents must face the fact that they're not as liberal as they had believed. "Sometimes there were objections," Kramer said. "Why did I have to make the black man so personable, so intelligent, so educated? Well, it was because I was trying to make the point that since Poitier's character had all those qualities, if there was an objection to him marrying a white woman, it could only be because he was black!"

In 1968, *Guess Who's Coming to Dinner* received ten Academy Award nominations: Best Picture (Kramer), Best Director (Kramer), Best Original Screenplay (William Rose), Best Actor (Spencer Tracy),

Best Actress (Hepburn), Best Supporting Actor (Cecil Kellaway), Best Supporting Actress (Beah Richards), Best Film Editing (Robert C. Jones), Best Art Direction–Set Decoration (Robert Clatworthy and Frank Tuttle), and Best Original Score (Frank De Vol). The film received two Oscars for Best Original Screenplay and Best Actress.

1. Who sings the film's theme song, "Glory of Love"?
2. The kinetic sculpture is who's favorite?
3. What is the name of the Drayton's distrusting maid?
4. Who is Matt Drayton playing golf with?
5. During filming, Sidney Poitier repeatedly forgot his lines, saying that he was distracted. What, according to Poitier, was distracting him?
6. What is John Prentice's middle name?
7. In what publication did Monsignor Ryan read an article about John Prentice?
8. John Prentice's wife and son died in 1959. How did they die?
9. Who does Matt Drayton call when looking for "dope" on John Prentice?
10. What did actor Spencer Tracy do fifteen days after filming concluded?
11. According to Joanna Drayton, how long did it take her to fall in love with John?
12. Matt Drayton has a framed photograph of a United States president sitting on his desk. Which one?
13. John Prentice was born in 1930. In what city was he born?
14. What does Monsignor Ryan say it's amusing to see a "broken-down old phony liberal" come face to face with?
15. Why does Matt conclude that John Prentice doesn't say much about himself?
16. According to Christina Drayton, what was Joanna "all through school and college"?
17. How many textbooks has John written?
18. What does Matt say that Joanna believes each of her children will be?
19. What is the name of Joanna's "best and oldest" friend?
20. When Christina fires Hillary, she tells her to cut herself a check. What is the amount of the check?

21. Who does Christina comment on having a "ruthless streak"?

22. Monsignor Ryan quotes a line from a song by the Beatles. What is this song?

23. What is Homer's occupation?

24. What is the "special flavor of ice cream" that Matt orders?

25. What does John's father say he cannot list in four hours?

Quiz No. 100:
YANKEE DOODLE DANDY (1942)

Screenplay by Robert Buckner and Edmund Joseph
Directed by Michael Curtiz
Starring James Cagney, Joan Leslie, and Walter Huston
Warner Bros.

> ***Before that it was more like a dream. I was just a kid, taking things as they came, the good roles, the bad ones. It was all new and a lot of fun. But in* Yankee Doodle Dandy *the idea of the whole thing began opening up. I realized that, or rather was starting to realize, where it was I wanted to go and how hard it was going to be to get there.***
>
> —ACTRESS JOAN LESLIE

Director Michael Curtiz's musical biopic of composer George M. Cohan features actor James Cagney in a rare song-and-dance performance. Film critic Dr. Edwin Jahiel observes, "Cagney can't really dance or sing by Hollywood standards, but he acts so vigorously that it creates an illusion, and for dance steps he substitutes a patented brand of robust, jerky walks, runs, and other motions."

In 1943, *Yankee Doodle Dandy* received eight Academy Award nominations: Best Picture (William Cagney, Hal B. Wallis, and Jack L. Warner), Best Director (Curtiz), Best Original Screenplay (Robert Buckner), Best Actor (Cagney), Best Supporting Actor (Walter Huston), Best Film Editing (George Amy), Best Sound (Nathan Levinson), and Best Scoring of a Musical Picture (Ray Heindorf and Heinz Roemheld). The film was awarded three Oscars for Best Actor, Best Scoring of a Musical Picture, and Best Sound.

1. On the first day of shooting, director Michael Curtiz announced to the film's crew, "Now boys and girls, we have had bad news, but we have a wonderful story to tell the world, so let's put

away sad things and begin." What was the "bad news" Curtiz was referring to?

2. In what 1955 film did James Cagney reprise his role as George M. Cohan?

3. In 1943, Michael Curtiz was nominated by the Academy for Best Director for two films. One of these is *Yankee Doodle Dandy*. What was the other film Curtiz was nominated for?

4. Who is the actress portraying George M. Cohan's sister?

5. On the theater marquee, who presents *I'd Rather Be Right*?

6. How many AFI Top 100 films does Walter Huston appear in, including *Yankee Doodle Dandy*?

7. What does George say he can never do in Boston?

8. The White House butler informs George that he saw him in *George Washington, Jr.* According to the butler, what president did he attend the performance with?

9. What is George Cohan's middle name?

10. What future filmmaker directed the montages in *Yankee Doodle Dandy*?

11. What holiday corresponded with George M. Cohan's birthday?

12. Who is billed as "America's youngest skirt dancer"?

13. Who was first offered the role of George M. Cohan, but declined to appear in the film?

14. What three elements must a show have before Schwab will invest in it?

15. What is the name of the theater in Buffalo, New York, where *Four of a Kind* appears?

16. In *The Four Cohans in Songs and Dances,* where do the Cohans state that they were born?

17. What play does the song "Harrigan" appear in?

18. When George throws Sam Harris out of his office, Harris is holding a script. What is the title of this script?

19. What does Josie liken to a "carriage with only three wheels"?

20. Where is Fay Templeton from?

21. Why is George rejected by the army?

22. Eddie Foy proclaims, "He certainly did give himself a billing, this George M. Cohan." Who is he speaking to?

23. George pens a musical for Fay Templeton. What is the title of this musical?

24. Director Michael Curtiz and actor James Cagney collaborated five times. One of these films is *Yankee Doodle Dandy*. What are the other four films the two made together?

25. What song does Sam Harris say is the best thing George has ever done?

Quiz No. 101:
Master Quiz: General Knowledge

The following questions cover various AFI Top 100 films. Think you're a movie whiz? See how many answers you know.

1. What AFI Top 100 film's theme song is sung by Roger O. Thornhill in *North By Northwest* (1959) and Alex in *A Clockwork Orange* (1971)?
2. Who directed more AFI Top 100 films than any other director, and how many of his films appear on the list?
3. One actor appears in seven AFI Top 100 films. Who is this actor?
4. What piece of music appears prominently in *The Birth of a Nation* (1915) and *Apocalypse Now* (1979), and is hummed by James Dean's character in *Rebel Without a Cause* (1955)?
5. In *Gone with the Wind* (1939), a horse throws Gerald O'Hara to his death. The horse that appears in this scene would later become a famous horse. Who was this?
6. How many of the films listed in AFI's top ten won the Oscar for Best Picture in their respective years?
7. *Gone with the Wind* producer David O. Selznick died on June 22, 1951, at exactly 2:22 P.M. What is the significance of the time?
8. In *The Best Years of Our Lives* (1946), a returning soldier played by Fredric March, and his wife, played by Myrna Loy, run down a long hallway and embrace. This scene was a reenactment of a World War II veteran's actual experience. Whose?
9. On January 3, 1939, *The New York Journal-American* cited "exclusive information" and announced that an actress had been cast to play Scarlett O'Hara in *Gone with the Wind.* Who was this actress?

10. What actress was paid a hundred dollars to sing one line in *The Wizard of Oz* (1939)?

11. When *Lawrence of Arabia* (1962) was released, Noel Coward commented that if Peter O'Toole had been any prettier, the film would have to be retitled What title did he suggest?

12. Who was *Taxi Driver* (1976) dedicated to?

13. What 1980 telefilm depicted producer David O. Selznick's difficulties in casting the role of Scarlett O'Hara in *Gone with the Wind*?

14. In 1964, MGM announced that *2001: A Space Odyssey* (1968) was rolling into production. However, the film had a different title at that time. What was this title?

15. Two Technicolor films from 1939—*Gone with the Wind* and *The Wizard of Oz*—appear on the AFI Top 100 list. How many color films were released in 1939?

16. When primary filming for *The Wizard of Oz* was completed, several scenes were reshot, costing the studio an additional sixty thousand dollars. Why were these scenes reshot?

17. Who called the 1940 Academy Awards ceremony a "benefit for David O. Selznick," suggesting that the producer wear skates to make his frequent trips to the stage easier?

18. In 1992, Harold Russell sold his Oscar for Best Supporting Actor in *The Best Years of Our Lives*. Why did Russell need the money?

19. True or false: *Fantasia* (1940) was dubbed "Disney's Folly" by the media.

20. Actor Robert Duvall appears in six AFI Top 100 films. What are these films?

21. Richard Dreyfuss stars in *American Graffiti* (1973), *Jaws* (1975), and *Close Encounters of the Third Kind* (1977). In addition, he also makes an uncredited cameo in another AFI Top 100 film. What is this?

22. James Stewart and director Alfred Hitchcock worked on three celebrated films in the 1950s. (Two of these, *Rear Window*, 1954, and *Vertigo*, 1958, appear on the AFI Top 100 list.) In this same decade, Stewart made eight films with another noted director. Who is this?

23. In *Rocky* (1976), Rocky tells Adrian that it may be Thanksgiving to her, but what does he say it is to him?

24. While in his makeup for *Tootsie* (1982), actor Dustin Hoffman sidled up beside his *Midnight Cowboy* (1969) costar Jon Voight at the Russian Tea Room. What was Voight's reaction?

25. Who directed the final scene of *Wuthering Heights* (1939)?

Quiz No. 102:
Master Quiz: Taglines

Below are twenty-five of the most memorable film taglines in the history of American cinema. Read each tagline, and see if you can guess which AFI Top 100 film it's from.

1. "Together for the first time!"
2. "This is Benjamin. He's a little worried about his future."
3. "The movie too hot for words!"
4. "A thousand hours of hell for one moment of love!"
5. "A powerful story of nine strange people!"
6. "The Civil War had ended, but one man's battle with himself was just beginning . . ."
7. "Where were you in '62?"
8. "On every street in every city, there's a nobody who dreams of being a somebody."
9. "If you come in five minutes after this picture begins, you won't know what it's all about! When you've seen it, you'll swear there's never been anything like it!"
10. "His whole life was a million to one shot!"
11. "The legendary epic that's as big as Texas."
12. "The greatest adventure a man ever lived . . . with a woman!"
13. "The ultimate trip."
14. "They're making memories tonight!"
15. "I'm in trouble, George. Bad trouble."
16. "It's all about women—and their men!"
17. "Movie-wise, there has never been anything like it—laugh-wise, love-wise, or otherwise-wise!"
18. "They're young, they're in love, and they kill people."

19. "A nervous romance."

20. "Being the adventures of a young man whose prinicipal interests are rape, ultra-violence, and Beethoven."

21. "Television will never be the same!"

22. "Don't give away the ending—it's the only one we have!"

23. "A homespun murder story."

24. "He is afraid. He is alone. He is three million light-years from home."

25. "This is it . . . the most compelling dramatic story ever unfolded on the screen . . . a tale of heartache and tragedy . . . love and ambition . . . told against the fabulous background of Hollywood."

Quiz No. 103:
Master Quiz: Quotes

Here are twenty-five of the most famous film quotes in the history of American cinema. Read each quote and see whether you know which AFI Top 100 film it's from.

1. "Don't be alarmed, ladies and gentlemen. Those chains are made of chrome steel."
2. "We all dream of being a child again, even the worst of us. Perhaps the worst most of all."
3. "If he'd just pay me what he's paying them to stop me robbing him, I'd stop robbing him!"
4. "No one needs to know about this except you, me, and mister-soon-to-be-living-the-rest-of-his-short-ass-life-in-agonizing-pain rapist here."
5. "One shot is what it's all about. A deer has to be taken with one shot."
6. "When you're slapped, you'll take it and like it."
7. "Look, you don't know me from Adam, but I was a better man with you as a woman than I ever was with a woman as a man. Know what I mean?"
8. "You know what you look like to me, with your good bag and your cheap shoes? You look like a rube. A well-scrubbed, hustling rube with little taste. Good nutrition has given you some length of bone, but you're not more than one generation from poor white trash."
9. "You know how to chicky race don't you?"
10. "Leave the gun, take the cannoli."
11. "I'm not going to waste my time arguing with a man who's lining up to be a hot lunch."

12. "I hate snakes, Jock! I hate 'em!"

13. "Every man on that transport died. Harry wasn't there to save them because you weren't there to save Harry."

14. "They've committed a murder, and it's not like taking a trolley ride where they can get off at different stops. They're stuck with each other, and they've got to ride all the way to the end of the line, and it's a one-way trip, and the last stop is the cemetery."

15. "Charging a man with murder in this place was like handing out speeding tickets at the Indy 500."

16. "Don't you see the rest of the country looks upon New York like we're left-wing, communist, Jewish, homosexual pornographers? I think of us that way sometimes, and I live here."

17. "No, I don't think I will kiss you, although you need kissing badly. That's what's wrong with you; you should be kissed and often, and by someone who knows how."

18. "No! No booze! Sex! I want sex! That one! The sultry bitch with the fire in her eyes! Bring her to me! Take her clothes off and bring her to me!"

19. "He may look like an idiot and talk like an idiot, but don't let that fool you. He really is an idiot."

20. "I remember Paris perfectly. The Germans wore gray, you wore blue."

21. "Ever pick your feet in Poughkeepsie?"

22. "Real diamonds! They must be worth their weight in gold!"

23. "Say, Lou, did ya hear about the guy who couldn't afford a personalized [license] plate, so he went and changed his name to J3L2404?"

24. "I'm a goddamn marvel of modern science!"

25. "Now it isn't that I don't like you, Susan, because, after all, in moments of quiet, I'm strangely drawn toward you, but, well . . . there haven't been any quiet moments."

Quiz No. 104:

Master Quiz: Name the Film

Here are twenty-five descriptions of the AFI Top 100 films covered within this volume. Think you're a film expert? See how many of these films you can name.

1. This film tells the story of cattleman Bick Benedict. What is this film?
2. An alien befriends a young boy. What is this film?
3. After returning home from Vietnam, Travis Bickle becomes a vigilante. What is this film?
4. An aged gunfighter-turned-pig farmer decides to hunt down two men who cut a prostitute's face. What is this film?
5. This film follows the exploits of two surgeons in the Korean War. What is this film?
6. This film tells the stories of two hitmen, a boxer, and two amateur robbers. What is this film?
7. C. K. Dexter Haven arrives in Philadelphia the day before his ex-wife's wedding. What is this film?
8. A wandering gunfighter comes to the aid of squatters who are being terrorized by a cattle baron. What is this film?
9. A struggling actor dresses as a woman to land a role on a daytime television drama. What is this film?
10. In this film, Alvy Singer analyzes his failed relationship with his ex-girlfriend, Annie. What is this film?
11. Judah is betrayed by his longtime friend Messala. What is this film?
12. Tony and Maria fall in love, but their gang alliances prohibit them from seeing each other. What is this film?

13. Popeye Doyle and his partner, Sonny, hunt drug smugglers in New York City. What is this film?

14. When seven thousand dollars is misplaced, George Bailey faces possible jail time. What is this film?

15. After stealing money from the realty office where she works, a young woman takes aimlessly to the highway. What is this film?

16. Two bank robbers flee to Bolivia with a posse on their trail. What is this film?

17. Characters named Quint and Hooper compare scars. What is this film?

18. Only hours after being married, Will Kane must face a gang of bandits. What is this film?

19. A pet leopard is accidentally switched with a ferocious leopard that has escaped from a traveling circus. What is this film?

20. After witnessing a gangland slaying, two musicians are forced to go into hiding disguised as women. What is this film?

21. A young FBI agent seeks assistance from a homicidal cannibal in the hopes of catching a serial killer. What is this film?

22. Needing money, Jerry Lundegaard arranges to have his wife kidnapped, forcing his father-in-law to pay a ransom. What is this film?

23. A struggling screenwriter befriends a washed-up silent-screen actress. What is this film?

24. Ringo asks Dallas to marry him. What is this film?

25. After their deaths, Heathcliff and Cathy are reunited as ghosts. What is this film?

Quiz No. 105:

Master Quiz: The Directors and Screenwriters

Here are twenty-five descriptions of AFI Top 100 directors and screenwriters whose works are covered within this volume. Think you know your movies? See how many of these filmmakers you can name.

1. He's the brother of Orson Welles's *Citizen Kane* (1941) cowriter, the producer of *The Philadelphia Story* (1940), and the director of *All About Eve* (1950). Who is this?
2. This screenwriter contributed to *Bonnie and Clyde* (1967), *The Godfather* (1972), and *Chinatown* (1974). Who is this?
3. This filmmaker served as a dialogue director on *All Quiet on the Western Front* (1930), was fired from *Gone with the Wind* (1939) because Clark Gable considered him a "woman's director," worked briefly on *The Wizard of Oz* (1939), and directed *My Fair Lady* (1964). Who is this?
4. He directed five films on the AFI Top 100 list, which is more than any other filmmaker. Who is this?
5. He was a producer on *The Manchurian Candidate* (1962) and directed the sequel to *The French Connection* (1971). Who is this?
6. He served as editor on *Citizen Kane* and later directed two AFI Top 100 films of his own. Who is this?
7. This son of a famous actor performed uncredited rewrites for *Wuthering Heights* (1939), directed three AFI Top 100 films, and appears as an actor in *Chinatown*. Who is this?
8. Years before becoming a legendary filmmaker in his own right, this man worked on *The Birth of a Nation* (1915) as an assistant director, editor, and actor. Who is this?

9. This director made what is now called *The American Trilogy.* All three of the films that comprise this trilogy appear on the AFI Top 100 list. Who is this?

10. This man served as editor on the 1938 adaptation of *Pygmalion,* which was later adapted as *My Fair Lady.* In addition, he also directed three AFI Top 100 films that feature actor Alec Guinness. Who is this?

11. This screenwriter contributed to both *The Philadelphia Story* and *Midnight Cowboy* (1969). Who is this?

12. This man was a producer and cowriter on both *Some Like It Hot* (1959) and *The Apartment* (1960), but did not direct them. Who was this?

13. This actor-turned-director appears in *Rebel Without a Cause* (1955), *Giant* (1956), and *Apocalypse Now* (1979). In addition, his 1967 directorial debut also appears on the AFI Top 100 list. Who is this?

14. This screenwriter-director contributed to both *Jaws* (1975) and *Apocalypse* (1979) *Now.* Who is this?

15. This screenwriter rewrote much of the dialogue for *The Third Man* (1949) and wrote an unproduced adaptation of Joseph Conrad's *Heart of Darkness* forty years before it was adapted as *Apocalypse Now.* Who is this?

16. This screenwriter contributed to both *Dr. Strangelove* (1964) and *Easy Rider* (1969). Who is this?

17. This nephew of Universal Pictures founder Carl Laemmle worked on both the 1925 and 1959 versions of *Ben-Hur.* Who is this?

18. The son of a former West Point aeronautics instructor performed an uncredited rewrite on the script for *Ben-Hur.* Who is this?

19. This man cowrote *Patton* (1970), executive-produced *American Graffiti* (1973), composed *Apocalypse Now* (1979), and directed a 1994 remake of *Frankenstein* (1931). Who is this?

20. This famed filmmaker appears as an actor in *The Godfather Part II* (1974) and *The Silence of the Lambs* (1991). In addition, a character is named after him in *Apocalypse Now.* Who is this?

21. She served as a location assistant on *The Godfather Part II,* worked as an executive assistant on *Apocalypse Now,* and wrote the screenplay for *E.T. The Extra-Terrestrial* (1982). Who is this?

22. He wrote *Taxi Driver* (1976) and was an uncredited screenwriter on *Close Encounters of the Third Kind* (1977). Who is this?

23. He was an uncredited extra in *All Quiet on the Western Front* be-

fore he directed *High Noon* (1952) and *From Here to Eternity* (1953). Who is this?

24. He produced *High Noon* and directed *Guess Who's Coming to Dinner* (1967). Who is this?

25. This filmmaker directed two AFI Top 100 films. One is about an insane asylum, and the other is about a jealous musician on the verge of a breakdown. Who is this?

THE ANSWERS

Quiz No. 1: Citizen Kane

1. William Randolph Hearst. 2. Xanadu. 3. Rosebud is the name of a sled. 4. Rosebud was the pet name Hearst used for his mistress Marion Davies's clitoris. 5. *RKO 281*. 6. *The Outlaw* (1943). 7. The Mercury Theatre Group. 8. Kane's own *New York Daily Inquirer*. 9. Thirty-seven. 10. $3 million. 11. "[N]o man can say." 12. Emily Norton and Susan Alexander. 13. John Singleton. 14. Thompson finds five sources: Bernstein, Jedediah Leland, Susan Alexander, Raymond the butler, and the deceased Walter Parks Thatcher (through memoirs). 15. 1871. 16. Twenty-five. 17. Fifty thousand dollars. 18. Crusader. 19. He thinks running a newspaper sounds like fun. 20. The declaration closely parallels comments made by Hearst to artist Frederic Remington regarding the 1896 Spanish-American War. 21. Sixty. 22. Principles. 23. *Stagecoach* (1939). 24. Craig. 25. This theory is false. According to the majordomo, he was present when Kane died.

Quiz No. 2: Casablanca

1. In real life, there was no such thing as a letter of transit. 2. All seventy-five. 3. Because the script was still being written even as the film was being shot, no one knew whether Ilsa would end up with Rick or her husband, Victor. When Bergman asked director Michael Curtiz whom she was supposed to be in love with, Curtiz told her to "play it in between." 4. Twenty-two. 5. According to screenwriter Julius Epstein, "Every studio in town turned it down!" 6. Because Turner's company colorized the rich black-and-white film. 7. The drums. 8. Hedy Lamarr was his first choice, and Ann Sheridan was the second. 9. "You asked for this, Major." 10. *Watch on*

the Rhine (1943). 11. The song "As Time Goes By." 12. George Raft and Ronald Reagan. 13. Paul Henreid, who feared that a supporting role might endanger his star status. 14. David Soul of "Starsky and Hutch" fame. 15. *As Time Goes By: A Novel of Casablanca.* 16. Despite the phrase's often being associated with the film, Bogart never once says this. Ilsa first instructs the piano player, "Play it, Sam. Play 'As Time Goes By.'" Later, Rick instructs him, "You played it for her. You can play it for me. Play it!" 17. In the German version of the film, Rick says, "I look into your eyes, little one." 18. In Albuquerque's recut, Ilsa does not take the plane. Instead, she runs back into Rick's arms. 19. The film was adapted from an unproduced play written by Murray Burnett and Joan Alison entitled *Everybody Comes to Rick's.* 20. *Passage to Marseilles.* 21. Don Siegel. 22. Stephani's treatment was titled *Brazzaville,* which is a reference to Renault's final lines in *Casablanca* in which he speaks of free French garrisons in Brazzaville. 23. All scenes or references regarding the Nazis or Major Strasser were removed. 24. Lena Horne. 25. That Rick and Ilsa had sexual relations in Paris.

Quiz No. 3: The Godfather

1. Zero. Mario Puzo and Francis Ford Coppola intentionally avoided using the words "Mafia" and "*la Cosa Nostra*" in the screenplay. 2. Commentator Russ Hodges's play-by-play of the October 3, 1951, Dodgers-Giants playoff game, in which Bobby Thompson hit his famed "shot heard 'round the world." 3. Because he felt that Hollywood discriminated against the American Indians. 4. A woman wearing faux Indian garb who called herself Sacheen Littlefeather. Later, she was discovered to be a little-known California actress named Maria Cruz. 5. *The Sicilian.* 6. Director Francis Ford Coppola's daughter, Sofia Coppola, who is one of only seven actors to appear in all three films. 7. Danny Thomas. 8. Vito's wife is the girl's godmother. 9. Tom Hagen is Vito's consigliere—his advisor. 10. Michael attended classes at Dartmouth University. 11. Carlo Gambino, the "boss of all bosses." 12. Johnny Fontane was modeled after crooner Frank Sinatra. As the story goes, godfather Carlo Gambino once made Sinatra's bandleader a real-life offer he couldn't refuse, resulting in Sinatra's release for one dollar. 13. After the bandleader turned down Vito's offer of ten thousand dollars, the godfather "persuaded" him to release the singer for a mere one thousand dollars. 14. Twelve directors turned down *The Godfather* before Coppola was approached about the project. For the producers, Coppola was their lucky thirteenth. Some of the other directors

approached included Fred Zinneman, Arthur Penn, Costa-Gavras, Peter Yates, Richard Brooks, and Sydney J. Furie. 15. Paramount Pictures lobbied for Robert Redford to play Michael. Before casting Pacino, the producers also considered Warren Beatty, Ryan O'Neal, Jack Nicholson, and Rod Steiger. 16. De Niro tested for the role of Michael Corleone. 17. De Niro was cast as the traitorous Paulie Gatto, but left the film when he was offered a leading role in *The Gang That Couldn't Shoot Straight* (1971). Humorously, that role (Mario) had become available because Al Pacino, who had already been cast, jumped ship to play Michael Corleone in *The Godfather*. 18. Luca Brasi, who would later "sleep with the fishes." 19. New Hampshire. 20. The veal. 21. A horse's head the producers had purchased from a New Jersey rendering plant. 22. A necklace. 23. Three times. 24. Fredo sides with parties who are "against the family." 25. Each time oranges appear in the film something bad happens to Vito Corleone. When Vito is purchasing oranges at the street market, he is gunned down. Later, he has an orange slice in his mouth when he suffers a fatal heart attack.

Quiz No. 4: Gone with the Wind

1. She was the first black person ever to be nominated or win an Oscar. 2. Because he was dead. Howard had been killed in a farming accident on August 23, 1939. 3. Sam Wood, William Cameron Menzies, George Cukor, and Reeves Easton. 4. Goldman's script was simply titled, "A Continuation of *Gone with the Wind*." 5. Symbolically, she throws dirt. "That's all of Tara you'll ever get!" 6. *They Knew What They Wanted,* which was adapted to film three times in *The Secret Hour* (1928), *A Lady to Love* (1930), and *They Knew What They Wanted* (1940). 7. Melanie. 8. Land. 9. She shoots him in the face. 10. Typhoid fever. 11. False; nearly fifteen hundred actresses were interviewed, and Leigh wasn't cast until after filming had already begun. 12. Timothy Dalton. 13. In 1939, the line "Frankly, Scarlett, I don't give a damn" was considered offensive. 14. Hattie McDaniel. These were racist times, and she was black. Although McDaniel won an Oscar for Best Supporting Actress, she wasn't allowed to attend the Academy Awards, either. 15. Because he doesn't want to leave the dying soldiers. 16. *Tap Roots* (1948). 17. Three o' clock. 18. *The Wizard of Oz* (1939). 19. $150. 20. Until she dies. 21. ". . . [O]nce they're really lost." 22. Reeves is credited with playing Stuart's brother, Brent; Fred Crane, who actually plays Brent, is credited with playing Stuart. 23. Gable disliked Cukor because he was gay and because he considered him a "woman's director." 24. A gentleman. 25. *Confederate Honey*.

Quiz No. 5: Lawrence of Arabia

1. Katharine Hepburn. 2. That they are one in the same. 3. *Revolt in the Desert.* 4. Producer Sam Spiegel. 5. The passionate. 6. Albert Finney. 7. *With Allenby in Palestine and Lawrence in Arabia* (1919) and *Lawrence of Arabia* (1935). 8. Not minding that it hurts. 9. Noel Howard and Andre De Toth. In addition, future filmmaker Nicholas Roeg served as second-unit photographer. 10. *Lawrence After Arabia* (1990). 11. *Nostromo.* 12. Gasim, the man whose life he has just saved. 13. General Allenby. 14. Twenty-three. 15. Mahatma Ghandi. 16. *Doctor Zhivago* (1965) and *Ryan's Daughter* (1970). 17. Gregory Peck, who was awarded for his performance in *To Kill a Mockingbird* (1962). 18. Lowell Thomas. 19. Marlon Brando. 20. Seventy-five. 21. *The Night of the Generals* (1967), *The Rainbow Thief* (1990), and *Gulliver's Travels* (1996). 22. Michael Wilson. 23. Director David Lean. 24. Zero. 25. His nose.

Quiz No. 6: The Wizard of Oz

1. *Gone with the Wind* (1939). 2. Richard Thorpe, George Cukor, and King Vidor. 3. L. Frank Baum's *The Wonderful Wizard of Oz* had already been adapted five times (1910, 1921, 1925, 1933, and 1938) before the most famous version was filmed in 1939. In addition, several other Oz-themed films existed: *The Land of Oz* (1910), *Dorothy and the Scarecrow in Oz* (1910), *The Patchwork Girl of Oz* (1914), *His Majesty, the Scarecrow of Oz* (1914), *The Magic Cloak of Oz* (1914), and *The Land of Oz: A Sequel to the Wizard of Oz* (1931). 4. $125 per week. 5. Shirley Temple and Deanna Durbin. 6. The Scarecrow and the Tin Woodsman. 7. Judy Garland, who plays Dorothy, and Jack Haley, who plays the Tin Woodsman, were the parents of Liza Minelli and Jack Haley, Jr., who were wed in the seventies. 8. *The Wiz.* 9. William Jennings Bryan. 10. Princess Betty of Oz. 11. *The Dark Side of the Moon.* 12. *Under the Rainbow.* 13. All five roles were played by actor Frank Morgan. 14. The Tornado that takes Dorothy to Oz. 15. *Twin Beds* (1942). 16. *Annie Get Your Gun* (1950). 17. Gale. 18. Dorothy's house lands on her, crushing her. 19. A lit match. 20. He's rusty. 21. Lions, tigers, and bears. 22. He's afraid of them. 23. At the Wash & Brush Up Company. 24. Courage. 25. The flying monkeys.

Quiz No. 7: The Graduate

1. Richard Dreyfuss. 2. *Who's Afraid of Virginia Woolf?* (1966). 3. "Jesus God" and "Oh, my God!" 4. Screenwriter Buck Henry. 5. "The Sounds of Silence" by Simon and Garfunkel. 6. *Jackie Brown.* 7. "Plastics." 8. In his fish tank. 9. In a car. When Benjamin presses her for details, she adds, "It was a Ford, Benjamin." 10. 568. 11. The Taft Hotel. 12. None; according to screenwriter Buck Henry, everything in the film was either the work of novelist Charles Webb or Henry. 13. Carl Smith. 14. The University of Southern California. 15. "Not for me." 16. Singleman. 17. It's his twenty-first birthday party. 18. *The Player.* 19. An hour. 20. Managing editor. 21. They envisioned a blond-haired man with a tan. 22. The glass of the picture frame. 23. Her purse. 24. A strip club. 25. Doris Day.

Quiz No. 8: On the Waterfront

1. Because he believed Elia Kazan might have named him as a Communist when he appeared before the House Un-American Activities Committee. 2. Fred Gwynne. 3. Malden Skulovich is actor Karl Malden's real name. 4. Martin Balsam. 5. This is the only nonmusical film Bernstein wrote the incidental music for. 6. Eight; Brando has been nominated for Best Actor seven times: *A Streetcar Named Desire* (1951), *Viva Zapata!* (1952), *Julius Caesar* (1953), *On the Waterfront*, *Sayonara* (1957), *The Godfather* (1972), and *Ultimo tango a Parigi* (1972). Brando has been nominated for Best Supporting Actor once for *A Dry White Season* (1990). 7. *A Streetcar Named Desire* and *One-Eyed Jacks* (1961). 8. In 1952, the duo had been nominated in the same categories for another Elia Kazan–directed film, *A Streetcar Named Desire.* Interestingly, Malden won for *A Streetcar Named Desire* and Brando won for *On the Waterfront.* 9. Fly. 10. Brando was annoyed that his monologue brought actual tears from Steiger. 11. In the basement of the church. 12. Teaching. 13. Charlie the Gent. 14. So he could see his psychoanalyst. 15. Thirty-nine pages. 16. Joey Doyle's. 17. Truck. 18. "It's the love of a lousy buck." 19. Billy Conn. 20. A boss-loader slot. 21. Palookaville. 22. That they were stolen the night before. 23. Frank Sinatra. 24. *The Daily Tribune.* 25. A fifty-dollar bill.

Quiz No. 9: Schindler's List

1. He was given the award in the category of fiction, despite it's being a true story. 2. *The Apartment* (1960). 3. Because he is a filmmaker who has

worked on many culturally themed films himself, Scorsese believed that only a Jewish filmmaker could do the film justice. 4. *Sophie's Choice* and *Shoah*. 5. The tatooed numbers on his forearm he had received as a prisoner in the Auschwitz concentration camp. 6. A method actor, Fiennes drank bottle after bottle of Guinness to put on the weight. 7. Coproducer Branko Lustig. 8. Twenty-four. 9. *Anna Christie*. 10. "I don't think Warren would have ever really worked on the accent," Spielberg said. "I think Warren would have played it like Oskar Schindler through Warren Beatty, but I don't think Warren would have taken on the accent." 11. Polish and German. 12. DIREKTOR. 13. *Class of '61* (1993). 14. Dom Perignon. 15. A good doctor, a forgiving priest, and a clever accountant. 16. Emilie Schindler. 17. To make money for him. 18. He is shot at point-blank range. 19. The University of Milan. 20. The liquidation of the ghetto. 21. Helen. 22. Schindler threatens to have her arrested. 23. The truth. 24. *Awakenings* (1990). 25. He was declared a righteous person.

Quiz No. 10: Singin' in the Rain

1. Gene Kelly. 2. Oscar Levant. 3. Codirector Stanley Donen's *Deep in my Heart* (1954). 4. 1927. 5. *The Hollywood Revue of 1929* (1929). 6. *The Royal Rascal*. 7. Billie Dawn from *Born Yesterday* (1950). 8. Betty Noyse. 9. He had a fever of 103 degrees. 10. *Screen Digest*. 11. *Say It with Music*. 12. R. F. Simpson. 13. Phoebe Dinsmore. 14. "His toeses are roses." 15. Making *The Jazz Singer* (1927). 16. The songs were already written, leaving Comden and Green the daunting task of having to fashion a storyline into which they could logically incorporate the songs. 17. *The Dancing Cavalier*. 18. "Broadway Melody Ballet." 19. *The Pirate* (1948), as "Be a Clown" performed by Gene Kelly. 20. Lina. 21. Jeanne Coyne. 22. A tarantula. 23. R. F. Simpson. 24. Because she cannot act, sing, or dance. 25. Stardust.

Quiz No. 11: It's a Wonderful Life

1. A rabbit. 2. *The Adventures of Tom Sawyer* by Mark Twain. 3. The Federal Bureau of Investigation, on the lookout for Communist activity in Hollywood, included *It's a Wonderful Life* in its list of eight films released in 1947 that it considered subversive. (*The Best Years of Our Lives* also appears on the list.) In addition, director Frank Capra was reported to have "associated with left-wing groups and, on one other occasion to have made a picture that was decidedly socialist in nature"—that was *Mr.*

Smith Goes to Washington (1939). 4. Switzer played Alfalfa on *The Little Rascals*. 5. *The Hunchback of Notre Dame*. 6. The Bailey Brothers Building and Loan. 7. *The Courtship of Andy Hardy* (1942). 8. He gives it to his brother Harry so he can go to college. 9. George's father, the druggist George saves from doom, and Uncle Billy. 10. Anchor chains, plane motors, and train whistles. 11. The story first appeared as a Christmas card that Van Doren Stern privately printed for his friends. 12. Fifty cents. 13. In the remake, George Bailey is a woman named Mary Bailey Hatch. 14. *The Gorgeous Hussy* (1935), *Navy Blue and Gold* (1937), *You Can't Take It With You* (1938), and *Malaya* (1949). 15. George Bailey. 16. Bert and Ernie. 17. *Winning Your Wings*. 18. Harry Bailey. 19. *Mr. Smith Goes to Washington*. 20. "American Gothic" by Grant Wood. 21. Cary Grant. 22. Dalton Trumbo, Clifford Odets, and Marc Connelly. 23. William Wyler and George Stevens. 24. Actor Lionel Barrymore. 25. Henry Travers.

Quiz No. 12: Sunset Boulevard

1. Mae West, Pola Negri, and Mary Pickford. 2. *Ninotchka* (1939), *Hold Back the Dawn* (1941), *The Lost Weekend* (1945), and *A Foreign Affair* (1948). 3. Montgomery Clift. After Clift quit, director Billy Wilder retorted, "If he's any kind of actor, he could be convincing making love to any woman!" However, Clift's real reason for backing out was revealed later: Clift, who was dating washed-up singer Libby Holman—twenty years his senior—believed the film was actually a sick parody of his own life. 4. *Queen Kelly* was directed by Erich von Stroheim, who appears in *Sunset Boulevard* as Max. 5. Billy Wilder and Max Kolpe. 6. Although Wilder intended the scene to be a serious one, screening audiences laughed hysterically. "It was a terrible night," Wilder would later recall. "I got sick to my stomach, and I was sitting on the steps leading to the restrooms, in despair. I looked up, and there was a lady coming from the theater, overdressed, and sees me sitting there and she says, 'Have you ever seen shit like this in your life before?' " 7. Mrs. J. Paul Getty, the estranged wife of the oil mogul. Some years later, to spite his ex-wife, Getty reportedly had the house torn down and built a Getty gas station in its place. Today, the twenty-two-story Getty Oil building sits on the land. 8. Dan Gillis. 9. *Rebel Without a Cause* (1955). 10. *Bases Loaded*. 11. Sheldrake. 12. MGM chief Louis B. Mayer. This caused such bad blood that Wilder never forgave him. In 1957, after hearing that Mayer's funeral was standing room only, Wilder remarked, "It just goes to show, give the public what it wants and they'll show up." 13. *Born Yesterday* (1950). 14. *Life*

magazine. 15. George Cukor. 16. The pictures. 17. *A Can of Beans*. 18. This was done because actor Erich von Stroheim didn't know how to drive. 19. Another ten thousand dollars. 20. *Samson and Delilah* (1949). 21. *All About Eve* (1950). 22. He strangled himself with them. 23. Jack Webb. 24. GREAT STAR KILLS HERSELF FOR UNKNOWN WRITER. 25. Gloria Swanson.

Quiz No. 13: The Bridge on the River Kwai

1. Michael Wilson and David Lean wrote the screenplay. Wilson did not receive credit because he was blacklisted, and Lean didn't receive credit simply because producer Sam Spiegel didn't want to give him credit. 2. *The Wind Cannot Read*. Although Lean didn't make the film, Ralph Thomas would later direct an adaptation in 1958. 3. "There isn't a single word of Foreman's in the picture," Lean said. 4. Johnny Walker–brand whiskey. 5. At the London Polytechnic. 6. John Ford, Howard Hawks, and William Wyler. 7. *Return from the River Kwai* (1988). 8. The oven. 9. During filming, Guinness repeatedly complained that the film would be horrible and that his character was boring. When he was nominated for Best Actor, Guinness opted not to go because he didn't believe he'd win. 10. Because the Geneva Convention forbids it. 11. Philip John Denton Toosey. 12. Charles Laughton. 13. Weaver. 14. *Sunset Boulevard* (1950), *The Wild Bunch* (1969), and *Network* (1976). 15. Kill himself. 16. Demoralization and chaos. 17. "Bless 'Em All." 18. The plastic explosives are exposed. 19. The Japanese defeat of the Russians in 1905. 20. Marlon Brando. 21. Nicholson and Saito. 22. He believed a captured officer would receive better treatment than an enlisted man. 23. Major. 24. *Lawrence of Arabia* (1962). 25. *The Prince and the Showgirl* (1957), which Olivier directed.

Quiz No. 14: Some Like It Hot

1. *Fanfares of Love*. 2. Adolf Hitler. 3. *Mister Roberts* (1955), *The Apartment* (1960), *Days of Wine and Roses* (1962), *Save the Tiger* (1973), *The China Syndrome* (1979), *Tribute* (1980), and *Missing* (1982). 4. This is a nod to *Scarface* (1932), in which Raft's character repeatedly flips a coin. 5. *Not Tonight, Josephine!* 6. *The Apartment*. 7. "The movie too hot for words!" 8. Bands for All Occasions Placement Agency. 9. Greased Lightning. 10. *Public Enemy* (1931). 11. *The Seven-Year Itch* (1955). 12. The University of Illinois. 13. Seven. 14. Frank Sinatra. 15. "I'll say! I had two

ponies drowned under me!" 16. *A Foreign Affair* (1948), *The Big Carnival* (1951), and *Sabrina* (1954). 17. Cinderella the Second. 18. *The Wall Street Journal.* 19. The story takes place in 1929. Grant's voice had yet to be heard in a film, so Jerry would not have known it, and if he had, no one would have recognized it. 20. Mitzi Gaynor. 21. Forty-seven; Monroe repeatedly said either, "Sugar, it's me" or "It's Sugar, me." 22. Kill himself. 23. Chicago. 24. "Security." 25. *Pepe* (1960) and *The Great Race* (1965).

Quiz No. 15: Star Wars

1. *The Hidden Fortress* (1958). 2. This is a continuity flaw because Red Six is the first pilot downed in the battle. 3. Cell Block 1138, which is a reference to George Lucas's film, *THX-1138* (1970). 4. The episode number and the subtitle, *The New Hope.* 5. Ewan McGregor, the actor who would later play Obi-Wan Kenobi. 6. Starkiller. 7. Greedo now fires his blaster just before Han guns him down. Lucas said he disliked the original version because it made Han look like a cold-blooded killer. 8. *Battle Beyond the Stars.* 9. Female advice. 10. "The Star Wars Holiday Special." 11. Parsecs are a measure of distance, not time. 12. "Let the wookie win." 13. Alderaan. 14. That there is no such thing. 15. Beru and Owen. 16. David Prowse. 17. *Patriot Games* (1992) and *Clear and Present Danger* (1994). 18. Bocce. 19. Jawas. 20. The Clone Wars. 21. Producer Rick McCallum. 22. A good blaster. 23. His T-16. 24. Mos Eisley. 25. Fisher wrote an episode entitled, "Paris, October 1916" for Lucas's *The Young Indiana Jones Chronicles* television series.

Quiz No. 16: All About Eve

1. *The Wisdom of Eve.* 2. *Best Performance.* 3. *The Fireball* (1950) and *Hometown Story* (1950). 4. *Titanic* (1997). 5. Davis appeared in the pilot for *Hotel,* but was ill when the series was finally picked up, making way for Baxter. 6. Gertrude Lawrence. 7. Anne Baxter, who plays Eve in the film. 8. McLean and Mankiewicz worked together three times, in *All About Eve, No Way Out* (1950), and *People Will Talk* (1951). 9. Ten days. 10. Gregory Peck. 11. Peter Pan. 12. Two; these are *All About Eve* and *Some Like It Hot* (1959). 13. Svengali. 14. *The Asphalt Jungle* (1950). 15. Her Sarah Siddons Best Actress of the Year trophy. 16. Eddie Fisher, whose only scene wound up on the cutting-room floor. 17. Jose Ferrer. 18. Look thirty-two. 19. Five hundred dollars. 20. Elisabeth Bergner. 21. *A Midsummer Night's Dream.*

22. Addison DeWitt. 23. It was the first screenplay ever published in book form. 24. The day she discovered she was different from little boys. 25. "It really pissed me off they called me a producer," Mankiewicz said.

Quiz No. 17: The African Queen

1. The Reverend Samuel Sayer. 2. *Beat the Devil* (1953) and *Sinful Davey* (1969). 3. Page Woodcock's Wind Pills. 4. Her brother's presence. 5. His gin. 6. Warren Oates. 7. In Shona. 8. Pumping water from the boat. 9. He suffers from a fever and has a nervous breakdown as a result of the Germans burning his church. 10. Two thousand. 11. That she "ain't no lady." 12. England. 13. That she knows nothing about boats. 14. The *Louisa*. 15. Death by hanging. 16. John Mills. 17. Eleanor Roosevelt. 18. "Never say die." 19. The crocodiles. 20. First Methodist Church of Kung Du. 21. James Mason. 22. Absurd ideas. 23. A screwdriver. 24. The Ulanga. 25. *Bringing Up Baby* (1938), *The Philadelphia Story* (1940), and *Guess Who's Coming to Dinner* (1967).

Quiz No. 18: Psycho

1. *Bates Motel.* 2. Francis. 3. *The Birds* (1963). 4. Twelve. 5. Alfred Hitchcock's daughter, Patricia Hitchcock. 6. A skull. 7. This is actually the sound of a knife cutting a melon. 8. Chocolate syrup. 9. "He must have noticed my wedding ring." 10. They're Norman's initials. 11. Ted Knight. 12. She poisoned herself. 13. Marie Samuels. 14. A lover. 15. *A Perfect Murder,* which is a remake of *Dial M for Murder* (1954). 16. Director Alfred Hitchcock. 17. *The Texas Chainsaw Massacre.* 18. "Transvestite." 19. Room 514. 20. *The Wrong Man* (1956). 21. The *Los Angeles Tribune.* 22. Vera Miles. 23. At a motel. 24. Milton. 25. The shower curtain.

Quiz No. 19: Chinatown

1. Howard W. Koch, Jr., the son of *Casablanca* (1942) cowriter Howard Koch. 2. J. J. Gittes & Associates. 3. *Bonnie and Clyde* (1967) and *The Godfather* (1972). (Towne's contributions to both films were uncredited.) 4. *The Two Jakes* (1990). 5. Jane Fonda. 6. "[H]e thought she was trouble." 7. Curly tells Jake he wants to kill his wife. Jake then tells him he's not rich enough to get away with murder. 8. *Frantic* (1988). (This was an uncredited rewrite for Towne.) 9. Roman Polanski and Jack Nichol-

son. 10. *The Last Detail* (1973), *The Missouri Breaks* (1976), *Reds* (1981), and *The Two Jakes*. 11. Director Roman Polanski. 12. His wife, actress Sharon Tate, was murdered by Charles Manson's cult. 13. "In the middle of a drought, and the water commissioner drowns!" 14. "Cheat." 15. *Prizzi's Honor*, which Huston directed. 16. Harry Dean Stanton. 17. He cut himself shaving. 18. *Bonnie and Clyde* and *Network* (1976). 19. At the time of Crabb's purchase, he had been dead for a week. 20. In Towne's screenplay, Evelyn kills Noah Cross. "We were arguing about the end and could not agree," Polanski recalls. "I was adamant about it. I did not believe in a happy ending in this type of movie." 21. Statutory rape. 22. "Forget it, Jake. It's Chinatown." 23. Noah Cross's bifocals. 24. Horse manure. 25. In the arm.

Quiz No. 20: One Flew Over the Cuckoo's Nest

1. Michael Douglas. 2. Producer Saul Zaentz. 3. James Caan. 4. *It Happened One Night* (1934). 5. Kirk Douglas. 6. Nothing; Kesey claims he has never viewed the film. 7. Salem, Oregon. 8. Thirty-eight-years old. 9. Danny DeVito. 10. Fifteen years old. 11. "Rocky Marciano got into forty, and he's a millionaire!" 12. Saltpeter. 13. Game one of the 1963 World Series. 14. *Goin' South* (1978), *Terms of Endearment* (1983), *Hoffa* (1992), and *Mars Attacks!* (1996). 15. Hard-on. 16. Nine. 17. A rigged game. 18. Candy. 19. Doctors from the mental hospital. 20. A fisherman. 21. A carton of cigarettes. 22. Two prostitutes, Candy and Rose. 23. *Goin' South*. 24. *The King of Marvin Gardens* (1972), *The Fortune* (1975), and *The Shining* (1980). 25. "Put the ball in the hole."

Quiz No. 21: The Grapes of Wrath

1. NO RIDERS ALLOWED. 2. The state penitentiary. 3. The crime he was imprisoned for. 4. Holy vessels. 5. *The Wizard of Oz* (1939). 6. Caterpillar tractors. 7. Muley. 8. A chicken. 9. Eight hundred. 10. If he broke out of prison. 11. Connie. 12. Gary Sinise. 13. If the truck holds everyone without breaking down. 14. Soothing syrup. 15. A dead man. 16. Connie. 17. *Young Mr. Lincoln* (1939), *Drums Along the Mohawk* (1939), *The Battle of Midway* (1942), *My Darling Clementine* (1946), *The Fugitive* (1947), *Fort Apache* (1948), *Mister Roberts* (1955), and *How the West Was Won* (1962). 18. Banana cream, pineapple cream, chocolate cream, and apple. 19. Because they're crossing the desert in a jalopy. 20. Oklaho-

mans. 21. *Drums Along the Mohawk.* 22. Grandpa. 23. The handbill advertising work in California. 24. The police officer was trying to shoot an innocent man. 25. The living.

Quiz No. 22: 2001: A Space Odyssey

1. "The Sentinel." 2. The Dawn of Man, Jupiter Mission 18 Months Later, and Jupiter and Beyond the Infinite. 3. "Thus Spake Zarathustra." 4. Alex North, who had composed Kubrick's *Spartacus* (1960). 5. January 12, 1992. 6. "Meddle." 7. Director Stanley Kubrick's daughter, Vivian Kubrick. 8. CRM-114. 9. Arthur C. Clarke and Stanley Kubrick. 10. Moonwatcher. 11. *The Making of 2001* by Jerome Angel. 12. He is Earth's chairman on the National Council of Aeronautics. 13. *The World Tonight.* 14. *Babylon 5.* 15. Three. 16. IBM. 17. "Heuristic" and "Algorithmic." 18. Seventy-two hours. 19. The 1913 Hamburg match between Roesch and Schlage. 20. Zero. 21. Martin Balsam. 22. They tell HAL they are checking a faulty transmitter. 23. HAL's statement that the 9000 series has a perfect record. 24. The three hibernating crewmen. 25. Urbana, Illinois.

Quiz No. 23: The Maltese Falcon

1. In *The Maltese Falcon* (1931), Ricardo Cortez appears as Sam Spade. In *Satan Met a Lady* (1936), Warren William appears in the role. 2. *The Great Lie* (1941). 3. He felt that it wasn't "an important picture" because it was a remake. 4. Walter Huston. 5. Cinematographer Arthur Edeson. 6. *In This Our Life* (1942). 7. *Swing Your Lady* (1938), which featured Humphrey Bogart. 8. Jacques Barzun and Wendell Hertig Taylor's *A Catalogue of Crime* defines gunsel as being a "young homosexual killer." 9. *Background to Danger* (1943), *Passage to Marseilles* (1943), *Casablanca* (1943), *The Mask of Dimitrios* (1944), and *Three Strangers* (1945). 10. *High Sierra.* 11. Room number 1001. 12. Sam Spade. 13. The Geary Theatre. 14. The Hotel Belvedere. 15. *The Great Lie.* 16. "When you're slapped, you'll take it and like it!" 17. A golden ram's horn. 18. *The Further Adventures of the Maltese Falcon.* 19. Kaspar Gutman. 20. *The Black Bird.* 21. To express his displeasure at the newly colorized version of the film, which had aired on Turner Broadcasting System the night before. 22. 1539. 23. 1730. 24. Wilmer. 25. *It Happened One Night* (1934), *Bringing Up Baby* (1938), *Gone with the Wind* (1939), *The Grapes of Wrath* (1940), *It's a Wonderful Life* (1946), and *The Searchers* (1956).

Quiz No. 24: Raging Bull

1. *Mean Streets* (1973), *Taxi Driver* (1976), and *New York, New York* (1977). 2. Tommy Como. 3. Girl's hands. 4. Screenwriter Jay Cocks. 5. Robert De Niro. 6. *Prize Fighter*. 7. "It means the game is over." 8. 1943. 9. Musician Robbie Robertson. 10. Martin Scorsese and Robert De Niro. 11. He pours ice-cold water down his pants. 12. Martin Scorsese's parents. 13. *Death Collector* (1975). 14. Pretty. 15. The Debonair Social Club. 16. Jackie Curtie. 17. In the final scene of Schrader's draft, Jake is shown masturbating in his jail cell. 18. *Father of the Bride* (1950). 19. *The Tales of Hoffman* (1951). 20. By kissing him. 21. Ten thousand dollars. 22. The stones. 23. Paddy Chayefsky, Rod Serling, William Shakespeare, Budd Schulberg, and Tennessee Williams. 24. *Rocky II*. 25. Martin Scorsese's New York University film instructor.

Quiz No. 25: E.T. The Extra-Terrestrial

1. Dungeons and Dragons. 2. Harvey. 3. John Sayles. 4. His father. 5. Reese's Pieces and Coca-Cola. 6. *The Empire Strikes Back* (1980). 7. He heals it. 8. Elliot belches, and then begins to act drunk. 9. *The Quiet Man* (1952). 10. Drew Barrymore and Erika Eleniak. 11. A Bell Telephone commercial. 12. A Speak-N-Spell. 13. Before E.T.'s arrival, it says ENTER. After E.T. shows up, Elliot changes it to DO NOT ENTER. 14. Keys. 15. Steve. 16. John Wayne kissing Maureen O'Hara. 17. Laurent Bouzereau. 18. His baseball. 19. Sally. 20. He warms a thermometer under the lamp, and then puts a heating pad on his face. 21. Divorce; "*E.T.* was a manifestation of my feelings about my mom and dad," Spielberg has said. "The whole movie is really about divorce." 22. Eat it. 23. "An accident." 24. He sets them free. 25. On *Tom and Jerry*, Tom's tail is on fire.

Quiz No. 26: Dr. Strangelove or: How I Learned to Stop Worrying and Love the Bomb

1. *Red Alert* by Peter George. 2. Dr. Strangelove, Merkin Muffley, and Group Captain Lionel Mandrake. 3. *Easy Rider* (1969). 4. Dan Blocker. 5. The Zhokhov Islands. 6. The bomb was named Lolita in the novel. Since Kubrick had directed a film of that title in 1962, he decided to change the name. 7. Major T. J. Kong. 8. Pies, which explain the large table of food visible in the War Room. 9. Kong originally said Dallas, Texas. However,

the filmmakers decided to change the line after John F. Kennedy's assassination there. 10. The name of the message decoder is the CRM-114 Discriminator. 11. "We'll Meet Again." 12. Tracy Reed, who appears in the film as General Turgidson's secretary, Miss Scott. 13. Fifty. 14. Goldie. 15. Burpelson Air Force Base. 16. Peace. 17. Trust no one, fire upon anyone who approaches within two hundred yards of the perimeter, and shoot first, ask questions later. 18. *One-Eyed Jacks* (1961). 19. The Generals. 20. World Targets in Megadeath. 21. Bucky. 22. *Candy*. 23. Kubrick was referring to Columbia Pictures, which he felt was distancing itself from the film before it was even finished. 24. Water. 25. He falls on his face.

Quiz No. 27: Bonnie and Clyde

1. "They kill people." 2. Robert Towne, who is credited as a "special consultant." 3. *From Here to Eternity* (1953). 4. *Dick Tracy*. 5. Warren Beatty. 6. William Daniel "W. D." Jones and Henry Methvin. 7. She served as Faye Dunaway's stand-in. 8. Clyde and C. W. 9. *The Other Side of Bonnie and Clyde* (1968). 10. A meat cleaver. 11. In the face. 12. A bluebird. 13. He is a minister. 14. The best. 15. Because the bank "failed three weeks ago," the bank holds no money. 16. He is a gas-station attendant and mechanic. 17. *The Gold Diggers of 1933* (1933). This is a continuity flaw as the scene takes place in 1931. 18. "We're in the Money." 19. John Dillinger. In fact, when Dillinger was gunned down, he was leaving the theater after viewing Loy's *Manhattan Melodrama* (1934). 20. Eva's Ice Cream Parlor. 21. "The Story of Bonnie and Clyde." 22. *Reruns: 50 Memorable Films*. 23. He shot off two of his toes. 24. Eighteen. 25. "I don't want no rich man."

Quiz No. 28: Apocalypse Now

1. *Heart of Darkness* by Joseph Conrad. 2. Orson Welles, who instead made *Citizen Kane* (1941). 3. *Eagle's Wing* (1979). 4. Robert De Niro. 5. Fourteen-years old. 6. The plan, conceived by Milius in 1971, was to shoot the film *in* Vietnam. By filming the actual soldiers and battles, the filmmakers believed they could reduce the budget and add realism to the film. 7. An air strike destroys Kurtz's compound as Willard and Lance start down the river. 8. He had a heart attack. 9. The general's name is "R. Corman," which is a nod to Coppola's mentor, Roger Corman. 10. Director Francis Ford Coppola. 11. There were no closing credits. 12. *Free Money*. 13. "The horror, the horror." 14. "The End" performed by the

Doors. 15. Charles Manson and his cult's murder of actress Sharon Tate. 16. Dismembered heads. 17. It smelled of "slow death, malaria, and nightmares." 18. "The Hollow Men" by T. S. Elliot. 19. According to Kurtz, it is "judgment that defeats us." 20. Director Francis Ford Coppola. 21. They chopped off the children's arms. 22. A typhoon destroyed them. 23. The director's father, Carmine Coppola. 24. He becomes stronger. 25. Handing out speeding tickets at the Indy 500.

Quiz No. 29: Mr. Smith Goes to Washington

1. *Casablanca* (1942) and *Lawrence of Arabia* (1962). 2. *Destry Rides Again*, *Ice Follies of 1939*, *Made for Each Other*, *It's a Wonderful World*, and *Hollywood Hobbies*, in which he appears in an uncredited cameo. 3. St. Vincent's. 4. Joseph Paine. 5. *You Can't Take It With You* (1938) and *It's a Wonderful Life* (1946). 6. *The Jackson City Star*. 7. Horace Miller. 8. The Lincoln Memorial. 9. Crooked men riding their backs. 10. *The Gentleman from Montana*. 11. The film was initially titled *Mr. Deeds Goes to Washington*, which would have starred Gary Cooper, reprising his character, Longfellow Deeds, from *Mr. Deeds Goes to Town* (1936). However, Capra was unable to get Cooper. 12. His father, Clayton Smith. 13. *Jeff's Boys Stuff*. 14. The Founding Fathers. 15. Daniel Boone. 16. Carrier pigeons. 17. He is a reporter. 18. The Milk Fund. 19. *Lady for a Day* (1933), *It Happened One Night* (1934), *Mr. Deeds Goes to Town*, *You Can't Take It With You*, and *It's a Wonderful Life*. 20. *Lost Horizon* (1937), *You Can't Take It With You*, and *It's a Wonderful Life*. 21. Diz Moore. 22. *Billy Jack Goes to Washington*. 23. Chick McGann. 24. Clarissa. 25. The Washington Press Corps.

Quiz No. 30: The Treasure of the Sierra Madre

1. John Huston won Oscars for Best Director and Best Screenplay, and his father, Walter Huston, won Best Supporting Actor honors. In doing so, they became the first father-son combination to win. 2. Director John Huston. 3. Go to a turkish bath and get cleaned up. 4. Eight dollars per day. 5. B. Traven actually visited the set himself under the guise of a pseudonym, claiming that he had been sent by the author. 6. After getting a haircut, his hat no longer fits. 7. "We don't need no stinkin' badges!" 8. "Comic strips and adventure stories." 9. The entire $175,000 worth of gold. 10. Howard. 11. Durango. 12. To the cemetery to dig their own

graves. 13. Curtin is a woman in Veloz's screenplay. 14. Twenty-five thousand dollars. 15. A gold watch and chain. 16. Kill him, run him off, or accept him as a partner. 17. Three. 18. Shoe polish. 19. The harmonica. 20. Half goat and half camel. 21. He tosses it to the ground. 22. Dallas, Texas. 23. Jimmy. 24. He claims to be a professional hunter. 25. "Right through the eyes."

Quiz No. 31: Annie Hall

1. "You can make a right turn on a red light." 2. Sigourney Weaver. 3. Diane Keaton, whose real name is Diane Hall. 4. Allen was playing the clarinet with his band, the New Orleans Funeral and Ragtime Orchestra, at their weekly appearance at Michael's Pub. 5. *The Dick Cavett Show*. 6. *The Sorrow and the Pity* (1971). 7. *Sister Mary Explains It All* (2001). 8. Murder mystery. 9. The morose type. 10. Groucho Marx. 11. It's Woody Allen's birthday. 12. A Coney Island roller coaster. 13. *The Turn of the Screw* by Henry James. 14. Robert Redford. 15. Chippewa Falls, Wisconsin. 16. Adlai Stevenson. 17. Federico Fellini. 18. *Sleeper* (1973). 19. *Ariel* by Sylvia Plath. 20. No one; the film has no score. Any music that appears in the film is source music. 21. Taking away her Bloomingdale's charge card. 22. The guitar and the bass. 23. "Getting raped by cossacks." 24. *The Misfits* (1961). 25. Warren Beatty, who was nominated as an actor, codirector, coscreenwriter, and producer on *Heaven Can Wait* (1978).

Quiz No. 32: The Godfather Part II

1. Lee Strasberg. 2. Hyman Roth. 3. Francis Ford Coppola's mentor, Roger Corman. 4. Sofia Coppola. 5. Melissa Mathison. 6. James Caan. 7. Two hundred dollars. 8. *Heat*. 9. The look is an order to kill Fredo. 10. Winning an Oscar for a primarily non-English-speaking role. 11. Michael's having Fredo killed. 12. Imbition. 13. Don Fanucci. 14. Tom Hagen. 15. Frank Pantangeli. 16. Danny Aiello. 17. Francis Ford Coppola's. 18. Paolo. 19. Andolini. 20. *Moshulu*. 21. Senator Pat Geary. 22. Make money. 23. Dominic Chianese. 24. The appearance of oranges foreshadows that something bad is about to happen: Senator Geary is framed for murder just after playing with an orange in Michael's office; Johnny Ola brings an orange to Michael's office just before the Corleone home is attacked; as Don Fanucci strides home where he will be killed by Vito, he picks up an orange. 25. The Capri.

Quiz No. 33: High Noon

1. "I do." 2. Die. 3. They have all had affairs with Helen Ramirez. 4. Van Cleef does not speak once in the entire film. 5. Jack Elam. 6. *Rio Bravo* (1959). 7. Hadleyville. 8. Grace Kelly. 9. Gregory Peck. 10. Coffins. 11. If he won't leave town with her, she'll leave alone. 12. Kill Will Kane. 13. *High Noon Part II: The Return of Will Kane.* 14. Helen left Miller for Kane. 15. Ralph Reed. 16. The town will die with him. 17. Tom Skerritt. 18. Get a gun and fight. 19. His badge. 20. *The Member of the Wedding.* 21. Because they haven't broken any laws. 22. Her brother and her father were gunned down. 23. Charlie. 24. Matt Howe. 25. Ben Miller.

Quiz No. 34: To Kill a Mockingbird

1. Maycomb, Alabama. 2. Six. 3. *The Stalking Moon* (1969). 4. Fight. 5. Robert E. Lee. 6. A pistol. 7. Author Harper Lee's father. 8. Zero; *To Kill a Mockingbird* is the only novel Lee ever published. 9. Because it's rabid. 10. Harper Lee's childhood friend, author Truman Capote. 11. Mr. Radley. 12. In the basement of the courthouse. 13. *The Spiral Road.* 14. "To Atticus, My Beloved Husband." 15. Tom Robinson's trial. 16. Atticus. 17. A ring and a necklace that belonged to her mother. 18. The dead. 19. "That all Negroes lie." 20. Boo Radley. 21. Because he felt sorry for her. 22. She tried to seduce a black man. 23. It was caught in a cotton gin. 24. A year. 25. *Captain Newman, M.D.* (1963).

Quiz No. 35: It Happened One Night

1. *You Can't Run Away from It* (1956). 2. "Night Bus." 3. *The Sure Thing.* 4. Ward Bond. 5. Myrna Loy. 6. *Men in White*, *Forsaking All Others*, *Chained*, and *Manhattan Melodrama.* 7. *Private Worlds* (1935) and *Since You Went Away* (1944). 8. The scene in which Gable chomps on a carrot reportedly served as inspiration for Bugs Bunny. 9. Ten thousand dollars. 10. $39.60 11. Four dollars. 12. *Boom Town* (1940). 13. King Westley. 14. Dunking doughnuts. 15. Ten cents. 16. Joe Gordon. 17. *For the Love of Mike* (1927). 18. The walls of Jericho. 19. Stubborn idiots. 20. "A high-class mama that can snap 'em back at ya." 21. A plumber's daughter. 22. *Broadway Bill.* 23. *One Flew Over the Cuckoo's Nest* (1975) and *The Silence of the Lambs* (1991). 24. Frank Capra. 25. Connie Bennett.

Quiz No. 36: Midnight Cowboy

1. *Midnight Cowboy* is the only "X"-rated film to win Best Picture. 2. *John and Mary*. 3. Michael Sarrazin, whose agent angered the producers when he tried to restructure his contract after being cast. 4. Miller's Restaurant. 5. *The Alamo* (1960). 6. Singer Harry Nilsson. 7. 1971. 8. Sunshine and coconut milk. 9. Enrico Salvatore Rizzo. 10. John Wayne. 11. His mother and his grandmother. 12. A slot machine paying off. 13. Tuberculosis. 14. Soliciting male customers. 15. Mr. O'Daniel. 16. Twenty dollars. 17. Ketchup. 18. He put a rock in his shoe. 19. Socks and cough syrup. 20. Because he was illiterate, he simply signed with an "X." 21. Because he shined shoes, and even the undertaker couldn't get his nails clean. 22. Sylvia Miles appears in the film for a mere six minutes, which is the shortest performance ever nominated by the Academy. 23. Because it's been condemned. 24. *Marathon Man* (1976). 25. Because she suggests that he's homosexual.

Quiz No. 37: The Best Years Of Our Lives

1. Blake Edwards. 2. *The Desperate Hours* (1955). 3. *Glory for Me*. 4. *Dr. Jekyll and Mr. Hyde* (1932). 5. To date, Harold Russell is the only actor ever to win two Oscars for the same role. 6. Five; Fred Derry, Al Stephenson, Homer Parrish, and two others. 7. *Diary of a Sergeant* (1945). 8. Wilma Cameron. 9. Farley Granger. 10. Six; *These Three* (1936), *Come and Get It* (1936), *Dead End* (1937), *Wuthering Heights* (1939), *The Westerner* (1940), and *The Little Foxes* (1941). 11. Director William Wyler's daughters, Judy and Cathy Wyler. The two girls also appear in *Roman Holiday* (1953). 12. Harold Russell. 13. Hortense. 14. At Grandview Arms on Pine Street. 15. On the body of a dead Japanese soldier. 16. General Douglas MacArthur. 17. Fay Bainter, who first accomplished this in 1939 when she was nominated for both *White Banners* (1938) and *Jezebel* (1938). Both Bainter and Wright won for Best Supporting Actress, and lost in their bids for Best Actress. 18. Her father. 19. He was a soda jerk. 20. *Returning Home*. 21. Mr. Milton. 22. His military-dress uniform. 23. $32.50 per week. 24. He sticks the prosthetic hooks through the windows, shattering the glass and frightening the children. 25. "Hey, where can I get a stick of dynamite?"

Quiz No. 38: Double Indemnity

1. *Three of a Kind.* 2. Richard Crenna. 3. July 16, 1938. 4. In the original ending, Walter Neff dies in the gas chamber as Barton Keyes observes. 5. Nettie. 6. "They said I had something loose in my heart." 7. Philadelphia. 8. Her name. 9. Twenty-six years. 10. False insurance claims. 11. *Trouble Indemnity.* 12. A smile. 13. The bowling alley. 14. In Ensenada. 15. Lola. 16. The insurance company. 17. One hundred thousand dollars. 18. Lola witnessing the signing of the insurance policy. 19. Ann Mathews. 20. At Jerry's Market. 21. Fifty dollars per check. 22. A claims inspector. 23. He fell from a train. 24. Ten. 25. Nino Zachetti.

Quiz No. 39: Doctor Zhivago

1. *Darling* (1965). 2. Moscow. 3. Lawyer. 4. Geraldine Chaplin is the daughter of Charles Chaplin. 5. They don't know the difference between right and wrong. 6. *The Big Parade* (1925). 7. Kaputkin Street. 8. Paper. 9. A pistol. 10. Nicolas Roeg. 11. *The Greatest Story Ever Told* (1965). 12. Lara. 13. Because Spain's dictator, General Francisco Franco, sent members of the secret police to observe filming and find out who knew the words to the revolutionary ballad. 14. Thirteen. 15. A clock. 16. History. 17. Sophia Loren. 18. Peter O'Toole. 19. Civic Instruction. 20. Turn it down. 21. Because she has learned that Yuri is alive. 22. *Doctor Zivengos.* 23. Pasha. 24. Strenilkov. 25. *Java Head.*

Quiz No. 40: North by Northwest

1. Nothing. 2. "I never make love on an empty stomach." 3. Director Alfred Hitchcock. 4. *High Anxiety.* 5. They couldn't find a logical way to incorporate it into the story. 6. A man's being mistaken for a nonexistent secret agent. 7. *Suspicion* (1941), *Notorious* (1946), and *To Catch a Thief* (1955). 8. Lester Townsend. 9. George Kaplan. 10. Clara. 11. Room 796. 12. She's dead. 13. *The Evening Star.* 14. Seven. 15. The brook trout. 16. Jack Philips. 17. R.O.T. 18. 3901. 19. "Singin' in the Rain." 20. 1212 N. Michigan Avenue. 21. The Actors Studio. 22. The FBI, CIA, and ONI. 23. "Like some people use a fly swatter." 24. Deliberate planning. 25. An old Gestapo trick.

Quiz No. 41: West Side Story

1. Maria was Jewish and Tony was Catholic. 2. This was the first time codirectors received the award. 3. The words were changed to "gay" and "today" as this scene became a daytime scene in the film. 4. Marni Nixon. 5. Riff and A-rab. 6. *Ben Hur* (1959) and *Titanic* (1997). 7. The Sharks. 8. Jimmy Bryant. 9. Lieutenant Shrank. 10. Tony. 11. He's Polish. 12. When you're a Jet. 13. Betty Wand. 14. VISITORS FORBIDDEN. 15. Doc. 16. Chino. 17. An orphan. 18. Maria. 19. Glad Hand. 20. The Sharks. 21. His skull. 22. When you're all white in America. 23. In front of the candy shop. 24. "My Daddy beats my Mommy, my Mommy clobbers me." 25. Doc.

Quiz No. 42: Rear Window

1. *Psycho* (1998). 2. *The Country Girl* (1954). 3. *To Catch a Thief* (1955). 4. Zero. 5. Put out their eyes with a red-hot poker. 6. "Eagle Head." 7. "It's always their Girl Friday who gets them out of trouble." 8. *To Catch a Thief*. 9. A neighbor's dog. 10. Yi Qiushui. 11. *Harper's Bazaar*. 12. Director Alfred Hitchcock. 13. *Rope* (1948), *The Trouble With Harry* (1955), *The Man Who Knew Too Much* (1956), and *Vertigo* (1958). 14. It was the largest indoor set ever built at Paramount Studios. 15. Harry. 16. Trouble. 17. Miss Lonely Hearts. 18. The number is never given. 19. Fish heads. 20. Meritsville. 21. Heckling. 22. William Irish. 23. *Rope*, *The Man Who Knew Too Much*, and *Vertigo*. 24. Five: *Mr. Smith Goes to Washington* (1939), *The Philadelphia Story* (1940), *It's a Wonderful Life* (1946), *Rear Window*, and *Vertigo*. 25. Miss Torso.

Quiz No. 43: King Kong

1. Director Ernest B. Schoedsack. 2. *Blind Adventure*. 3. *Creation* (1931). 4. Skull Island. 5. *Gone with the Wind* (1939). 6. SS *Venture*. 7. Twenty dollars per person. 8. Beauty. 9. Eighteen inches tall. 10. A bother. 11. Two, in the films *Horse Feathers* (1929) and *The Most Dangerous Game* (1932). 12. *The Beast*, *Kong*, *King Ape*, and *The Eighth Wonder of the World*. 13. *Mighty Joe Young*. 14. Kong battling the Tyrannosaurus rex. 15. Rabbit fur. 16. *The Most Dangerous Game*. 17. Jim Thorpe. 18. One million dollars. 19. According to Cooper the scene "stopped the picture cold." After the sailors were eaten by the spiders, test audiences either left the theater

or talked about the scene for the remainder of the film. 20. Cary Grant. 21. *King Kong Lives.* 22. A pretty face. 23. Captain Englehorn. 24. Three. 25. A captive.

Quiz No. 44: The Birth of a Nation

1. *The Clansman.* 2. According to official records, somewhere between eighteen- and twenty-million dollars. However, because of poor tabulation and outright sales of the picture in some states, this is inaccurate. It is believed that the film might have made four or five times that. 3. The National Organizatin for the Advancement of Colored People (NAACP). 4. President Woodrow Wilson. 5. *Judith of Bethulia* (1914). 6. He was a minister. 7. *Birth of a Race.* 8. Abraham Lincoln and Jesus Christ. 9. Pennsylvania Republican Senator Thaddeus Stevens. 10. Elsie, Phil, and Tod. 11. *Duel in the Sun* (1945). 12. Piedmont, South Carolina. 13. His sexual feelings for his mulatto maid, Lydia Brown. 14. Tod Stoneman. 15. He is shot and killed. 16. Parched-corn kernels. 17. Abraham Lincoln is assassinated. 18. Adolf Hitler. "I went to the opera one night years later when I was in Germany, and Hitler was sitting in the box, right up there, just as Lincoln was sitting in the box when I played John Wilkes Booth," Walsh said. "If I had a gun or something, I could have walked around and pumped him full of lead. What the hell is one life compared to twenty million?" 19. Silas Lynch. 20. Twenty-three. 21. Five thousand dollars. 22. His castration. 23. Twice. 24. "Ride of the Valkyries." 25. War.

Quiz No. 45: A Streetcar Named Desire

1. Ann-Margaret. 2. *An American in Paris* (1951). 3. Edgar Allan Poe. 4. Scotch. 5. *The Evening Star.* 6. Alan killed himself. 7. Shep Huntleigh. 8. The Napoleonic Code. 9. Belle Reve. 10. The Hotel Flamingo. 11. The Moon Lake Casino. 12. She was a prostitute. 13. Humphrey Bogart for *The African Queen* (1951). 14. Scarlett O'Hara. "I'm not Scarlett O'Hara! I'm Blanche DuBois!" 15. Her name. 16. An animal's habits. 17. A bus ticket to Laurel. 18. Huey Long. 19. Deliberate cruelty. 20. Stanley's raping Blanche. 21. The doctor who takes her to the mental institution. 22. Eunice. 23. Stanley breaking the lightbulb with her slipper. 24. The radio. 25. He was seventeen years old.

Quiz No. 46: A Clockwork Orange

1. Mick Jagger. 2. *A Clockwork Orange.* 3. *The French Connection* (1971). 4. "A bit of the old ultraviolence." 5. *Earthly Powers* (1981). 6. Nadsat. 7. The number twenty-one represents the age of human maturity. In the final chapter of Burgess's novel—which does not appear in Kubrick's film—Alex matures and leaves his violent ways behind him. 8. The Korova Milkbar. 9. Staja No. 84F. 10. *Vinyl* (1965). 11. A ripped-out eyeball. 12. A Durango. 95. 13. He becomes physically ill. 14. Violence. 15. Post-Corrective Advisor. 16. The soundtrack from *2001: A Space Odyssey* (1968). 17. *The William Tell Overture.* 18. Joe. 19. A serum known only as Number 114. This is the director's trademark; the number 114 appears in many of Kubrick's films. 20. "It was the only song I know." 21. Deodorant. 22. He grabs the policeman's crotch. 23. Miss Weathers. 24. The Ludovico Clinic. 25. Rossini's *The Thieving Magpie.*

Quiz No. 47: Taxi Driver

1. The Marines. 2. *Return of the Dragon* (1972). 3. Charles Palantine. 4. *Alice Doesn't Live Here Anymore* (1974). 5. George Memmoli. 6. Jeff Bridges. 7. Herrmann liked it when Travis Bickle pours peach brandy over his cornflakes. 8. *The Last Detail* (1973). 9. Because she had a "big ass." 10. Twenty dollars. 11. *Swedish Marriage Manual* (1969). 12. Brian De Palma. 13. Steven Spielberg. 14. *Cape Fear* (1991). In this remake, Scorsese used Herrmann's original 1962 score. 15. Neil Diamond. 16. Director Martin Scorsese's mother. 17. Wizard. 18. Killer. 19. *The Wrong Man* (1956). 20. That Robert De Niro appear in the film. 21. "Easy" Andy. 22. $875. 23. Two thousand dollars. 24. Henry Krinkle. 25. *Jennifer on My Mind* (1971).

Quiz No. 48: Jaws

1. *Stillness in the Water.* 2. Sterling Hayden. 3. Robert Shaw. 4. Author Peter Benchley. 5. Steven Spielberg's. 6. Robert Redford, Paul Newman, and Steve McQueen. 7. *Stakeout* (1987). 8. "Coroner." 9. July 4 through 10. 10. *The Deep* (1977). 11. Cape Cod, the Hamptons, and Long Island. 12. Bad Hat Hari Productions. 13. Pippet. 14. Three thousand dollars. 15. Lorraine Gary. 16. *Chasing Amy.* 17. One hundred to one. 18. Water. 19. Ben Gardner's head. 20. That the shark is a man-eater. 21. Ringing the dinner bell for the shark. 22. Five people were attacked

and chewed up by a shark. 23. Killer Shark. 24. The *Orca.* 25. When the man falls overboard, he has no shoes on. However, the leg that surfaces is wearing a shoe.

Quiz No. 49: Snow White and the Seven Dwarfs

1. Doc and Dopey. 2. *Seven Wise Dwarves* (1941). 3. A song that was written for the film, but not used. 4. Prince Charming. 5. "I'm Wishing." 6. He tries to stab her. 7. A bluebird. 8. Snow White's heart. 9. Will Rogers. 10. Marguerite Clark. 11. Louis Hightower. 12. The multiplane camera. 13. Dig. 14. His animation staff. 15. They believe someone has stolen the dishes. 16. Poison. 17. The Queen. 18. Snow White. 19. She makes them wash up. 20. To make her old. 21. "The Sleeping Death." 22. Doc. 23. A skull. 24. John Barrymore. 25. The animals of the forest.

Quiz No. 50: Butch Cassidy and the Sundance Kid

1. *The Sting* (1973). 2. *The Towering Inferno* (1974). 3. *Butch and Sundance: The Early Days* (1979). 4. *The Only Game in Town* (1970). 5. The Wild Bunch, who were also immortalized onscreen the same year in Sam Peckinpah's *The Wild Bunch* (1969). 6. Percy Garris. 7. Robbing a few banks. 8. Prayer. 9. She was a prostitute. 10. Woodcock. 11. Ray Bledsoe. 12. Lord Baltimore. 13. *The Hot Rock* (1972), *The Great Waldo Pepper* (1975), *All the President's Men* (1976), and *A Bridge Too Far* (1977). 14. Butch Cassidy's sister, Lula Parker Bentenson. 15. The Hole-in-the-Wall Camp. 16. Joe Lefors. 17. Butch. 18. B. J. Thomas. 19. *The Three Outlaws.* 20. *Way of the Gun.* 21. Harry Longbaugh. 22. Jack Lemmon. 23. Experience, maturity, and leadership. 24. *Wanted: The Sundance Woman* (1976). 25. News.

Quiz No. 51: The Philadelphia Story

1. Clark Gable and Spencer Tracy. 2. *A Bill of Divorcement* (1932), *Little Women* (1932), *Sylvia Scarlett* (1936), and *Holiday* (1938). 3. Complete Surrender. 4. Joseph Cotten. 5. *Susan and God.* 6. *Sylvia Scarlett*, *Holiday*, and *Bringing Up Baby* (1938). 7. Samantha. 8. Fifteen cents. 9. Tina Mara. 10. Waldo Salt. 11. An intellectual snob. 12. Mike Connor carrying

Tracy. 13. *High Society*. 14. Ginger Rogers for *Kitty Foyle* (1940). 15. *People Will Talk* (1951). 16. Red. 17. Junius. 18. *The Animal Kingdom* (1932) and *Holiday,* which also stars Cary Grant and Katharine Hepburn. 19. *Kitty Foyle*. 20. That something "smells." 21. Sidney Kidd. 22. "Lydia the Tattooed Lady." 23. French. 24. Himself. 25. Gig Young.

Quiz No. 52: From Here to Eternity

1. Prew. 2. Two days. 3. Natalie Wood. 4. A lone wolf. 5. The Mafia. This rumor served as the inspiration for a similar story in *The Godfather* (1972). 6. "Strangle in his own spit." 7. Twenty years. 8. Thirty years. 9. Eli Wallach. 10. The latrines. 11. The New Congress Hotel. 12. Aldo Ray. 13. Liquor. 14. Two flower leis. 15. Fatso. 16. Dixie Wells. 17. He spit in Judson's eye. 18. "The Reenlistment Blues." 19. Six months. 20. From a line in Rudyard Kipling's poem, "Gentleman Rankers." 21. The Treatment. 22. Put his head in a noose. 23. Prewitt's. 24. The Kalakaua Inn. 25. Because he hates officers.

Quiz No. 53: Amadeus

1. Cynthia Nixon. 2. "Leave me alone." 3. That God make him a great composer. 4. Emperor Joseph. 5. A crucifix. 6. "Will you marry me, yes or no?" 7. Love. 8. Talent. 9. He believes it has "too many notes." 10. *One Flew Over the Cuckoo's Nest* (1975). 11. Composition. 12. God. 13. Simon Callow. 14. Beloved of God. 15. Salieri. 16. *The Marriage of Figaro*. 17. The emperor's yawn. 18. "Salieri." 19. Mozart. 20. Albert Finney for his turn in *Under the Volcano* (1984). 21. Nipples of Venus. 22. *One Flew Over the Cuckoo's Nest*. 23. Because he thought Salieri didn't like him. 24. To torture him. 25. His music.

Quiz No. 54: All Quiet on the Western Front

1. George Cukor. 2. *The Road Back*. 3. He is a postal worker. 4. "To make him famous." 5. The first bombardment. 6. Fred Zinneman. 7. Sergeant Stanislaus Katczinsky. 8. His right leg. 9. Because he's dead. 10. Being "alive or dead." 11. Ernest Borgnine. 12. Yellow Rat. 13. Zasu Pitts. 14. Erich Maria Remarque's *All Quiet on the Western Front*. 15. Director Lewis Milestone's. 16. Because Behm was already dead. 17. The boots are passed along from soldier to soldier as each new owner is killed. 18. Katczinsky. 19. German veterans living in California. 20. *Two Arabian*

Knights (1927) and *The Front Page* (1931). Milestone also received a fourth Oscar nod as a producer for *Of Mice and Men* (1939). 21. A confession. 22. Because he can't run away. 23. Women. 24. Music that had been added against his wishes. 25. Die.

Quiz No. 55: The Sound of Music

1. *The Von Trapp Family Singers* (1966). 2. *Die Trapp Familie*. 3. *Gone with the Wind* (1939). 4. In Wise's *West Side Story* (1961), Nixon had provided the singing voice for Natalie Wood. 5. The sound of music. 6. Twelfth. 7. Franz. 8. *Grease*. 9. Discipline. 10. Max Detweiler. 11. The drapes. 12. Ugly German threats. 13. Maria von Trapp. 14. Yul Brynner. 15. William Wyler. 16. The Reverend Mother. 17. Maria. 18. "Something Good." 19. The captain. 20. At the convent. 21. They have demobilized the Nazi vehicles. 22. Sister Margaretta. 23. Seven. 24. Singing. 25. Her money.

Quiz No. 56: M*A*S*H

1. Sex. 2. Painless and Jawbreaker. 3. "Suicide is Painless." 4. On February 15, 1996, actor McLean Stevenson, who played Lieutenant Colonel Henry Blake on the television series, died of a heart attack. The following day, Roger Bowen, the actor who played Blake in the film, died of the same cause. 5. O'Houlihan. 6. A microphone. 7. Frank attacked him. 8. A pornographic magazine. 9. *To Kill a Mockingbird* (1962), *The Godfather* (1972), *The Godfather Part II* (1974), *Network* (1976), and *Apocalypse Now* (1979). 10. Having no olives for his martini. 11. Army morale. 12. The disrespect shown to Frank. 13. Because he punched Frank. 14. Pierce's being addressed as "Hawkeye." 15. Generals. 16. The army. 17. The loudspeaker broadcast of O'Houlihan and Frank Burns's sexual escapades. 18. Three. 19. That he's homosexual. 20. "M-U-S-H." 21. Walt. 22. Blondes. 23. Blackmail photographs of him with a prostitute. 24. Fred Williamson. 25. Gary Burghoff.

Quiz No. 57: The Third Man

1. American, British, Russian, and French. 2. *The Lives of Harry Lime*. 3. Novels written by Holly Martins. 4. Dying. 5. That "you can pick them up or put them down whenever you want to." 6. *Too Much Johnson* (1938), *Citizen Kane* (1941), *Journey Into Fear* (1942), *The Magnificent Ambersons* (1942), *Duel in the Sun* (1946), *Othello* (1952), *Touch of Evil* (1958), and *F*

for Fake (1975). 7. Holly Martins. 8. Director Carol Reed's. 9. Orson Welles. 10. *Othello*. 11. Penicillin. 12. Twenty percent. 13. Human beings. 14. The professionals. 15. Causes of death. 16. "The Modern Novel: The Crisis of Fate." 17. A group of soldiers. 18. Fun. 19. The three-card trick. 20. Croatia. 21. A parrot bites him. 22. *The Third Man*. 23. The porter. 24. To his speaking engagement. 25. Joseph Harbin's.

Quiz No. 58: Fantasia

1. Deems Taylor. 2. Hugh Douglas. 3. Walt Disney, who is uncredited. 4. Stereotypical Aunt Jemima–like black servants. Disney has since denied the existence of these scenes. However, Jim Korkis and John Cowley's book, *Cartoon Confidential,* contains actual cell photographs from *Fantasia* containing these servants. 5. This was Mickey Mouse's first appearance with pupils. 6. *Clair de Lune*. 7. Mickey Mouse's. 8. Entertainment. 9. Music that tells a definite story, music that paints a series of pictures, and absolute music that exists for its own sake. 10. Trained musicians. 11. Violin bows. 12. Tchaikovsky's *The Nutcracker Suite*. 13. A nutcracker. 14. Dewdrop fairies and dragonfly sprites. 15. The collision of three sprites. 16. Chinamen. 17. Nearly two thousand-years old. 18. Eight minutes. 19. A broom. 20. Two. 21. "To express primitive life." 22. Legs. 23. The Sixth Symphony. 24. Mount Olympus. 25. A bolt of lightning thrown by Zeus.

Quiz No. 59: Rebel Without a Cause

1. She is visiting her sister. 2. The film, which had already begun shooting, was being filmed in black and white. After early screenings of *East of Eden* (1959) indicated that James Dean was about to become a phenomenon, Warner decided to shoot the film in color. 3. Dennis Hopper. 4. Jim Backus. 5. *Rebel Without a Cause: The Hypnoanalysis of a Criminal Psychopath*. 6. A homosexual relationship between Plato and Jim, which appeared in early drafts of the screenplay. 7. The police mistake her for a prostitute. 8. John Crawford. 9. Jimbo. 10. Malaria. 11. A monkey. 12. Alan Ladd. 13. It's his birthday. 14. Knock her out cold. 15. A chicky run. 16. Clifford Odets, Leon Uris, and Irving Shulman. 17. "The Blind Run." 18. He hitchhiked. 19. Continue moving from place to place. 20. *The James Dean Story* (1957). 21. His father. 22. Stepping on the school insignia. 23. Comic books. 24. A cigarette. 25. *Medic*.

Quiz No. 60: Raiders of the Lost Ark

1. Three days. 2. He wraps the bullwhip around his hand, throwing the pistol away. 3. *Indiana Jones and the Raiders of the Lost Ark*. 4. Forrestal's. 5. Producer Frank Marshall. 6. Tom Selleck. 7. The idol. 8. Satipo. 9. His gun. 10. The words "love" and "you." 11. R2D2 and C3PO. 12. Jock. 13. The tablets that the Ten Commandments are written on. 14. Invincible powers. 15. The Staff of Ra. 16. Dr. Abner Ravenwood. 17. Reggie. 18. Marcus Brody. 19. OB-CPO, which is a reference to the characters Obi-Wan Kenobi and C3PO from *Star Wars* (1977). 20. Hovitos. 21. Five thousand dollars—three grand up front, and another two thousand dollars when he gets back home. 22. "Six kadams high" or seventy-two inches. 23. Top men. 24. Indy throws the hot poker away with his bullwhip. 25. It burns his flesh.

Quiz No. 61: Vertigo

1. Terror and tension. 2. *Bell, Book, and Candle*. 3. *Les Diaboliques* (1955), which was later remade by Jeremiah Chechik as *Diabolique* (1996). 4. Because he has attacks of vertigo, caused by his acrophobia. 5. Director Alfred Hitchcock. 6. John Ferguson. 7. Salina, Kansas. 8. None; Coppel was credited for contractual reasons only. When Samuel A. Taylor wrote his draft, he read neither Coppel's script nor the novel the film is based on. Instead, Taylor wrote only from Alfred Hitchcock's notes of the storyline. 9. Vera Miles. 10. Between 1958 and 1960, Barbara Bel Geddes appeared in four episodes of *Alfred Hitchcock Presents*: "Foghorn," "Lamb to the Slaughter," "The Morning of the Bride," and "Sybilla." 11. A man trying to get fresh with her. 12. *Obsessed with Vertigo*. 13. Most Distinguished Reissue. 14. *The Ring* (1927) and *Secret Agent* (1936). 15. Painting. 16. San Francisco, California. 17. He was a police officer. 18. A brassiere. 19. In reality, the mission does not have a bell tower. This appearance was given in the film through trick photography. 20. Nineteen thousand dollars. 21. Hitchcock shot the new scene that tells of the police tracking down Gavin Elster because European laws prohibited the release of any film in which the "bad guy" got away in the end. 22. The Argosy Bookshop. 23. The McKittrick Hotel. 24. Color, excitement, power, and freedom. 25. The birth of Carlotta Valdez.

Quiz No. 62: Tootsie

1. Stephen Bishop. 2. Die. 3. Age. 4. "What acting is all about." 5. *Frances* (1982). 6. Enrage her. 7. Director Sydney Pollack. 8. Barry Levinson. 9. Logic. 10. *Would I Lie to You?* 11. Ron. 12. The Tongue. 13. "Southwest General." 14. Dorothy. 15. "I don't write the shit, you know." 16. Garr and Coleman both appear in the 1986 miniseries *Fresno,* as well as *Short Time* (1990). 17. Andy Warhol. 18. She throws her drink in his face. 19. Hell. 20. The Beatles. 21. Gene Shalit. 22. Dwayne and Alma Kimberly. 23. As a man to a woman. 24. *Oh, God!* (1977). 25. *King Kong* (1976).

Quiz No. 63: Stagecoach

1. Three thousand dollars. 2. Social prejudice. 3. Josiah Boone. 4. The telegraph was down. 5. Because he wanted to "do it right." 6. Henry. 7. They were murdered by Jake Plummer. 8. Kansas City, Kansas. 9. Luke Plummer. 10. A businessman. 11. Josiah Boone. 12. Kris Kristofferson. 13. The Apaches leave him alone. 14. At Superstition Mountain. 15. His horse. 16. Lloyd Nolan. 17. Doc Boone. 18. Five. 19. When he was sixteen years old. 20. Apache war signals. 21. He tries to kill her 22. Aces and eights, which are commonly known as the "dead man's hand." 23. "Because that would have been the end of the movie." 24. *The Treasure of the Sierra Madre* (1948). 25. *Drums Along the Mohawk* (1939).

Quiz No. 64: Close Encounters of the Third Kind

1. Francois Truffaut. 2. Paul Schrader. 3. Robert De Niro. 4. Francois Truffaut. 5. *Watch the Skies.* 6. *The UFO Experience* (1972). 7. Close encounter of the first kind: a UFO sighting; close encounter of the second kind: physical evidence; close encounter of the third kind: contact. 8. Walter Cronkite. 9. It sang to him. 10. Brian De Palma. 11. *The Ten Commandments* (1956). 12. Excessive cocaine usage. 13. *Jaws* (1975) and *Always* (1989). 14. Paul McCartney and George Clinton. 15. CE3K. 16. Orange. 17. *The Muncie Star.* 18. *Firelight* (1964). 19. Carl Weathers. 20. According to Lacombe, he is the man who created the hand signs he uses during his explanation of the breakthrough. 21. Random numbers. 22. Richard Dreyfuss's cousin, Justin Dreyfuss. 23. "Chances Are" by Johnny Mathis. 24. This is a nod to Peter Benchley, the author of *Jaws.* 25. That a train carrying chemical gas derailed in the area.

Quiz No. 65: The Silence of the Lambs

1. Roger Corman. 2. HAL, the killer computer from *2001: A Space Odyssey* (1968). 3. *It Happened One Night* (1934) and *One Flew Over the Cuckoo's Nest* (1975). 4. Frankie Faison and Dan Butler. Oddly enough, both actors play different characters in the two films. Faison appears as Lieutenant Fisk in *Manhunter* and as Barney in *The Silence of the Lambs.* Butler appeared as an FBI fingerprint expert in *Manhunter* and as an entomologist in *The Silence of the Lambs.* 5. Psychology and criminology. 6. BILL SKINS FIFTH. 7. Valentine's Day. 8. Eight years. 9. A gun. 10. An insect cocoon. 11. He weighted the body down. 12. Discourtesy. 13. The lambs were screaming. 14. Three days. 15. Brian Cox. 16. Lamb chops, extra rare. 17. "He would consider that rude." 18. "American Girl." 19. Benjamin Raspail. 20. Julianne Moore. 21. Catherine. 22. The death of her father. 23. "Love your suit." 24. A poodle. 25. *Instinct.*

Quiz No. 66: Network

1. *A Streetcar Named Desire* (1951). 2. *Marty* (1955) and *The Hospital* (1971). 3. The University of Missouri. 4. Henry Fonda. 5. The United Broadcasting System (UBS). 6. Because he was dead. 7. "The Death Hour." 8. A fifty share. 9. A whorehouse network. 10. Howard Beale. 11. This is a reference to *Love is a Many-Splendored Thing* (1955), which also stars William Holden. 12. Bullshit. 13. $33 million. 14. "To impugn his cocksmanship." 15. A thirty share and a twenty rating. 16. A bucket of Kentucky Fried Chicken. 17. Twenty-five years. 18. He fires his pistol into the air. 19. Less than 3 percent. 20. *The Six-Million Dollar Man, All in the Family,* and *Phyllis.* 21. Caroline. 22. Bugs Bunny. 23. Archie Bunker. 24. *The Dykes.* 25. A psychiatrist.

Quiz No. 67: The Manchurian Candidate

1. President John F. Kennedy. 2. Eighteen months. 3. Frank Sinatra. 4. One year. 5. They are all named after cast members of *The Phil Silvers Show.* 6. She looks at a bottle of Heinz catsup, which causes her to think of the steak sauce, Heinz 57. 7. Frank Sinatra's. 8. Director John Frankenheimer. 9. Hydrangeas. 10. He dresses as a priest. 11. Marco "and fifty-two queens." 12. Himself. 13. His Congressional Medal of Honor. 14. Fu Man Chu. 15. If they disagree with her "about anything." 16. He gave it to the American Civil Liberties Union. 17. Abraham Lincoln. 18. Impossible to

like. 19. Those who walk into a room and turn the television off and those who walk into a room and turn the television on. 20. Senator John McCain, who was shot down and captured in North Vietnam, where he was held captive for five years. 21. The Pavlov Institute of Moscow. 22. Reading. 23. Guilt and fear. 24. "He smelled like a goat." 25. Two.

Quiz No. 68: An American in Paris

1. *The Red Shoes.* 2. Gene Kelly. 3. The Freed Unit. 4. *An American Werewolf in Paris.* 5. Charisse discovered she was pregnant and could not make the film. 6. *The Playhouse* (1921). 7. *Till the Clouds Roll By.* 8. Zero. 9. Henri Baurel. 10. At the time Freed was considering the picture, Warner Bros. went into production on a Gershwin biopic, *Rhapsody in Blue* (1945). 11. A red rose. 12. He read an article about expatriate American soldiers in *Life* magazine. 13. *Ziegfield Follies* (1946), *The Pirate* (1948), and *Brigadoon* (1954). 14. *Royal Wedding* (1951). 15. Seventy-two. 16. Gene Kelly. 17. He introduces himself as a concert pianist. 18. Henri. 19. Dave Diamond. 20. The Montmarte. 21. Five hundred thousand dollars. 22. Paris. 23. Modesty. 24. Maurice Chevalier, who was embroiled in controversy at the time over his political activities during the German occupation of France. Because of this, casting Chevalier was an impossibility. 25. *Lust for Life* (1956).

Quiz No. 69: Shane

1. *A Place in the Sun* (1951) and *Giant* (1956). 2. "The Quilting Party." 3. Guns. 4. Somewhere he has never been. 5. "The Call of the Faraway Hills." 6. "Put Your Little Foot." 7. Sweden. 8. Gunfighters. 9. Independence Day. 10. Sears and Roebuck. 11. *Rope of Sand* (1949). 12. That he will make his mark someday. 13. Ask them to please go around to the gate. 14. Lemon, strawberry, and lilac. 15. One of Ryker's men. 16. A friend of Starrett's. 17. Cheyenne, Wyoming. 18. Elisha Cook, Jr. 19. How to shoot. 20. When the "snow flies." 21. His father. 22. A .38-caliber pistol. 23. Joe Starrett. 24. Pig Farmer. 25. Sody Pop.

Quiz No. 70: The French Connection

1. Ed O'Neill of *Married with Children* fame. 2. Paul Newman and Ben Gazarra. 3. Eddie Egan and Sonny Grosso, the real-life detectives the film

is based upon. 4. *To Live and Die in L.A.* 5. According to legend, she was not a paid actress, but rather, a real pedestrian with a real baby in the stroller. The scene is said to have been shot on location with real pedestrians wandering around during the chase. 6. They were all real New York City cops. 7. John Frankenheimer. 8. That the film's chase scene had to be better than the chase scene in *Bullitt* (1968), which he also produced. 9. The store would not press charges. 10. Sal and Angie's. 11. Arrests. 12. That Burt Lancaster portray him in the film. 13. After receiving praise for his performance in the film, Egan became an actor. Grosso became a producer. 14. *The Seven-Ups*. 15. To move calmly and cautiously. 16. Jimmy. 17. At age twenty-five, Friedkin was the youngest director ever to receive the award. 18. The New York Yankees. 19. Hackman objected to a scene in which his character had to slap a suspect to make him confess. "Gene couldn't do that," Friedkin says. "Fifteen takes, and the black kid finally says, 'Listen, just hit me in the face and get it over with. Let's go home.' And while this would be going on, Eddie Egan would be standing right next to the camera, and Egan would finally, when he saw it work, turn to the crew and say, 'Look at him! This guy's more me than me!' 20. Hockey. 21. The license plate of the brown Lincoln the detectives watch. 22. He is a film director. 23. He waves at him. 24. Sal Boca. 25. In real life, Egan was never shot.

Quiz No. 71: Forrest Gump

1. Seventy-five. 2. Director Robert Zemeckis's son, Alex. 3. *Through the Eyes of Forrest Gump* (1994). 4. *Apollo 13* (1995). 5. *As Summers Die* (1986). 6. His brother, Jim Hanks. 7. Carla and Laura. 8. Susan. 9. Bobbi Dillon. 10. Saturday. (However, March 22, 1982, was actually a Monday.) 11. "Take good care of your feet" and "try not to do anything stupid, like get killed." 12. Lennon's song was released in 1971. However, Lennon did not appear on "The Dick Cavett Show" until the following year. 13. Alpha Company. 14. Haley Joel Osment. 15. Because the team did not travel to China until after Richard Nixon's historic trip to Beijing in February 1972. 16. Gary Sinise's brother-in-law, Jack Treese. 17. Five. 18. *Rosemary's Baby* (1968). 19. *Midnight Cowboy* (1969), in which Ratso Rizzo does the same thing. In addition, the Harry Nilsson song, "Everybody's Talkin' "—the theme song to *Midnight Cowboy*—plays on the soundtrack. 20. *Gump & Co.* 21. *Cast Away* (2000). 22. Hurricane Carmen. 23. Tom Hanks's daughter, Elizabeth. 24. *Punchline* (1988). 25. Taylor.

Quiz No. 72: Ben-Hur

1. *A Tale of the Christ.* 2. *Titanic* (1997). 3. *The Ten Commandments* (1956). 4. *The Agony and the Ecstasy* (1965). 5. *The Greatest Story Ever Told.* 6. *The Big Country* (1958). 7. Two. These versions were produced in 1907 and 1925. 8. A Roman world. 9. Hate. 10. Charioteering. 11. Malluch. 12. Pontius Pilate. 13. Czechoslovakia. 14. Eight weeks. 15. Burt Lancaster. 16. Messala. 17. The 1925 version of the film. 18. Gregory Peck. The two had gotten into a heated argument while filming *The Big Country.* 19. To the Valley of the Lepers. 20. Simonides and Malluch. 21. Director William Wyler. 22. Legendary stuntman Yakima Canutt. (Canutt is credited with creating the profession of stunt man.) 23. Despite popular legend, no one was killed during the filming of this sequence. One extra cut his chin and received stitches, and a 65-millimeter camera was destroyed, but no one was killed. 24. The Star of David. 25. The merciful.

Quiz No. 73: Wuthering Heights

1. The bridal chamber. 2. Dancing and singing. 3. Heathcliff. 4. *Dodsworth* (1936). 5. *Intermezzo* (1939). 6. Ellen Dean. 7. Heathcliff. 8. Hindley. 9. A race to the barn on horseback. 10. Milton Rosmer. 11. "Withering Heights." 12. Actress Vivien Leigh. 13. *Pretty World.* 14. Edgar Linton's. 15. Cathy. 16. Heathcliff. 17. The final scene in which the ghosts of Cathy and Heathcliff are reunited. In Wyler's cut, the film ended with a shot of Heathcliff's corpse. Goldwyn wanted a happier ending, but the cast and crew had already been released. 18. Peter Kominski. 19. He freezes to death searching for Cathy's ghost. 20. The Lintons. 21. New Orleans. 22. Joseph Earnshaw. 23. "A girl who died." 24. *Carrie* (1952). 25. *Three Comrades.*

Quiz No. 74: The Gold Rush

1. *Benny & Joon.* 2. *The History of the Dinner Party.* 3. Charles Chaplin. 4. Chaplin hired vagrants, paying each of them a day's wage. 5. Sixty-three. 6. Licorice. 7. Alexander Woolcott. 8. A bear. 9. Douglas Fairbanks. 10. A wanted poster. 11. The wind keeps blowing him back inside the door. 12. The barrel of the rifle is aimed at him, following him around the room as the two men fight. 13. The Tramp hiccups. 14. Two of spades.

15. He shoots them both, killing them. 16. Nails. 17. A chicken. 18. Douglas Fairbanks. 19. An axe. 20. A skunk. 21. At the dance hall. 22. Georgia. 23. The Tramp. 24. It's tied to a dog. 25. Lita Grey.

Quiz No. 75: Dances with Wolves

1. Graham Greene. 2. *Stacy's Knights.* 3. Cisco. 4. Timmons. 5. Two Socks. 6. Kicking Bird. 7. Christine. 8. The killing of the white hunters. 9. Buffalo. 10. Three. (Dunbar, Stands with a Fist, and Major Fambrough, who succeeds.) 11. Kicking Bird. 12. His horse. 13. He is the medicine man. 14. The doctor on the left is producer Jim Wilson, and the doctor on the right is director Kevin Costner. The actor lying on the table is actually Costner's stunt double. Other actors' voices were later dubbed for Costner's and Wilson's. 15. "Fire lives on the prairie." 16. Smiles A Lot. 17. Horseback. 18. Stands with a Fist's deceased husband. 19. Black Shawl. 20. To watch over his family while he is away fighting the Pawnee. 21. The trail of a true human being. 22. More than can be counted; like the stars. 23. The winter camp. 24. His journal. 25. Stone Calf.

Quiz No. 76: City Lights

1. *A Comedy Romance in Pantomime.* 2. The Tramp. 3. He becomes a street cleaner. 4. A whistle. 5. Eddie Mason. 6. Midway through the film the movie stopped and the lights came on. The manager then announced that he wanted "to take five minutes of your time and point out to you the merits of this beautiful new theatre." 7. Albert Einstein. 8. False. *City Lights* is a synchronized film. Although it has no spoken dialogue, it has sound effects and a musical score. 9. "Peace and Prosperity." 10. *The New York Times.* 11. Because Clive refused to jump into cold water. 12. His cane. 13. She throws a bucket of water on him. 14. He is nearly drowned. 15. Down the Tramp's pants. 16. He tries to shoot himself with a revolver. 17. Alfred Newman, David Riskin, and Edward Powell. 18. A limousine. 19. His Rolls-Royce. 20. A cat. 21. He's driving a limo. 22. Georgia Hale, who had appeared with him in *The Gold Rush* (1925). 23. Twenty-two dollars. 24. Jean Harlow. 25. Fifty dollars.

Quiz No. 77: American Graffiti

1. Toni Basil. 2. THX 138, which is a reference to director George Lucas's independent film *THX-1138* (1970). 3. Bill L. Norton. 4. He was killed by a drunk driver. 5. John Phillips of the Mamas and the Papas. 6. "C. S." 7. At University of Southern California Film School. 8. When Buddy Holly died. 9. Producer Francis Ford Coppola's *Dementia 13*. 10. Harrison Ford's character, Bob Falfa. 11. Mr. Beeman. 12. "Because he's a Negro." 13. Wilson's Appliance Store. 14. "Johnny B. Goode." 15. A 1958 Edsel. 16. A goat's head. 17. The film was reissued in 1978 with the intentions of cashing in on the later successes of the cast members, most of whom were unknown when the film was initially released. 18. Carol. 19. Bo Hopkins. 20. He is an insurance agent. 21. "Where were you in '62?" 22. Two thousand dollars. 23. Toad. 24. College girls. 25. Mel's Drive-in.

Quiz No. 78: Rocky

1. Actor Burgess Meredith. 2. Muhammad Ali. 3. *Rocky V* (1990). 4. *Rocky Marciano*. 5. Rocky's life. 6. The scene in which Rocky admits his fears to Adrian. 7. Joe Frazier. 8. Moby Dick. 9. Fifty dollars. 10. Grunt and smell. 11. "Crap thunder." 12. In his hat. 13. $40.75. 14. The Lucky Seven Tavern. 15. "Because I can't sing or dance." 16. $1.1 million. 17. Mack Lee Green's. 18. "Apollo Creed Meets the Italian Stallion." 19. Cuff and Link. 20. Muhammad Ali versus Chuck Wepner. 21. The film originally featured a downbeat ending in which Rocky enters an empty-boxing arena where he is consoled by another boxer. He then takes Adrian's hand and walks away with her. 22. *The Italian Stallion*. 23. *The Lords of Flatbush* (1974). 24. Gloria. 25. Ryan O'Neal.

Quiz No. 79: The Deer Hunter

1. Costar Meryl Streep. 2. Michael. 3. Socks. 4. Three. 5. *Heaven's Gate* (1980). 6. *The Young and the Restless*. 7. *The Thin Red Line*. 8. Welsh's Lounge. 9. Mustard. 10. *Mistress* (1992). 11. *Dear America: Letters Home from Vietnam* (1987). 12. John Welsh. 13. Starve himself. 14. His knees. 15. Chevoteravich. 16. *Falling in Love* (1984) and *Marvin's Room* (1996). 17. Zero. 18. Sun dogs. 19. "Michael Chipino." 20. John Cazale died of cancer. 21. One shot. 22. *Pulp Fiction* (1994). 23. That the Eagles' quarterback wears a dress. 24. "Can't Take My Eyes Off You." 25. Three: *The Godfather* (1972), *The Godfather Part II* (1974), and *The Deer Hunter*.

Quiz No. 80: The Wild Bunch

1. No other Technicolor film had ever had as many cuts. 2. *The Hellbenders.* 3. San Rafael. 4. Five cents. 5. He sticks his tongue in her ear. 6. The Rio Nazas. 7. Yuma Territorial Prison. 8. *Major Dundee* (1965). 9. The Mexican Revolution of 1914, around which the film is loosely based. 10. Metal washers. 11. *The Split* (1968). 12. Crazy Lee. 13. Mexicans. 14. Stay out jail. 15. *Major Dundee.* 16. Generalissimo Mapache. 17. The worst. 18. Sixteen. 19. Family ties. 20. He shot Pike in the leg and ran. 21. Deke Thornton. 22. A machine gun. 23. Ten thousand dollars. 24. Accidental death. 25. A small child wearing an army uniform.

Quiz No. 81: Modern Times

1. Charles Chaplin. 2. *The Masses.* 3. Sheep. 4. Oil. 5. *The Great Dictator* (1940). 6. On *Modern Times,* Chaplin used a shooting script for the first time, rather than filming improvisationally. 7. Excitement. 8. A Communist leader. 9. Cocaine. 10. His costar, Paulette Goddard. 11. Smoking a cigarette. 12. Gloria DeHaven, the daughter of Chaplin's assistant director, Carter DeHaven. 13. Her father. 14. To remain in jail. 15. The inventor of the Billows Feeding Machine. 16. *A Nous la Liberte* (1931). 17. It is holding up a half-finished ship. When the Tramp removes it, the ship slides into the water and sinks. 18. Cigars. 19. They worked together at the steel mill. 20. The Electro Steel Corporation. 21. *Chaplin* (1992). 22. Metal bolts. 23. The sheriff. 24. A loaf of bread. 25. *The Bohemian Girl.*

Quiz No. 82: Giant

1. *The Mirror Crack'd* (1980). 2. He pulled out his penis and urinated. "I'm a method actor," Dean would say later. "I figured if I could piss in front of those two thousand people, man, and I could be cool, I could do just anything, anything at all." 3. Jordan. 4. *Somebody Up There Likes Me* (1956). 5. Nick Adams. 6. In a scene in which Jett Rink visits the Benedicts and fixes himself a drink, Dean had suggested that Rink pour the liquor from his own flask rather than drink the Benedicts'. 7. Jetexas. 8. Juana. 9. Hang Bick. 10. Alan Ladd. 11. The scene in which Bick arrives in Virginia to take his wife home. 12. James Dean, who died on September 30, 1955, in an automobile accident. 13. Grace Kelly. 14. Texas. 15. Glenn McCarthy. 16. Forty-four days. 17. Marfa, Texas. 18. Appeared in a Western. 19. He wants to be a doctor. 20. A meager (in comparison) fifteen hundred dol-

lars per week. 21. Actress Elizabeth Taylor discovered that she was pregnant. 22. Audrey Hepburn. 23. Sarge's Place. 24. Marcus. 25. Dennis Hopper.

Quiz No. 83: Platoon

1. Sidney Lumet. 2. Innocence. 3. Hell. 4. Forrest Whitaker. 5. *Wall Street* (1987). 6. *Salvador* (1986). 7. Barnes and Elias. 8. Chris Taylor. 9. Three. 10. First Assistant Director H. Gordon Boos. 11. *Born on the Fourth of July* (1989) and *Heaven & Earth* (1993). 12. *Letters Home from Vietnam* (1987) and *Born on the Fourth of July* (1989). 13. "Go around a village cuttin' off heads." 14. The next person who falls asleep during guard duty. 15. Director Oliver Stone. 16. *Apocalypse Now* (1979). 17. The world will turn. 18. Himself. 19. Johnny Depp. 20. Kyle MacLachlan. 21. He is killed and hung on a tree. 22. That the new guy's life isn't worth as much because he hasn't put his time in yet. 23. Chris Taylor. 24. He stabs himself. 25. "He thinks he's George Freakin' Washington!"

Quiz No. 84: Fargo

1. Director Joel Coen. 2. *Mystery Train* (1989). 3. Shep Proudfoot. 4. "Eat a breakfast." 5. *The Big Lebowski* and *Armageddon*. 6. *How to Talk Minnesotan* (1987). 7. Jose Feliciano. 8. *The Tonight Show*. 9. Drink milkshakes. 10. Director Joel Coen and screenwriter Ethan Coen. 11. As spring was approaching, the snow kept melting. 12. The International House of Pancakes. 13. *The Shawshank Redemption* (1994). 14. *Blood Simple* (1984). 15. Bruce Campbell. 16. *High and Low* (1963). 17. *Barton Fink* (1991) and *The Hudsucker Proxy* (1994). (The duo won for *Barton Fink*.) 18. $320,000. 19. Stan Grossman. 20. Ecklund and Swedlin's. 21. Nobody's; despite the film's claim to the contrary, this is not a true story. 22. Hooker Number 1. 23. J3L2404. 24. Bill Deal. 25. *A Clockwork Orange* (1971).

Quiz No. 85: Duck Soup

1. Italy. 2. Chicolini. 3. "He gets mad because he can't read." 4. Pinkie. 5. Director Leo McCarey. 6. *The Love Parade*. 7. He shortens their lunch hour to twenty minutes. 8. Because he's already paid a month's rent on the battlefield. 9. "Change the name of your town. It's hurting our picture." 10. Clamping devices that were used on the first atomic bombs.

11. Zero. 12. One. 13. They didn't show up. 14. Mata Hari. 15. Zero. 16. A Union soldier's uniform, a Confederate soldier's uniform, a Boy Scout troop leader's uniform, a Revolutionary War British general's uniform, and a Davey Crockett outfit. 17. To save money on chairs. 18. The stove. 19. She is pelted with fruits and vegetables. 20. Gummo Marx. 21. His dog. 22. On the Fireflys. 23. The Balkan State of Freedonia. 24. Twelve dollars. 25. *The Cocoanuts* (1929) and *Animal Crackers* (1930).

Quiz No. 86: Mutiny on the Bounty

1. Cary Grant. 2. Laughton had it made by the same tailor shop where Bligh had his uniforms made. 3. He was hanged. 4. Their captain, their judge, and their jury. 5. Glenn drowned when a barge carrying fifty-five crew members capsized while filming exterior scenes. 6. *Mutiny on the Bunny*. 7. The law of fear. 8. Their hearts. 9. He is keel-hauled. 10. This was the last time Gable appeared on-screen without his trademark mustache. 11. *In the Wake of the Bounty* (1933). 12. Victor McLaglen for *The Informer* (1935). 13. Dr. Bacchus. 14. Tahani. 15. James Cagney. 16. His name. 17. The *Pandora*. 18. Marlon Brando. 19. A snake. 20. He was seasick. 21. Timor. 22. A midshipman. 23. Three. 24. Anthony Hopkins. 25. *Forever and a Day* (1943).

Quiz No. 87: Frankenstein

1. *Bride of Frankenstein* (1935). 2. "Now I know what it feels like to be God!" 3. Heaven. 4. Vincent Price. 5. Charles Ogle. 6. A statue of the Grim Reaper. 7. To create life. 8. Evil. 9. Preview audiences were unhappy with the original ending, in which the film closed with a long shot of the burning mill. Thus, a happy ending was attached. 10. *Frankenstein 1970*. 11. God. 12. The burgomaster. 13. Heaven. 14. The monster is alive. 15. *Frankenstein Meets the Wolf Man*. 16. The monster strangles him, and then impales him. 17. Fire. 18. The records of his experiments. 19. Robert Florey. 20. *Young Frankenstein*. 21. Abnormal brain. 22. His sanity. 23. Henry. 24. Goldstadt Medical College. 25. *House of Dracula* (1945).

Quiz No. 88: Easy Rider

1. *Love and a .45*. 2. *The Last Movie* (1971). 3. "The Pusher." 4. Animal Teeth. 5. *The Trip* (1967). 6. *Biker Heaven*. 7. Nowhere; "A man went looking for America and couldn't find it anywhere." 8. Parading without a per-

mit. 9. Pisces. 10. *Motorcycles: Born to Be Wild.* 11. Hopper claimed that Torn pulled a knife on him. However, Torn and several witnesses say Hopper pulled the knife on Torn. Shortly after Hopper made the statement, he was sued by Torn in two separate lawsuits and ordered to pay approximately $950,000 in damages. 12. A handful of mud. 13. Porky Pig. 14. *Head.* 15. Rock producer Phil Spector. 16. He's a lawyer. 17. Country witticisms. 18. Forty. 19. Yul Brenner. 20. Toni Basil. 21. *Rebel Without a Cause* (1955), *Giant* (1956), *Easy Rider* (1969), and *Apocalypse Now* (1979). 22. Venus. 23. A women's cell. 24. A Mardi Gras queen. 25. *The Magic Christian.*

Quiz No. 89: Patton

1. The day of his funeral. 2. Because he loves it. 3. *A Soldier's Story* by Omar Bradley (1951) and *Patton: Ordeal in Triumph* by Ladislas Farago (1970). 4. Omar Bradley. 5. *The Hanging Tree* (1959). 6. Willie, his dog. 7. Because he did not feel that he was in competition with other actors and felt the award served no purpose. 8. *The Last Days of Patton.* 9. Give them each a medal. 10. All scenes featuring the Nazis. 11. Self-inflicted wounds. 12. "The worst of everything." 13. *Patton: Salute to a Rebel.* 14. A bordello. 15. "Every goddamn day." 16. Because Zanuck left the studio. 17. Spain. 18. The Bible and Hollywood. 19. Palermo, Italy. 20. A pimp from a cheap New Orleans whorehouse. 21. Pacifists. 22. Because actor George C. Scott disagreed with using Patton's speech as the film's intro. Therefore, the only way the producers could convince Scott to do the scene was by telling him it would appear at the end of the film. 23. Laughed. 24. Dying for his country. 25. By the last bullet of the last battle of the last war.

Quiz No. 90: The Jazz Singer

1. The role of Al Jolson in *The Jolson Story* (1946). "He sang every song as if he were going to drop dead at the end of it," Parks remembers. 2. Danny Thomas. 3. *Day of Atonement.* 4. A cantor. 5. *Mammy* (1930). 6. In Salt Lake City. 7. Yussel Rabinowitz. 8. Sam Warner, who had overseen the film, died of a sinus infection the night before. Rather than attend the premiere, his brothers headed back east for his funeral. 9. $250. 10. *The Singing Fool* (1928). 11. Vitaphone. 12. Run away. 13. Cantor Rosenblatt. 14. Eddie Cantor and George Jessel, who originated the role on

Broadway. 15. GI Jolson. 16. "My Gal Sal." 17. Jack Robin. 18. Neil Diamond. 19. A tear. 20. Myrna Loy. 21. Expression. 22. "Ragtime" Jakie. 23. Sara. 24. "Dirty Hands, Dirty Face." 25. *The Beloved Rogue, When a Man Loves,* and *Old San Francisco.*

Quiz No. 91: My Fair Lady

1. Marni Nixon. 2. Marni Nixon. 3. Shakespeare, Milton, and the Bible. 4. Higgins's home. 5. Wendy Hiller. 6. Because he cannot afford them. 7. In Spain. 8. They pronounce it properly. 9. A birdcage and a Chinese fan. 10. Henry Daniell. 11. The cast and crew were informed that President John F. Kennedy had been assassinated. 12. Sell flowers. 13. A temptation. 14. Influenza. 15. *Paris—When It Sizzles.* 16. Keats and Milton. 17. He is executed. 18. The Spanish Inquisition. 19. Alfred Doolittle. 20. *An American in Paris* (1951). 21. Bill Shirley. 22. A damned nuisance. 23. "Why Can't the English Learn to Speak?" 24. Lisson Grove. 25. Julie Andrews.

Quiz No. 92: A Place in the Sun

1. Sergei Einstein. 2. His uncle's business card. 3. Because she can't swim. 4. Mrs. Roberts. 5. Ivan Moffat. 6. Earl Eastman. 7. "The second happiest." 8. Mrs. Hamilton. 9. Friday, September 1. 10. Montgomery Clift. After Clift wrecked into a tree near Taylor's house, she discovered the wreckage beside the road. When Taylor found him, Clift was choking on his own broken teeth. She cleared his airway and sent for help. 11. Bathing suits. 12. That he's an Eastman. 13. Her parents. 14. A picture of them appears in the Society section of the newspaper. 15. *Red River* (1948). 16. *Now and Forever* (1934). 17. VICKERS. 18. This was prohibited by the Hays Code. 19. Dr. Wyeland. 20. *The Diary of Anne Frank* (1959). 21. The Internal Revenue Service. 22. HOW LONG SINCE YOU'VE WRITTEN YOUR MOTHER? 23. Thirty-five dollars. 24. Hitch-hiking. 25. *The Only Game in Town.*

Quiz No. 93: The Apartment

1. A *mensch.* 2. Consolidated Life of New York. 3. Wednesday. 4. In the knee. 5. *Some Like It Hot* (1959), *Irma la Douce* (1963), *The Fortune Cookie* (1966), *Avanti!* (1972), *The Front Page* (1974), and *Buddy Buddy* (1981).

6. Thirty seconds. 7. That she cannot spell and that she will hate herself for having written it. 8. Housekeeping. 9. Miss Olsen. 10. The Marx Brothers. 11. "Yeah, it's me." 12. Natchez. 13. $94.70. 14. The executive washroom. 15. *Brief Encounter* (1946). 16. *The Crowd.* 17. Mr. Dobisch. 18. Because she installed an air conditioner. 19. The nineteenth floor. 20. *Irma la Douce.* 21. Mascara. 22. Ordinary Policy Department. 23. "NOT TOO LOUD! THE NEIGHBORS ARE COMPLAINING." 24. The cracked mirror in her compact. 25. *Schindler's List* (1993).

Quiz No. 94: GoodFellas

1. *Wise Guy* (1985). 2. John Gotti. 3. Scorsese feared that *Wise Guy* would be too similar to Brian De Palma's comedy *Wise Guys* (1986), and the television series *Wiseguy,* confusing viewers. 4. "The good half." 5. Jimmy "the Gent." 6. *Jules et Jim* (1961). 7. *Double Indemnity* (1944) and *The African Queen* (1951). 8. Stacks Edwards. 9. Janice Rossi. 10. Billy Batts. 11. Sammy Davis, Jr. 12. Rats. 13. Sonny's Bamboo Lounge. 14. A one-hundred-dollar bill. 15. "Never rat on your friends, and always keep your mouth shut." 16. Handguns. 17. Seven. 18. He "wasted eight fucking aprons" to assist a wounded man. 19. For keeping the ice cubes cold. 20. He believes Vinnie uses too many onions. 21. A mink coat for his wife. 22. His mother. 23. She calls from the house. 24. "Roses Are Red." 25. Michael Imperioli.

Quiz No. 95: Pulp Fiction

1. *Pandemonium Reigns.* 2. *Psycho* (1960). 3. Red Apple Cigarettes. 4. The monologue appeared in Tarantino's original draft of *From Dusk Till Dawn* (1995). 5. 6-6-6. 6. The monologue was originally performed by Chiba in *The Bodyguard* (1974). 7. Divine intervention. 8. Tarantino claims that the two characters are brothers. However, this would seem to be an afterthought as Tarantino first attempted to cast Madsen to portray Vincent Vega. 9. Sarah Kelly. 10. *Modesty Blaise* (1965). 11. *Black Mask.* 12. Esmerelda of the Wolves. 13. Tarantino wanted to cover an ugly scar on the back of actor Ving Rhames's head. 14. A medical textbook. 15. Five dollars. 16. Steve Buscemi. 17. Jayne Mansfield. 18. *Neon Jungle.* 19. Knives. 20. In the throat. 21. The scene appears in very early drafts of *True Romance* (1993). 22. Blueberry pancakes with maple syrup. 23. Big Kahuna Burger. 24. "Bad Motherfucker." 25. The character Kane from *Kung Fu.*

Quiz No. 96: The Searchers

1. Actor John Wayne's son, Patrick Wayne. 2. 1868. 3. "[A] Texican is nothing but a human man way out on a limb." 4. Because he found Lucy's dead body. 5. The Bible. 6. A Texas Ranger captain. 7. He loses her first romantically to his brother and later to Chief Scar. 8. "Shall We Gather at the River." 9. According to Ethan, the Comanches believe that a dead man without eyes cannot enter the "spirit land" and is forced to "wander forever between the winds." 10. "That'll be the day." 11. *High Lonesome* (1950). 12. Bond and Wayne were good friends. On a hunting trip, Wayne accidentally shot Bond. Although Bond recovered from this, he never allowed Wayne to live it down—even after his death. 13. *The Wings of Eagles* (1957). 14. Five. 15. Ken Curtis. 16. To prevent the Comanches from eating. 17. John Ethan Wayne. 18. Because it's "blood money." 19. Look. 20. *Reap the Wild Wind* (1942). 21. One thousand dollars. 22. "A bunch of dead man's clothes to wear." 23. Wayne appeared in 142 leading roles. 24. The University of Southern California. 25. *The Conqueror*.

Quiz No. 97: Bringing Up Baby

1. *What's Up, Doc?* 2. The eighteenth hole. 3. Harold Lloyd. 4. *The Awful Truth,* which also stars Cary Grant. 5. Baby is three years old. 6. "Crazy." 7. The skeletal brontosaurus David is restoring at the museum. 8. Grant and his canine costar first appeared together in *The Awful Truth* (1938). 9. "Don't let it throw ya." 10. Walter Catlett. 11. When Susan rips out the back of her dress, David covers her exposed derriere with his hat. She asks, "What are you doing?" He answers smugly, "Oh, I feel a perfect ass." 12. Grant's character asks, "What happened to the bone?" Hepburn's reply was scripted, "It's in the box." 13. He was concerned that all the characters were off-center. "There were *no* normal people in it," he observed. 14. Conflict. 15. Boopie. 16. Alice Swallow. 17. Brazil. 18. "Finish my brontosaurus and get married at three o' clock." 19. She says its fun—"just like a game." 20. A loon. 21. "I Can't Give You Anything But Love, Baby." 22. A rock. 23. "Nothing. I just thought it was funny." 24. Ward Bond. 25. *Carefree*.

Quiz No. 98: Unforgiven

1. Sergio Leone and Don Siegel. 2. Claudia. 3. Alice. 4. THIS IS WHAT HAPPENS TO ASSASSINS AROUND HERE. 5. "Clear out through the back door."

6. Boston. 7. Five ponies. 8. Pete Sothow. 9. They're feverish. 10. *Absolute Power* (1997). 11. *A Perfect World.* 12. Because he carries a Schofield-model Smith and Wesson pistol. 13. "Yeah." 14. He urinates on himself. 15. The Bar-T. 16. Because of the size of his penis. 17. "*The Duck of Death.*" 18. "I'll fart on them." 19. English Bob. 20. He "busted his leg with a shovel." 21. Little Bill. 22. The carrying of firearms. 23. Sally Two Trees. 24. "Killin' folks." 25. *Star in the Dust* (1956).

Quiz No. 99: Guess Who's Coming to Dinner

1. Jacqueline Fontaine. 2. Hillary's. 3. Matilda "Tilly" Binks. 4. Monsignor Ryan. 5. He was intimidated by his legendary costars, Spencer Tracy and Katharine Hepburn. Several scenes were filmed with Poitier actually saying his lines to empty chairs. 6. Wade. 7. *Common Reader.* 8. They were killed in a train wreck. 9. Edie. 10. He died. 11. Twenty minutes. 12. Franklin Delano Roosevelt. 13. Los Angeles. 14. His own principles. 15. Because no one would believe him. 16. Happy. 17. Two. 18. President of the United States. 19. Judy. 20. Five thousand dollars. 21. Joanna. 22. "We Can Work It Out." 23. He is a lawyer. 24. Fresh Oregon Boisenberry Sherbet. 25. His objections to John and Joanna's plans to marry.

Quiz No. 100: Yankee Doodle Dandy

1. President Franklin Delano Roosevelt had just declared war against Germany and Japan. 2. *The Seven Little Foys.* 3. *Casablanca* (1942), for which he won the Oscar. 4. Actor James Cagney's sister, Jeanne Cagney. 5. Sam H. Harris. 6. Three: *The Maltese Falcon* (1941), *Yankee Doodle Dandy*, and *The Treasure of the Sierra Madre* (1948). 7. Anything wrong. 8. Teddy Roosevelt. 9. Michael. 10. Don Siegel. 11. Independence Day. 12. Josie Cohan. 13. Fred Astaire. 14. "Songs, dances, and a lot of girls." 15. Robinson's Theatre. 16. Virginia. 17. *Little Johnny Jones!* 18. *Wildfire.* 19. The Four Cohans sans George. 20. New Rochelle, New York. 21. He's too old. 22. George M. Cohan. 23. *Forty-five Minutes from Broadway.* 24. *The Mayor of Hell* (1933), *Jimmy the Gent* (1934), *Angels with Dirty Faces* (1938), and *Captains of the Clouds* (1942). 25. "Mary."

Quiz No. 101: Master Quiz: General Knowledge

1. *Singin' in the Rain* (1952). 2. Steven Spielberg directed five films on the AFI Top 100 list. These are *Jaws* (1975), *Close Encounters of the Third Kind* (1977), *Raiders of the Lost Ark* (1981), *E.T. The Extra-Terrestrial* (1982), and *Schindler's List* (1993). 3. Ward Bond appears in *It Happened One Night* (1934), *Bringing Up Baby* (1938), *Gone with the Wind* (1939), *The Grapes of Wrath* (1940), *The Maltese Falcon* (1941), *It's a Wonderful Life* (1946), and *The Searchers* (1956). 4. Wagner's "Ride of the Valkyries". 5. Silver of *The Lone Ranger*. 6. Six: *Casablanca* (1942), *The Godfather* (1972), *Gone with the Wind* (1939), *Lawrence of Arabia* (1962), *On the Waterfront* (1954), and *Schindler's List* (1993). 7. The longest film ever made at the time it was released, *Gone with the Wind*'s running time is 222 minutes. 8. Director William Wyler's. 9. Jean Arthur. 10. Adriana Caselotti. 11. *Florence of Arabia*. 12. Composer Bernard Herrmann. 13. *The Scarlett O'Hara War*. 14. *Journey Beyond the Stars*. 15. Eight. 16. In the scenes featuring the rusty Tin Woodsman, he didn't *look* rusty, so the filmmakers decided to redo them. 17. Bob Hope. 18. To pay for his wife's cataract surgery. 19. False; this label was applied to *Snow White and the Seven Dwarfs* (1937). 20. *To Kill a Mockingbird* (1962), *M*A*S*H* (1970), *The Godfather* (1972), *The Godfather Part II* (1974), *Network* (1976), and *Apocalypse Now* (1979). 21. he played a boardinghouse neighbor in *The Graduate* (1967). 22. Anthony Mann. 23. Thursday. 24. Voight didn't recognize him. 25. H. C. Potter.

Quiz No. 102: Master Quiz: Taglines

1. *It Happened One Night* (1934). 2. *The Graduate* (1967). 3. *Some Like It Hot* (1959). 4. *Mutiny on the Bounty* (1935). 5. *Stagecoach* (1939). 6. *Dances With Wolves* (1990). 7. *American Graffiti* (1973). 8. *Taxi Driver* (1976). 9. *The Manchurian Candidate* (1962). 10. *Rocky* (1976). 11. *Giant* (1956). 12. *The African Queen* (1951). 13. *2001: A Space Odyssey* (1968). 14. *It's a Wonderful Life* (1946). 15. *A Place in the Sun* (1951). 16. *All About Eve* (1950). 17. *The Apartment* (1960). 18. *Bonnie and Clyde* (1967). 19. *Annie Hall* (1977). 20. *A Clockwork Orange* (1971). 21. *Network* (1976). 22. *Psycho* (1960). 23. *Fargo* (1996). 24. *E.T. The Extra-Terrestrial* (1982). 25. *Sunset Boulevard* (1950).

Quiz No. 103: Master Quiz: Quotes

1. *King Kong* (1933). 2. *The Wild Bunch* (1969). 3. *Butch Cassidy and the Sundance Kid* (1969). 4. *Pulp Fiction* (1994). 5. *The Deer Hunter* (1978). 6. *The Maltese Falcon* (1941). 7. *Tootsie* (1982). 8. *The Silence of the Lambs* (1991). 9. *Rebel Without a Cause* (1955). 10. *The Godfather* (1972). 11. *Jaws* (1975). 12. *Raiders of the Lost Ark* (1981). 13. *It's a Wonderful Life* (1946). 14. *Double Indemnity* (1944). 15. *Apocalypse Now* (1979). 16. *Annie Hall* (1977). 17. *Gone with the Wind* (1939). 18. *M*A*S*H* (1970). 19. *Duck Soup* (1933). 20. *Casablanca* (1942). 21. *The French Connection* (1971). 22. *Some Like It Hot* (1959). 23. *Fargo* (1996). 24. *One Flew Over the Cuckoo's Nest* (1975). 25. *Bringing Up Baby* (1938).

Quiz No. 104: Master Quiz: Name the Film

1. *Giant* (1956). 2. *E.T. The Extra-Terrestrial* (1982). 3. *Taxi Driver* (1976). 4. *Unforgiven* (1992). 5. *M*A*S*H* (1970). 6. *Pulp Fiction* (1994). 7. *The Philadelphia Story* (1940). 8. *Shane* (1953). 9. *Tootsie* (1982). 10. *Annie Hall* (1977). 11. *Ben-Hur* (1959). 12. *West Side Story* (1961). 13. *The French Connection* (1971). 14. *It's a Wonderful Life* (1946). 15. *Psycho* (1960). 16. *Butch Cassidy and the Sundance Kid* (1969). 17. *Jaws* (1975). 18. *High Noon* (1952). 19. *Bringing Up Baby* (1938). 20. *Some Like It Hot* (1959). 21. *The Silence of the Lambs* (1991). 22. *Fargo* (1996). 23. *Sunset Boulevard* (1950). 24. *Stagecoach* (1939). 25. *Wuthering Heights* (1939).

Quiz No. 105: Master Quiz: The Directors and Screenwriters

1. Joseph L. Mankiewicz. 2. Robert Towne. 3. George Cukor. 4. Steven Spielberg. 5. John Frankenheimer. 6. Robert Wise. 7. John Huston. 8. Raoul Walsh. 9. George Stevens. 10. David Lean. 11. Waldo Salt. 12. I.A.L. Diamond. 13. Dennis Hopper. 14. John Milius. 15. Orson Welles. 16. Terry Southern. 17. William Wyler. 18. Gore Vidal. 19. Francis Ford Coppola. 20. Roger Corman. 21. Melissa Mathison. 22. Paul Schrader. 23. Fred Zinneman. 24. Stanley Kramer. 25. Milos Forman.

Bibliography

Print Materials

Alexander, Paul, *Boulevard of Broken Dreams: The Life, Times, and Legend of James Dean,* Penguin Books, 1994.

Amburn, Ellis, *The Most Beautiful Woman in the World: The Obsessions, Passions, and Courage of Elizabeth Taylor,* HarperCollins Publishers, 2000.

Baer, William, "*North by Northwest*: Interview with Ernest Lehman," *Creative Screenwriting,* November/December 2000.

———, "*American Graffiti*: An Interview with Gloria Katz and Willard Hyuck," *Creative Screenwriting,* January/February 1999.

———, "*Psycho*: An Interview with Joseph Stefano," *Creative Screenwriting,* September/October 1998.

Barnes, Alan, and Marcus Hearn, *Tarantino: A to Zed,* BPC Consumer Books, 1996.

Bauer, Erik, "Don't Tread on Me: An Interview with John Milius," *Creative Screenwriting,* March/April 2000.

Bauer, Erik, "Ten Years, Ten Films: Interview with Oliver Stone," *Creative Screenwriting,* Fall 1996.

Benedetto, Robert, "The Two *Chinatowns*: Towne's Screenplay versus Polanski's Film," *Creative Screenwriting,* November/December 1999.

Bernard, Jami, *Quentin Tarantino: The Man and His Movies,* Simon & Schuster, 1995..

Bjorkman, Stig, *Woody Allen on Woody Allen,* Grove Press, 1993.

Bogdanovich, Peter, *Who the Devil Made It?,* Ivy Moon Company, 1997.

Brennan, Mary, "Interview: John Schlesinger," *Mr. Showbiz,* 1996.

Brode, Douglas, *The Films of Robert De Niro,* Citadel Press, 1993.

Brunette, Peter, *Martin Scorsese Interviews,* University Press of Mississippi, 1999.

Burr, Ty, *Entertainment Weekly: The 100 Greatest Movies of All Time,* Time Inc. Home Entertainment, 2000.

Capra, Frank, *The Name Above the Title,* The Macmillan Company, 1954.

Carr, Charmaine, *Forever Liesl: A Memoir of The Sound of Music,* Viking-Penguin, 2000.

Chaplin, Charles, *My Autobiography,* Simon & Schuster, Inc., 1964.

Chaplin, Jr., Charles, *My Father, Charlie Chaplin,* Random House, Inc., 1964.

Clarke, Gerald, *Get Happy: The Life of Judy Garland,* Random House, 2000.

Clarkson, Wensley, *Quentin Tarantino: Shooting from the Hip,* The Overlook Press, 1995.

Culhane, John, *Fantasia,* Harry N. Abrams, Inc., 1983.

Dalton, Mary, and Steve Jarrett, "*Platoon*: The Fiction of History," *Creative Screenwriting,* Fall 1996.

Davis, Bette, *This 'N That,* G. P. Putnam's Sons, 1987.

Dawson, Jeff, *Quentin Tarantino: The Cinema of Cool,* Applause Books, 1995.

DeMille, Cecil B., *Autobiography,* Prentice-Hall, 1959.

Desmond, John, "A Good Joke Retold: John Huston's Adaptation of B. Traven's *The Treasure of the Sierra Madre,*" *Creative Screenwriting,* January/February 1999.

De Vries, Hillary, David Hiltbrand, Damian Holbrook, Michael Scheinfeld, and Ray Stackhouse, "The 50 Greatest Movie Moments of All Time," *TV Guide,* March 24–30 2001.

Divine, Christian, "Keeping the Flow: An Interview with David and Janet Peoples," *Creative Screenwriting,* November/December 1998.

Dougan, Andy, *Martin Scorsese: Close Up,* Thunder's Mouth Press, 1997.

———, *Untouchable: A Biography of Robert De Niro,* Thunder's Mouth Press, 1996.

Edwards Anne, *Vivien Leigh: A Biography,* Simon & Schuster, Inc., 1977.

Edwards, Colin, "Between the Bolts: A Found Interview with Boris Karloff," *Monster Scene,* March 1995.

Emery, Robert J., *The Directors: Take One,* Media Entertainment, Inc., 1999.

Fine, Marshall, *Harvey Keitel: The Art of Darkness,* Fromm International, 1997.

Fleming, Robert, "BookPage Mario Puzo Interview," *Bookpage,* 1996.

Garceau, Jean, and Inez Cocke, *Dear Mr. G: The Biography of Clark Gable,* Little, Brown, and Company, 1961.

Gish, Lillian, *The Movies, Mr. Griffith, and Me,* Prentice-Hall, Inc., 1969.

Gore, Chris, *The Fifty Greatest Movies Never Made,* St. Martin's Press, 1999.

Haun, Harry, *The Cinematic Century,* Applause Books, 2000.

Hepburn, Katharine, *Me: Stories of My Life,* Ballantine Books, 1991.

Heston, Charlton, *In the Arena: An Autobiography,* Simon & Schuster, Inc., 1995.

Heymann, C. David, *Liz,* Birch Lane Press, 1995.

Higham, Charles, *Bette,* Macmillan Publishing Co., Inc., 1981.

Hinson, Hal, "*The Manchurian Candidate,*" *The Washington Post,* Februrary 13, 1988.

Huff, Theodore, *Charlie Chaplin,* Henry Schuman, Inc., 1951.

Hutchinson, Tom, *Rod Steiger,* Fromm International Publishing Corporation, 1998.

Kanfer, Stefan, *Groucho: The Life and Times of Julius Henry Marx,* Alfred A. Knopf, 2000.

Kapsis, Robert E. and Kathie Coblentz, *Clint Eastwood Interviews,* University Press of Mississippi, 1999.

Karney, Robyn, *Chronicle of the Cinema,* Dorling Kindersley Limited, 1995.

Kelly, Mary Pat, *Martin Scorsese: A Journey,* Thunder's Mouth Press, 1991.

Lardner, Jr., Ring, *I'd Hate Myself in the Morning: A Memoir,* Thunder's Mouth Press, 2000.

Leaming, Barbara, *Marilyn Monroe,* Three Rivers Press, 1998.

Levine, Josh, *The Coen Brothers,* ECW Press, 2000.

Lobranno, Alexander, "Catching Up with the Players," *TV Guide,* December 23–29, 2000.

Maltin, Leonard, *Leonard Maltin's Movie and Video Guide,* New American Library, 1998.

———, *Leonard Maltin's Movie Encyclopedia,* New American Library, 1994.

Manvell, Roger, *Chaplin,* Little, Brown, and Company, 1974.

McGilligan, Patrick, *Film Crazy: Interviews With Hollywood Legends,* St. Martin's Press, 2000.

McGilligan, Patrick, *Jack's Life: A Biography of Jack Nicholson,* W. W. Norton & Company, Inc., 1994.

Menendez, Francisco, "Coppola's Transformation of *Apocalypse Now,*" *Creative Screenwriting,* March/April 2000.

Morris, Gary, "An Interview With Sylvia Miles," *Bright Lights Film Journal,* April 1996.

Nashawaty, Chris, "Oscar Goes Cuckoo," *Entertainment Weekly,* February 23, 2001.

Peary, Danny, *Cult Movies,* Random House Value Publishing, Inc., 1998.

Peary, Gerald, *Quentin Tarantino Interviews,* University Press of Mississippi, 1998.

Phillips, Julia, *You'll Never Eat Lunch in This Town Again,* Random House Inc., 1991.

Poitier, Sidney, *The Measure of a Man: A Spiritual Autobiography,* HarperCollins Publishers, 2000.

———, *This Life,* Alfred A. Knopf, Inc., 1980.

Quirk, Lawrence J., *Paul Newman,* Taylor Publishing Company, 1996.

Roberts, Randy and James S. Olson, *John Wayne: American,* Simon & Schuster Inc., 1995.

Schickel, Richard, *The Men Who Made the Movies,* The Educational Broadcasting Corporation, 1975.

Schirmer, Mary J., "*Dances With Wolves*: An Interview with Michael Blake," *Creative Screenwriting,* Fall 1996.

Silver, Alain and James Ursini, *David Lean and His Films,* Silman-James Press, 1974.

Silverman, Stephen M., *David Lean,* Harry N. Abrams, Inc., 1992.

Singer, Kurt, *The Laughton Story,* The John C. Winston Company, 1954.

Singer, Michael, *A Cut Above: Fifty Film Directors Talk About Their Craft,* Lone Eagle, 1998.

Spaugh, Terry, "*The Silence of the Lambs*: An Interview with Ted Tally," *Creative Screenwriting,* September/October 1998.

Spignesi, Stephen J., *The Official Gone with the Wind Companion,* Penguin Books, 1993.

———, *The Woody Allen Companion,* Andrews & McMeel, 1992.

Spoto, Donald, *Rebel: The Life and Legend of James Dean,* Cooper Square Press, 1996.

Stein, Eliot, "Howard Koch, Julius Epstein, Frank Miller Interview," Stein Online, May 1995.

Stern, Lesley, *The Scorsese Connection,* British Film Institute, 1995.

Sullivan, Robert, *Remembering Sinatra,* Time Inc., 1998.

Taylor, Elizabeth, *Elizabeth Taylor,* Harper & Row, 1964.

Thompson, David, *Rosebud: The Story of Orson Welles,* Alfred A. Knopf, Inc., 1996.

Thompson, David, and Ian Christie, *Scorsese on Scorsese,* Faber and Faber Limited, 1989.

Truffaut, Francois, *Hitchcock/Truffaut,* Editions Ramsay, 1983.

Variety, The Editors of, *The Variety Portable Movie Guide,* Berkley Boulevard Books, 2000.

Victor, Adam, *The Marilyn Encyclopedia,* The Overlook Press, 1999.

Walker, Alexander, *Bette Davis,* Conundrum Ltd., 1986.

———, *Audrey: Her Real Story,* St. Martin's Press, 1994.

Welles, Orson and Peter Bogdanovich, *This Is Orson Welles,* Da Capo Press, 1992.

Wilson, Earl, *Sinatra,* Macmillan Publishing Co., Inc., 1976.

Woods, Paul A., *King Pulp: The Wild World of Quentin Tarantino,* Thunder's Mouth Press, 1996.

———, *Quentin Tarantino: The Film Geek Files,* Plexus Publishing Limited, 2000.

Web Sites

Actor's Bone: *Birth of a Nation*
<http://www.actorsbone.com/Movies/TopFilms/BirthofaNation.htm>

An American in Paris: Interview
<http://www.rhino.com/features/liners/71961lin.html>

Animation History: *Snow White and the Seven Dwarfs*
<http://animationhistory.com/snowwhite/>

David Lean: An Online Guide to References and Resources
<http://www.davidlean.com>

Film Site
<http://www.filmsite.com>

The *Godfather* Trilogy: A Web site You Can't Refuse
<http://www.jgeoff.com/godfather.html>

Hidden Mickeys
<http://www.hiddenmickeys.org.>

The Internet Movie Database
<http://www.imdb.com>

Joan Leslie Page
<http://www.picturegoer.com>

Olivier
<http://www.murphsplace.com/olivier/main.html>

The Original *Midnight Cowboy* Homepage
<http://www.geocities.com/BourbonStreet/Bayou/3385/MidnightCowboy.html>

Reel Classics
<http://www.reelclassics.com>

Reexamining *The Birth of a Nation*
<http://www.mdle.com/ClassicFilms/FeaturedVideo/birth.htm>

The Robert Altman Appreciation Page
<http://www.geocities.com/Hollywood/Set/4815/>

Turner Classic Movies
<http://www.turnerclassicmovies.com>

The Ultimate Frankenstein Site
<http://meineseite.i-one.at/frankenstein/frankenstein-frames.htm>

The Ultra Fab Official Homepage of Terry Southern
<http://www.terrysouthern.com/>

West Side Story Web site
<http://www.geocities.com/Broadway/4243/west-side-story.html>

Documentaries

Bouzereau, Laurent, *The Making of* Jaws, Universal Pictures, 1995.

Bouzereau, Laurent, *The Making of* American Graffiti, Universal Pictures, 1998.

Bouzereau, Laurent, *The Making of* Close Encounters of the Third Kind, Columbia Pictures, 1998.

Coppola, Francis Ford, *The Destruction of the Kurtz Compound* (with director's commentary), Paramount Pictures, 1998.

Epstein, Michael and Thomas Lennon, *The Battle Over* Citizen Kane, Lennon Documentary Group/PBS, 1996.

Haley, Jr., Jack, *The Wonderful Wizard of Oz: The Making of a Movie Classic,* Metro-Goldwyn-Mayer, 1999.

Hickenlooper, George, *Hearts of Darkness: A Filmmaker's Apocalypse,* Paramount, 1991.

Meer, Van der, *Giant Stars Off to Texas,* Warner Bros., 1956.

———, *The* Giant *Premiere,* Warner Bros., 1956.

———, "History versus Hollywood: *Butch Cassidy and the Sundance Kid,*" The History Channel, 2000.

———, "History versus Hollywood: *The French Connection,*" The History Channel, 2000.

———, "History versus Hollywood: *Patton,*" The History Channel, 2000.

———, *The Making of* Giant, Warner Bros., 1956.

———, *Reflections on* Citizen Kane, 1991.

Original Interviews Conducted by Author

Avary, Roger, 1999. (Conducted in Avary's home.)

Corman, Roger, 1999. (Conducted in Corman's office.)

Henry, Buck, 2000. (Conducted via telephone.)

Hickenlooper, George, 2000. (Conducted via telephone.)

Kelly, Sarah, 1999. (Conducted via telephone.)

Milius, John, 1999. (Conducted in Milius's office.)

Towne, Robert, 2000. (Conducted via telephone.)

Zaillian, Steven, 2000. (Written correspondence interview.)

About the Author

Andrew J. Rausch is a freelance writer and film critic whose articles, essays, reviews, and celebrity interviews have appeared in numerous publications, including *Film Threat, Ain't It Cool News, Bright Lights Film Journal, Shock Cinema, Micro-Film, The Joe Bob Briggs Report, Creative Screenwriting,* and *Images: A Journal of Film and Popular Culture. The 100 Greatest American Films: A Quiz Book* is his first book. He resides in Parsons, Kansas, with his wife, Mary, their three daughters, Jordan, Jaiden, and Jalyn, and their two pets—a dog named Kesey (after novelist Ken Kesey) and a cat named Tyger (after Stephen King's short story, "Here There Be Tygers").

Jami Bernard (foreword) is a film critic for *The New York Daily News* and is the author of *First Films: Illustrious, Obscure and Embarrassing Movie Debuts, Total Exposure: The Movie Buff's Guide to Hollywood Nude Scenes, Chick Flicks: A Movie Lover's Guide to the Movies Women Love,* and *Quentin Tarantino: The Man and His Movies.* Her most recent book is *Breast Cancer, There and Back: A Woman-to-Woman Guide.* She was formerly the film critic for *The New York Post.* She is a member of the National Society of Film Critics and a member and former chair of the New York Film Critics Circle. Her articles on film celebrities, pop culture, humor, and travel have appeared in numerous national publications.

Acknowledgments

I would like to thank the following individuals for assisting me, encouraging me, and listening to my ramblings: God, my wife, Mary, Dan and Sherry Rausch, Norman and Marion Leistikow, Steve Spignesi, John White, Richard Ember, Michael Dequina, George Beahm, Jami Bernard, Sean Westhoff, Fred Rosenberg, Josh Barnett, Cherie Fitzwater, Henry Nash, Peter Modesitt, Mike White, Brent Bates and Mike Brotherton. I would also like to thank my three children, Jordan, Jaiden, and Jalyn, for occasionally allowing me to work on this project.